Liar, Alleged: A Tell-All: Celebrities, Sex, and All the Rest

Copyright © 2023 by David Vass

All rights reserved.

Permission to reproduce or transmit in any form or by any means, electronic or mechanical, including photocopying, photographic and recording audio or video, or by any information storage and retrieval system, must be obtained in writing from the author.

Liar, alleged: A Tell-All: Celebrities, Sex, and All the Rest is a registered trademark of David Vass.

First printing September 2023

Library of Congress Cataloging-in-Publication Data

Vass, David
liar, alleged: a tell-all: celebrities, sex, and all the rest / by david vass

Paperback ISBN: 979-8-989-0745-0-1
Hardcover ISBN: 979-8-9890745-1-8

Published by AR PRESS, an American Real Publishing Company
Roger L. Brooks, Publisher
roger@incubatemedia.us
americanrealpublishing.com

Edited by: Sabrina Young
Interior design by Eva Myrick, MSCP

Printed in the U.S.A.

LIAR,

ALLEGED
A TELL-ALL: CELEBRITIES, SEX, AND ALL THE REST

DAVID VASS

READER DISCRETION IS ADVISED – ADULT MATERIAL

This book contains explicit sexual content, adult themes, and is suitable only for mature audiences eighteen and older.

This work may be considered profane, vulgar, unsettling, inappropriate and/or offensive; it may be too graphic or explicit for some readers.

Reader discretion is advised.

LEGAL DISCLAIMER

This work depicts actual events in the life of the author as truthfully as recollection permits and with due diligence to attempt to verify dates and places as accurately as is possible. All memoirs are subjective by their nature. I am recounting my present recollections of experiences over time. The author's long-term memory is good for his age, but not perfect.

Some names and characteristics have been changed, some events have been compressed and some conversations have been recreated, based on written notes, diaries and long-term memory, in an effort to be as accurate as is possible. This is a book of memories, and I've done my best to make it tell my story in as truthful a way as I know how.

These are my personal recollections, opinions and observations and they may not reflect other opinions, observations or recollections of conversations. Neither the publisher, myself or any associated parties shall be held responsible for any opinions, interpretations or consequences arising from different recollections relating to all of the above.

<u>If you do not accept all of the terms and disclaimers as written above, please stop reading this book now.</u> The author will not be held liable or responsible for any perceived or actual loss or damage to any person or entity, caused or alleged to have been caused, directly or indirectly, by anything written or implied in this memoir. Again, if you do not accept this term, please stop reading now.

DEDICATION

For stagehands, road managers, tech directors, spotlight operators, light and sound board runners and designers. For stage managers, agents, box-office personnel, theatre, nightclub and cabaret managers, talent bookers, make-up and hair artists, pit musicians, conductors and all the many other unsung, hard-working, and usually underpaid *behind-the-scenes* teams that allow the audience to come in, take their seats, and relish in what they paid for—the magic and authenticity of a live show.

To the women and men who made and make their livings onstage, with or without props, poles, or clothes: to the strippers, exotic dancers, burlesque queens, bar top go-go dancers, and sex workers. An honorable profession, and one maligned by so many with such regularity. I admire and am inspired by your bravery.

To The Mafia, The Mob—in so many ways my *real* family; the ones who taught me more about honesty and the importance of keeping your word than all the psychiatrists, psychologists, and twelve-step meetings put together. You really made me feel special, nurtured my sense of self-worth, and had my back.

To my courageous brothers and sisters who seeded and participated in The Mattachine Society, The Gay Activists Alliance, The Gay Liberation Front, and in later years, ACT-UP. All of the political activists, then and now, some still imprisoned for standing up for the First Amendment, and for genocides disguised as wars, fighting for social justice and trying to correct endless wrongs. Heroes and patriots, all.

A shout-out to my prison buddies—thank you for raising my political consciousness, teaching me how to grow tomatoes and pot, and for 'taking it like a man'—my pleasure!

For every single LGBTQ+ person who, while walking down the street, hears a word used towards them as a slur, turns their ass around, and confronts the offender—there is no braver or more dangerous action. I have the scars to prove it, and I am humbled by yesterday's and today's generations for not putting up with any shit, anymore.

And to my beloved Paul—my partner, soulmate and husband, as we enter our forty-seventh year together. He stood by me when I thought there was no hope for a scoundrel, an addict, a liar, a louse, and a handful like me. Slowly and patiently he brought me back to a sane and balanced reality. My very own handsome hero.

MANTRA / EPIGRAPH:

"And if I laugh at any mortal thing, 'tis that I may not weep."

— *Lord Byron*

Table of Contents

A Note from the Author vii

1. Tongue-Tied, Out, Proud 1
2. Anita O'Day: Jezebel of Jazz and the Mother I Never Had 19
3. Are You a Butch or a Fem? 37
4. A Gay Walks into a Strip Club 57
5. Welcome to the Firehouse 79
6. A Foursome on Jane Street 101
7. First Love, Worst Love 121
8. Lights, Cameras, and so Much Action 143
9. Mafia Mule, Carnegie Debut, and a Shitty Avery Fisher 169
10. The Fog Lifts 189

Epilogue 210

11. Celebrity Profiles (Bonus Chapter) 213

A NOTE FROM THE AUTHOR

I've never cared much for memoirs and biographies that begin with childhood and work their way up the sequential ladder. I usually skip forward to when 'whoever' develops pubic hair. I dig in *then*, because that's usually when it becomes interesting, at least for me. I share this to lubricate you, the reader, so my over-sized narrative slides right in, like those books about handsome ice hockey players or bull riders (my newest addiction).

This is my book—warts, cock sucking, bubble butts, strippers, addictions, legendary and horrible celebrities, and all the rest. If I've lost your attention for a few pages in the 'necessary' beginning, take a break and scoot to the "Celebrity Profiles Bonus Chapter" at the end, for a little gossip about said legendary and horrible celebs, then come back to where you left off. Think of the memoir as great sex and the bonus chapter profiles as quick jerk-offs in the bathroom, okay?

My chosen writing approach is minimalist, the essence of what I experienced, without loads of gilded descriptive paragraphs—a 'just the facts, please' slant. Where more intimate descriptions are required, I opt to use dialogue, both from my diaries and my memory. Two of my favorite writers are Dominic Dunne and Truman Capote, both of whom also embraced a tailored approach to their work. They give me hope.

1.

Tongue-Tied, Out, Proud

I knew from birth. I just did. I was only seven years old when I decided to come out to my mother, but I knew well before then I was different, and not just because I'd been born to a dirt-poor family and raised in a downtown, white trash neighborhood in Baltimore near the B&O train garage. I'd arrived ten years after my last sibling—a 'the condom broke' mistake in 1950. That's not what made me different, not really. Yes, I had a severe stutter and a significant speech impediment, and I talked funny and was an unwanted child. (I knew I was unwanted instinctively. Little kid radar, I guess. This was later proven true.) When I was seven, I overheard my married-but-closeted uncle (who, while sleeping in the same bed as me at his house one time groped my crotch, realized I didn't have pubes, and went back to sleep) use the word "gay" while whispering on the phone to his friend. I asked one of my older sisters what gay meant, lying and telling her I'd heard it at school. "It's another word for fag, David," Anne said, giving me a funny look.

See, back then, "homo," "deviant," "fag," "sissy," "pansy," and "queer" were the words people commonly used for a man who liked being with a man. It was 1957, and the word "gay" was only *just* gaining in popularity. Before that, it meant a straight man who slept with a lot of prostitutes. ("He lives a gay life!") One time, when I was watching the Cary Grant movie *Bringing Up Baby* on late-night TV, starring an actor I already had a crush on—I heard the word "gay" being used in a different way. In the film, Grant loses his clothes and has to put on a woman's feathery bathrobe. When Aunt Elizabeth asks him why he's wearing such a ridiculous outfit, he prances effeminately and shouts, "Because I just went *gay* all of a sudden!" (To be fair, Hollywood had been using the word "gay" in movies to suggest homosexuality from the mid-30s, since the censor board wouldn't allow them to use other terms.)

Anyway, I realized this was the perfect word to describe me. I liked the term so much that I decided to try it out on my mother. Now, in my run-down neighborhood in Baltimore, and in my family in particular, every other word was usually "fuck" or "shit," so cuss words weren't shocking to us. By the time I was four years old, I cursed like a sailor and certainly knew more than one word for what happened when you got a boner. This is what I declared to my mom:

"Mom, whenever I see a guy I think is cute, I stare at his crotch and get a hard-on. I think I'm gay."

She paused and decided to test me.

"What's gay?"

"A homosexual."

"You think you're a homo at *your* age? David, do you even have pubic hair yet?"

I shook my head. I was only in the third grade, for Christ's sake!

"Then you can't know what you are yet. Let's put this conversation off until you have pubic hair."

I must have agreed, but I knew exactly what I was and who I was. Probably because I absolutely loved staring at boys' crotches, which, looking back, was certainly my first addiction. I didn't know then there would be so many more to come.

———•———

My stutter and lisp didn't exactly make me a popular kid. I often heard other kids laughing at me on the playground and the streets, but

I didn't connect it with the fact that I had speech issues. Because get this: I lived for six years with five siblings and two parents and not once did *any* of them mention to me that I sounded funny. Maybe, it was because my brothers and sisters were a decade or more older and spent most of their time trying to figure out how to get married or join the military to escape a house where they were physically and emotionally abused by my father. In essence, I was an only child, a completely different generation to theirs, so I didn't really have close siblings or any friends. When the other kids laughed at me, I just assumed it was because I was gay.

One day I went up to my teacher and said, "A lot of the kids are laughing at me, and I think it's because I'm gay." She asked me what I meant by that. "A homosexual," I clarified. She decided that we needed to go talk to the principal about this matter, so off we went to his office where she told him what I'd said.

"You're a fag?" Mr. Fry asked me.

I said that wasn't a very nice word—even at seven, I was inspired to defend my community, something that would come in handy years later when I started the Baltimore Gay Liberation Front. The principal shook his head. "That's not why people are laughing at you, David," he said. "It's because when you talk, you stutter and don't say your S's properly. You have a serious speech impediment." I basically sounded exactly like the Daffy Duck cartoons I watched on Saturday mornings. "Is that silk?" became "Ift that thilk?" When he said it, I knew in my mind that he was right, and I felt like a freak. So, I ran. I ran until I couldn't run anymore and had used up all my physical energy, collapsing under a tree where I curled up into a ball and sobbed. It was a loud and dangerous sound. I saw a few women walk by on the sidewalk and start to head over to see if I was okay. Then, thinking better of it, they kept on walking. It was not the cry of a child. I'd never felt so alone.

After I exhausted myself with tears, I wondered why my family, all eight of them—whom I lived with in a space of less than eight hundred square feet—never told me that I sounded broken. Maybe they never truly really *heard* me. My siblings were busy morphing into adults. My mother lived in a stupor of hopelessness and tranquilizers and beers. My father was rarely home, and when he was, he trotted me out like a prize pony for the neighborhood women to ooh and ahh over, and he didn't let me talk. (It's possible he didn't want to admit I was a product of his inferior sperm that snuck through a hole in a rubber.) But it occurred to me when he took me out in public, he always talked over me; if I tried to say something, he closed me down. I was his prop, and props don't talk.

I didn't speak to my family for several days after that, and they never noticed. It only validated my belief—that I didn't exist to them. Returning to school a day later, my teacher sent me to a speech therapist who traveled between several schools. During our first meeting, the therapist sat me down and recorded me while I spoke. Then she played it back for me, and I immediately burst into tears again. I *hated* the way I sounded; it was the first time I actually heard myself, my voice coming out of this machine. I had a stutter, and it was hard for me to get a sentence out without saying the same word over and over, like a broken record. She explained that with breathing exercises I could learn to overcome my stutter but that I was also "tongue-tied." Which meant a piece of skin under my tongue (the frenum) kept me from being able to say my S's. I needed to give my mom a note, which she wrote, and then a doctor would take care of clipping the skin, which would give my tongue full movement. Then she could work with me on fixing the rest of my broken speech.

I came home and told my mother that I needed my tongue clipped. Despite never acknowledging that I sounded broken, she took me to a doctor at Johns Hopkins. The doctor assured us the procedure I was about to undergo was quick, easy, and wouldn't hurt. Then he took a pair of scissors, made me open my mouth, and cut through that fucking piece of skin. It was barbaric, scary, and it hurt like hell. Blood was spurting everywhere. My mother was freaking out, calling him a son of a bitch and asking him what he'd done. He gave me a piece of gauze to hold in my mouth and two little blue pills. "Take one if you have pain," he advised. When I made it home, I took one of those little blue pills and suddenly felt a lot better. So, I took the other pill to see what that would do. I felt the best I'd felt in weeks—so free! I was high as a kite. (This would be the first but not the last time I found thrills in pills.) I later tried to go to the school nurse to con her out of more of those blue pills, which she did not give to me. Had anyone been noticing, they would have seen my addictive personality had already started to blossom.

After my tongue was clipped, I went ahead and made the firm decision to never speak to anyone again. Ever. I met my speech therapist and handed her a note that said as much. She made a deal with me that I only had to speak to her during our sessions, and she didn't care what I did elsewhere. "I'll give you the corrections you need so you sound like a normal person, and then people will stop laughing at you," she said. That sounded like a decent arrangement, so I agreed. Starting that day, I literally didn't speak out loud to anyone else for six months. I only wrote things down. I also began to write in diaries, which I would shoplift from various dime stores. (Pilfering what I couldn't afford was another early addiction.) I had things to say and no one who cared to say them to, so I started jotting down what happened to me and what I thought. Several months later, the therapist played a new tape of me talking, and my stutter was much better, but my tongue was not cooperating the way it needed to. I thought, *This isn't working*. Mrs. Fisher encouraged me to try speaking out loud at home to practice, which I did only when I was alone. Everyone else? They got notes, written on pieces of school paper.

My vow of silence didn't exactly win over any friends at school. (My mother sent in a note telling my teachers that I didn't have to speak out loud if I didn't want to—that was her contribution.) But there was one other kid in class who also didn't speak to anyone. She was really tall, much bigger than anyone else, and she not only didn't talk, she also didn't do her schoolwork or engage with anyone. Every time she entered the room, she'd take her elbow and knock it on the wall twice and then say, "Unga Bunga." She'd do it again when she left the room. That's all she ever said. "Unga Bunga." One day I was walking down the hallway, and three older boys came up and started to push me around; they acted like they were going to shove me into a locker or worse. Out of nowhere, the silent girl came up behind those boys and pushed them hard up against the wall. They all ran off, scared to death. She looked over her shoulder at me and smiled. It was the only time I ever saw her smile. From that day and until school ended a few months later, wherever I went in school she walked about six feet behind me. I never asked her to, but she became my bodyguard. We never talked—neither of us were talking to anyone—but whenever I looked behind me, there she would be, and boy did everyone leave me the fuck alone after that.

I remained silent for almost two full years, until all the hard work I'd put into speech therapy paid off and I finally sounded perfect. When the therapist played the tape of me saying my words the correct way, I couldn't believe it. I sounded like the movie stars I heard on television, nothing like my family or neighbors—no Baltimore accent whatsoever! I had rediscovered myself and I couldn't wait to start talking again. The first person I chose to go up to was this really cute boy, who I had a crush on and whose crotch I loved to stare at. I went up to him and said, "I don't have a speech impediment anymore. I sound like me now, so we can talk." He shoved me and said, "You're still a fag and you still keep staring at my dick, and I still don't give a fuck if you can talk or not; stay the fuck away from me." At least he touched me—okay, so he pushed me—but that still counted in my head. It was the first time I was touched by a boy.

———•———

I was born September 26, 1950, at Johns Hopkins Hospital in downtown Baltimore. It was known as a teaching hospital and one of the best in the USA, even then. How my mother managed to have me there, I don't know, as we didn't have any insurance and we weren't on welfare. (Maybe in 1950 it was cheap to have a baby?) I was the youngest of seven kids, ten years younger than my youngest brother. I was truly a different generation from the rest of my siblings, but I was a cute little boy—blond hair, dimples, big eyes. My older sisters would pretend I was another of their dolls and dress me in little outfits, and I savored the attention.

Between my entrance into the world and the time I went to school, my mother and father were actually still together, even though they were fighting all the time. My older sisters were each born eleven months apart, and my two brothers came two years after them, born just a year apart. My parents were from a small town called Beckley, West Virginia, which is where they had the first six of their kids, before moving to Baltimore in 1948. My mother wasn't an educated woman. She got married at seventeen and became pregnant by her very first romantic partner, my father. (I once asked her why she had so many kids, and she said back then there was only one pharmacy in town, and only prostitutes went inside to ask for condoms. Those were pre-diaphragm days.) My father was a car mechanic, and when they moved to Baltimore, he also sold cars at Johnny's New & Used Cars, a mafia-owned lot.

It wasn't a happy household—but it was certainly a cramped one. My parents rented a row house in center Baltimore, and all eight of us lived hand-to-mouth in this narrow, itty-bitty, three-story home. It wasn't more than nine feet wide, and it had one window in front and one window in the back, with identical row houses on each side. My three sisters slept in one room, two to a bed and the other on a cot, and my two brothers shared a bed in a tiny room that had once been a closet. I slept in a dresser drawer for the first year of my life, and once I outgrew it, I just bounced around to wherever was open. There was one toilet for eight people, which never worked very well. One day my father decided he was going to fix it, so he took it off the floor. He couldn't figure out what was wrong with it or how to reconnect it, so for some months everyone in the family had to shit through a hole in the floor—a literal shithole. Eventually my Aunt Penny stopped by, saw the mess in the bathroom, and called the health department, who made my dad fix the toilet.

My father wasn't a 'good dad.' He *was* incredibly handsome, and truth be told, I grew the occasional 'Little David' erection when I stared at his crotch. I knew he could be charming around women, but he was also mean. He enjoyed playing mentally abusive games with his children and the occasional physical slap. When I was being born, he gave each of my sisters and brothers a toothbrush, a candle, and a can of Ajax and made them scrub every inch of all the floors with the toothbrush before they could eat. "To make sure the house is clean for your new brother," he said. The candle? That was their illumination source, since he didn't allow the lights to be turned on. Maybe he was mean because, like my mother, he felt trapped by the constraints of family life. He was only seventeen when he got married, and they very quickly had six kids. Their first child, a boy, was born sickly and died at six months old. I once heard that when he was dying, they had to cut his diapers off with scissors because he was too weak to be lifted. Neither of my parents spoke of him again.

My father didn't make much money fixing cars, and my mother did what she could with what money he gave her, but she was at his mercy. There were nights when nobody ate. My brothers took to dumpster diving behind grocery stores, which they later taught me to do as well. You'd be surprised at how much perfectly good food is wasted! I have no shame about it, and in fact I thought it was fun, like unwrapping Christmas gifts, except ones with flies and water bugs on them. (Quick tip—if you need to dumpster dive, always wear closed-toe shoes.)

When I was about four years old, my father blew up our house. He'd come home from work in his grease-stained coveralls. He liked to look sharp, so he'd go to the basement, where we had a washer with a ringer, and try to take the spots out. He rinsed the coveralls in gasoline, because that broke down the oils better than soap and water. My father, like my mother, was a chain-smoker. I was upstairs in the living room, banging on my little red toy piano, which I just loved, and suddenly there was a boom that blew everyone in the house in different directions. The blast blew me off the floor and into the wall; it blew one of my sisters right off the toilet and threw my brother halfway out a window, cutting him all up. Yes, my father had dropped a lit cigarette onto his clothes soaking in gasoline. How he survived, I'll never know. He was in the hospital for weeks with serious burns. The house was pretty much destroyed. Somehow, it got rebuilt. To this day, whenever I hear a sudden loud boom—a car backfiring, fireworks, a loud sneeze—it sends me back to the day my father very nearly killed us all.

After the last of my five siblings left the house, my mother finally decided to end her abusive marriage and divorced my dad. She was determined that, with only me, she would find a way to make a living and to some degree become independent. She had never had any real freedom, somehow managing to feed and clothe five children, and she was determined to find a job, a small apartment, and provide a home for us. Even though I was only about seven years old, I knew the fact that she still had to raise that last 'mistake child' wasn't exactly a thrill.

My mother always cared for me, but she never cared *about* me— she had used up all that energy. After eighteen years of raising six kids back-to-back in white trash poverty, she was tired; she wanted her life back. I was the last speed bump she needed to navigate before she could finally have total freedom. So at night, all she wanted to do was drink a few beers, smoke her cigarettes, and swallow a couple Miltown pills while watching TV. (Miltown was the best-selling tranquilizer back then, before everyone started popping Valium instead.) She wasn't really interested in what I was doing. She washed my clothes in the sink and kept me clean, but in a way, we were more like roommates than mother and son. The upshot was that I had total freedom to do as I pleased. Ride buses, take walks, hook school, wander where my feet took me, stay up late—I was completely off her radar. In bingo, there's a term called 'waiting to wait,' which means just two numbers away from winning. With me, she was 'waiting to wait'—just a couple more years, and at last, her freedom from all that parenting.

She got a secretarial job, and I was old enough to wonder how a woman with no typing, shorthand, spelling, or prior experience could land that kind of job. I decided, without quite being old enough to know how such things worked, that it must have been magic. It was only much later that I learned from a sister that the job also required her getting on her knees for the executive VP.

At home, we'd already started to develop a rhythm that certain things "just were," and we didn't question each other. It was a kind of precursor to "don't ask, don't tell." She would leave the house an hour before I left for school and return at 6:00 p.m. after taking the two buses (each way) she needed to reach her job. I had my own key, so I would come home from school and mostly read. When she walked through the door, she put together the easiest, fastest, and cheapest food we could have for dinner—mostly soup and toast or very rarely, if money allowed, a TV dinner. Poverty was still a way of life for both of us. Sometimes she'd give me a dime and send me across the street to the little store run by Polish ladies, where I'd buy her three cigarettes. That's how hand-to-mouth we were. But no matter our dire financial state, she always managed to have her three beers a night. (By the time I started high school, three beers had turned into six.) I always stayed up later than her, just to make sure she didn't pass out on the couch with a lit cigarette in her mouth. (To this day, I keep a fire extinguisher in every room, both from the PTSD of my dad blowing up our old row house and from my mom's chain-smoking while only half awake.) I'd make sure she staggered into bed before I went to sleep myself. She always woke up and went to work, even if she was hungover. Even though we kept out of each other's way, I instinctively knew that so long as she still had me in the house as a responsibility, she didn't feel free.

My mother didn't have a car, so we took the bus or we walked to get to wherever we needed to, which never included a visit to the dentist until I left home. I also never saw a doctor for illness, not once that I can remember. I guess my mother determined I was healthy, plus the school nurse looked at everyone once a year, primarily for ringworm and lice.

One day at school, we all lined up and walked through the gymnasium, where we were given a little white paper cup with a sugar cube in it. The liquid polio vaccine was eye-dropped onto the cube. We had to chew it up and swallow it and open our mouths to show the nurse it was gone. The line continued to a smaller room, where another nurse sat atop a ladder with a "bright blue light" to check our hair/head for lice and ringworm. The blue light made everything that was white glow blue, including my blond hair, and I was hypnotized and intrigued by the effect—I'd never seen anything quite like it before. I promised myself that one day I would get one of those lights and make 'dramatic effects' everywhere. That promise, of course, came true when I went into show business as a lighting designer.

After my mother left my dad, we moved a lot. We must have lived in eight different apartments by the time I (barely) graduated high school. They were generally in brick and stone buildings that had at one time been mansions and were then cut into different apartments. They were in parts of the urban center of Baltimore that are now very trendy neighborhoods, but back then this was the bottom rung for people like us. Most apartments had a dumbwaiter—a small box that ran on a rope pulley from the top of the house to the bottom, where the trash cans were stored. The small door to cover this contraption was always in the kitchen. You would put your garbage in the dumbwaiter, and the super would pull it down once a day and empty it into the trash cans. After one of my brothers was kicked out of the military and came back to live with us for a bit, he used to ride that dumbwaiter up and down into other apartments while most people were at work, sneak into their kitchens, and steal food. My mother never asked him where he got it, but we sure did eat it.

My father was somewhat in the picture in the earliest days of the split, but just barely. When they were still together, he used to like to take me to the ice-cream store for a sundae and show me off (aka use me as chick-bait). Occasionally he'd walk away with a random woman's phone number. I always felt guilty when he took me out for ice cream while my siblings were at home going hungry. One time, I tried to sneak some ice cream home by putting most of my banana split into my pockets to share with them. Of course, it melted and got everywhere and made a huge mess. I cried myself to sleep that night.

After the divorce, my dad would show up at the schoolyard with a chocolate milk for me, but when I saw him, I'd run back into the school and hide. I wanted nothing to do with that man, not so much for how he treated me but for his violence and abuse towards my brothers, sisters, and mother. After three tries, I never saw him again. (Seems lazy, considering he'd made me with his own semen.) He got a trailer somewhere and found other people to abuse, I guess. When he died in 1972, a family member somehow contacted one of my brothers to let him know. He'd had a heart attack and a stroke and been dead in his trailer for ten days before anybody knew, except his cat. (I hope the cat wasn't hungry?) One sibling went to his funeral and became executor of his 'estate.' When everything was said, done, and sold, we each got $11. That was his legacy to us. That, and the skills to scrub floors with a toothbrush in the dark.

When I was eleven, I got pubes. They were sprouting up like corn, that summer of '61! I remembered how my mother told me to talk to her about my sexuality when I 'pubed,' and she decided I needed to see a psychiatrist, as I was still telling her I was gay. She figured that since I was going through puberty, it was only a matter of time before

I acted on the thoughts that come with it. We went back to Johns Hopkins, where the psychiatrist asked me tons of questions. When I got home, I wrote them all down in my (stolen) diary:

Doc: "David, why do you think you're homosexual?"

Me: "Because I stare at boys' crotches and get a hard-on."

Doc: "Do you ever have fantasies about sex with boys?"

Me: "Never!"

This was true. I had loads of fantasies about kissing and feeling up boys, but I didn't know the specifics of sex or what a climax was, so I didn't really know what he meant by that.

Doc: "Have you ever lied?"

Me: "Never!"

Doc: "David, everyone lies sometimes. I'm sure you do too. Tell me about a lie you've said that you remember."

Me: "Um, OK. I went to school one morning and told the teacher I threw up and didn't feel good. She sent me to the school nurse, who took my temp and told me I'd be all right and gave me a spoon of Pepto Bismol and sent me back to class. Before leaving her office, I asked for some blue pills, and she just gave me the fish-eye. I was trying to get out of school because I *really* wasn't in the mood to pretend to listen that day."

Doc: "Have you ever stolen anything?"

Me: "Never!"

Doc: "David, everybody takes things sometimes. Maybe you took some money out of your mother's purse or saw something small you liked at a friend's house and put it in your pocket?"

Me: "I don't have any friends, and I never took money out of her purse."

The truth was that I had taken money out of her purse, and also a few of her Miltowns. My mother had been on Miltowns since her pregnancy with me until the early 60s, when she switched to Valium. I would steal a few pills when she was passed out from beer, and she never seemed to know. The pills were blue, the same color as the two pills that asshole doctor who snipped my tongue gave me. For a long time, I thought that all blue pills made you feel good, relaxed, leveled-out.

Doc: "David, do you love your mother?"

Me: "She's nice to me and lets me do what I want. So, I like that. And she keeps my clothes clean. Is that love? I don't really know what love means, how it's supposed to feel. No one has taught me how to 'love.' Do people just know what love is, doctor, or do they have to learn it? I haven't had any lessons and I don't think I have ever loved anyone, at least not yet. I don't like her passing out every night on the couch from drinking beer and smoking, drunk, and me worrying about her setting the house on fire."

At the end of my session with the doctor, he called my mother into his office, told her to put out her cigarette, and said, "Mrs. Vass, your son has a lot of problems, but being gay isn't one of them." My mother was quiet during the bus ride home until she turned to me and said, "Okay, you're gay. And you have pubic hair now, so we have to find you a boyfriend."

Upon reflection, if that isn't love, I'm not sure what is.

I left home the day I graduated high school, and my mother did get her life back. She changed jobs and started working downtown for the city of Baltimore. She bought herself a used car so she could drive back and forth to work. She'd been a beautiful woman when she was younger—she looked like the actress Jane Wyman, with a little button nose and high cheekbones—and suddenly had more money than she'd ever had before. She was by no means rich, but she bought herself some nice clothes and would regularly get her hair done. My mom, with all she had been through, was still 'a looker' for her age. She was also, according to my older sister, incredibly horny. (My entire family was oversexed, if we're being honest. When one of my sisters was in an assisted living home, she was constantly threatened with eviction because she would have sex with any man that would let her. She died happy.)

At this point, my middle sister had been stripping in mafia-owned clubs on the infamous 'Block' in Baltimore for several years under her stage name, "Devil Delicious, Satan's Slut." She loved this job. She was an exhibitionist, loved being naked, loved people flirting with her, and she loved the money. She started inviting my mom down to the clubs to score free drinks off the men who came in. So my mom's finally having a ball (literally) and just fucking whoever and doing whatever she wanted. One night a guy comes into the club, they have some drinks, and my mother sleeps with him. (Men came to The Block for two reasons: to watch the strip shows and to hit on women, because a few of them, like my mom, hung out at the bars in the clubs just looking for a fun night.) A few nights later, that same man came back and the same thing happened—he and my mother went home together. My sister told my mother, "I think that guy likes you." My mother said, "Find out what you can about him." My sister investigated and told her, "Good job. Travels a lot. Works for B&O Railroad. His wife just died nine months ago, and he has a nice house outside of Philly."

My mother got it in her head that she was going to marry this guy, which would get her a nice house and the financial security not to have to work anymore. He'd be traveling most of the time with the railroad job, and she could sit around and drink and watch TV and finally do whatever the fuck she wanted to do. And that's exactly what happened. He was happy with the arrangement. Neither one of them loved each other, but she cleaned the house and did his laundry and made him dinners when he was home and generally looked after him and had sex with him a lot. And that's all he was looking for—sex, food, and somebody to keep his house clean and groceries in stock. So they were a pretty good match. They were together for about five years, until my mother got lung cancer in 1974. While in the hospital, my mother called her sister, my aunt, to come to their house and help care for her husband. Six weeks after her funeral, B&O guy married my mom's sister. Never look a meal ticket in the mouth, I guess.

By the time I was twenty-four, both of my parents were dead. I was well into my career working as a lighting and sound tech in cabarets and nightclubs in New York by then, and I remember when I went to my mother's funeral, I had to get a sub because I had a gig that day. The funeral was the last time as I recall that all three of my sisters and one of my brothers (the other was recovering from being shot in the head while working the graveyard shift as a security guard in a graveyard) were all in the same room, and we took some time to share "mom" stories. I recall mine very well. It took me back to when I was around eight.

It was spring in Baltimore, and my mom had planted some seeds to grow a few vegetables in a backyard at one of the many apartments we rented while I was in elementary school.

I had just barely listened that day to a teacher drone on about the importance of vegetables and salads for our young, growing bodies, and when I got home, there was some leaf lettuce poking up in the yard that looked tall enough, at least to me, to harvest. Also, there was a big cucumber in the fridge, and an onion, and a few slices of bologna, so I thought as a treat for my mom I'd whip up a healthy salad for dinner and save her having to make something after she got home from work.

Working diligently, I chopped up the lettuce leaves, sliced big chunks of the cuke, cut up some onion, added the meat, and soaked all of it in whatever oil we had. It was a masterpiece, for sure, and I was quite proud that I took the burden off her having to make dinner for that night at least. She would come home and be served a healthy dinner!

I proudly showed it off to her the minute she walked through the door. Grabbing two plates I portioned us up—and even put it on our two TV trays, with the wash rags we used in our shower as napkins. While I ate with gusto, mom pushed it around her plate and had a look like she really didn't want to have anything to do with my salad. My feelings were really hurt, and I made a note that my efforts in the kitchen would not be repeated, and we could go back to *her* making some kind of dinner every night.

Why this story popped up in my head escapes me, but it did, so I shared. All three of my sisters started laughing while I scratched my head and thought, *What the fuck, we're all grown-ups now and they're still laughing at me?* My sister Anne said, "David, Mom didn't eat that salad because she had been using that cucumber as a dildo for the last week, and she was pretty sure you hadn't washed it." Okay, then I laughed too and shuddered at the thought of accidentally getting my mom's pubes stuck in my teeth that night.

After the funeral and later that week, I realized I felt nothing about her dying—and I felt bad that I felt nothing. Friends asked me if I was alright, and I said, "What the fuck are you talking about? Everybody's mother dies." I was very matter-of-fact about it. Of course, it probably helped that we'd never truly had a mother-and-son relationship; and besides, by this point I'd already met the woman who became a surrogate mother to me: jazz legend Anita O'Day.

2.

Anita O'Day: Jezebel of Jazz and the Mother I Never Had

Anita O'Day was more important to me than any other celebrity I worked with throughout my career. The two of us seemed to connect intimately and immediately; maybe it's because we were so similar in many ways and maybe, because I didn't feel like I had a real mother, I connected with her mothering tendencies towards me. She often told me I was like the son she'd never had. (Which was a weird thing to say, as she'd had nine abortions and I wondered "which son, which one?") More importantly, I think we were way more alike than we were different.

Anita knew from the age of thirteen that she wanted to make money—she called it 'dough' her entire life. She spoke in a kind of pigeon jazz or 'hip' talk, so she made up her last name, which is based on pig latin for dough. (She absolutely *loved* talking in pig latin; when she found out that I spoke it, it became the way we'd converse with each other.) Like me, Anita came from nothing. She had no mentors and her mother didn't have an emotional attachment to her. She was also highly critical of her only child. When Anita told her mom she wanted to be a singer and a dancer, her mother laughed and said, "That will never happen." And when Anita quit school at age fourteen to join danceathons, her mother threatened to have her arrested. Like me, Anita didn't have any higher education; she didn't go to a performing arts school. Everything she learned was self-taught, based on her instincts.

We connected in other ways. We both had addictive personalities; issues with alcohol and drugs took over our lives at times. We were both on our own from age thirteen onward; we lied about our age to work in clubs. We stole when we needed to. We understood the mafia and its role in the music business and learned to do what we did on the job. We both spent time in prison, fucked whomever we wanted, ran from our love affairs, and struggled with feeling worthy. Anita told me because she lived life as a gypsy, crashing wherever she could, that those nine abortions over three decades were the right decision; she didn't think she'd be a good mother. In the 70s, a gay man having a baby just wasn't on the radar as we were not allowed to adopt or foster, and the use of surrogates for us gay folks was illegal. I had never felt the calling to be a parent either, mostly because I wanted to do whatever the fuck I wanted—my *baby* was always freedom, baby. That was Anita's take, too.

Anita and I first met at Reno Sweeney, the trendiest, hottest, 'now' nightclub in 1970s New York City. I was a technical director awaiting her arrival for a tech rehearsal the opening day of her two-week gig. I'd been teching there, running the lights and sound and hand-holding the celebs at Reno, for nearly three years. Honestly, if the first time we'd met each other had gone any differently, I doubt she would have become a lifelong friend and mentor. She was scheduled to come in at three o'clock to do a sound check and give me an opportunity to hear her voice live. Then I would set the sound levels and focus the lighting system after seeing how she moved around the stage. Reno Sweeney had a very low ceiling and, as a result, I couldn't use a spotlight; it would have lit the back heads of the audience more than the performer. So I manually focused and gelled the lights based on how the performer liked to move around onstage.

In saunters Anita, wearing a mink coat in the middle of summer. I introduced myself and told her I was happy to wait for her trio to arrive before we got started.

"Oh, uh, right. About that, David. I have a little problem."

"What's that?" I asked.

"I don't have a trio," she said. "They all quit in Boston because my gig there last night didn't cough up the dough after the last show, and I couldn't pay them, and they said, "No pay, no play." So, do you think you can find me a pianist, bass player, and drummer? I don't care if they're Broadway pit musicians or rock and rollers, they just need to be able to read music charts."

I was floored. I told her I wasn't sure I'd be able to find a jazz trio on such short notice (an understatement as the first show was in five hours) and honestly, good jazz musicians weren't that easy to come by.

"David," she advised, "I'd rather work with young guys who don't know shit about jazz, because I can teach them how to play for the way I sing easier than I can with a jazz trio that's been around for ten years."

I could see at this point that she was eyeballing the bar, so I said, "Let's have a drink to take the edge off this conversation." She gives me a big crooked grin and says, "Scotch, double, no ice."

I called Louis Friedman, the owner of Reno Sweeney, and explained the problem. He looked through his Rolodex and somehow managed to find three musicians who were able to play the 9:00 o'clock and 11:00 o'clock shows, which was hard because so many of the good musicians in New York played in the orchestra pits for Broadway shows. They'd be able to pick up an 11:00 p.m. gig afterward to make extra money, but that 9:00 p.m. slot was difficult to fill. I told Anita the good news and said the new trio could be here in two hours for a sound check.

"No need, just have them come in at 8:30," she said. I reminded her that there would already be people in their seats by then.

"Yeah, and I'm going to teach 'em, the trio, how to play jazz as part of the show. This is going to be a jazz class, David. The people will love it! I'll teach them my hand movements, because if you work with me as a musician, you know what to do by the way I move my hands. I'll just stop the musicians if they fuck it up, explain it to them, and have them start again. They'll leave the gig with some money and knowing how to play jazz. It'll be cool." She put on her coat to leave, but I stopped her and said I at least wanted a sound check on her voice.

"David, do you know what you're doing?" she asked. I said I did.

"So let me get this straight. You've got three musicians coming. The first show is at nine. You know what you're doing, and I know what I'm doing. So, I'll see you at 8:30. Just be cool." She walked out the door and all I could think about was that at nine o'clock, there was going to be an Anita O'Day show no matter what, sold out for both sets. She needed to pull it out of her ass and I needed to help make that happen.

When the musicians got there, we all crammed into her dressing room. She told them, "If you're nervous, have a fucking drink and look through the song charts, but just know that if I move my hands fast [demonstrates], it means speed up the tempo and never mind what the chart says. If I move my hands slow [demo], it means slow down the tempo and never mind what the charts say. Got it? Cool." When it was showtime, there were 120 people packed in the Paradise Room, expecting to see the Anita O'Day they heard on her albums. But Anita was no longer a big band singer, a 'canary.' She was a jazz stylist and the most improvisational singer on the jazz circuit. She turned to the audience and told them about her Boston gig and her trio flaking on her. Again, with that big-toothed, crooked grin.

"So, we got these cats about three hours ago, and *you* cats are in for a real treat. You're getting double your money's worth because I'm going to teach a jazz lesson while I'm singing, and you get to be part of the fun. So, you're going to leave here knowing a lot more about jazz than when you walked in. Cool, yes?" she said. The musicians started playing and she'd occasionally stop cold and school them.

"Hey piano, this time when you play, you're only going to play chords, don't play melody, 'cause that's what I'm singing for those six bars. Bass man, only pluck the strings, don't bow—never bow on an up tune for me. Hey drums, take it easy on the snare, keep the rhythm with the brushes on the top hat." By the fourth night, the guys sounded like professional jazz musicians. She was putting them through the hoops and was having a blast and it just...worked. On the second night of her performance, the *New York Times* came to review the show, and the review came out the next morning. It said, "Run, don't walk, to Reno Sweeney to get a once-in-a-lifetime jazz lesson. Some people pay four years tuition at Juilliard to get this type of instruction, but what Anita O'Day is doing, you will never see again, and she is at the height of her vocal uniqueness."

We had a line halfway down the street for the rest of her gigs, all of which were sold out with long waiting lists. The bar area of the Cabaret Room was packed; people stood just to hear her performance through the arched doorway entrance. (The fire marshal even came a few times to clear the area down to code.) By this point, I knew Anita really liked me because I listened to what she was doing with her voice and matched the lighting to her cadences. In essence, I was becoming another one of her musicians. She could feel what I was doing on her face and on the trio, lighting things in a way to match the mood of the tune; she could tell I was musical. I didn't put reverb on her voice, knowing she would hate it because she couldn't sustain notes. (Her uvula was cut out during a tonsillectomy gone wrong when she was twelve years old. Without an uvula, a singer can't create vibrato, and without vibrato, breath is used up more quickly. You can just wave bye-bye to sustaining notes.) So, after one of her sets, she pulled me aside and said, "Let's go and have some drinks after the show, somewhere where none of these note-chasers [what she called all audience members] will be." I thought for a minute and said, "I know the place." I walked her to a West Village gay bar, the Ninth Circle, which is where I hung out. I knew the bartenders and was sure they'd treat her well. We could find us a little corner where we could sit and talk and the gay guys wouldn't bother her; most of them wouldn't even know who she was. So that's where we went.

After we walked in, she said, "David, this is a gay bar!" I explained that it's where I went to calm down after shows because they were open until four in the morning. I asked if it bothered her.

"No, no, not at all. I love gay cats. Except for some lesbians, they can get on my nerves. I've always been suspicious of women who don't understand how wonderful it is when you get just the right cock."

We started talking and she said something in pig latin and I answered back. She seemed surprised that I knew how to speak it—it was one of the few things my mother had taught me—and asked if I was any good at it. I replied, "Yes, of course, I'm fluent!" And from that point on, whenever she wanted to say something to me and didn't want anyone else to know what she was talking about—where she could get a joint, whether there was a bar around where she could throw back drinks between shows—she'd say it in pig latin. And that's how our friendship began. Soon after that first gig together, whenever she felt like it, she'd call me (late, always late) and tell me little stories about her life, all while calling me Avid-day, pig latin for David.

———————•———————

During one of our calls, she told me about her childhood. Her mother was extremely strict until Anita was twelve years old. And then, she didn't care about her anymore. It was the Great Depression and Anita, who was living in Chicago, had read about "walkathons," or "danceathons." This was where a man and woman, usually tethered at the feet, would walk or dance together in a large sports venue or ballroom; the last couple standing won money. Contestants only got two two-hour breaks and six hours of sleep each day. (They slept on folding cots at the edges of the stage; even when they were sleeping, the audience could see them 24/7). This meant they also had to piss and shit while tied together. Luckily, the audience was unable to see into the primitive backstage port-a-john. Anita told me that she was good at these danceathons; she was good-looking and looked older than fourteen, so no one questioned her or asked for proof of age. She said the male danceathon guys liked her because she didn't weigh much. If she reached the point where she was exhausted, they could pick her up and throw her over their shoulder while they continued to dance. She could take little naps that way. People came to watch and bet money on them. "Oh, I think couple forty-two is going to pass out in two hours." Or, "I think eighty-three is going to go for two more days." They'd place all these bets on who was going to make it to the end, just like at a horse race. The last couple standing got a bunch of prize money. Anita was part of the last couple standing many times.

"I just wouldn't let my guys pass out," she said. "I can't tell you how often I would make them put their feet on my feet so they wouldn't have to move, and I would move their feet for them and hold on to them so they could just sleep in my arms." She was winning money this way, and in the beginning she would send some dough back to her mother, but she never once got a thank-you.

"I thought, if I'm going to send her money and not even get a thank-you, I'm not going to send her money. So that was pretty much the end of my relationship with my mother."

Anita was sixteen and on her own after her danceathons. She told me how she'd stand outside famous jazz joints in Chicago, freezing in a thin coat, and just listen through the window and the doors to the music. These were the kinds of clubs where all the pro jazz players would go when they were done with their gigs; they'd go to one of these clubs and jam with each other, playing until five or six in the morning. And Anita would be right outside the club, listening. After a couple of months, one of the guys at the Downbeat Club offered her a job at coat check so she could come inside and stay warm. And that's how she truly learned jazz.

"I don't read music, but I hear it. I could hear what they were doing, hear what each instrument was playing, and break each instrument up and put them into layers. So, I started practicing while I was hanging up coats—some nights I would sing piano, or bass, or just the drums. I could sing on the beat, against the beat, I could do downbeat, I could back phrase, forward phrase. I could do anything I wanted. I was like a vocal trapeze artist, except without the chops to be a singer. A canary maybe, but not a singer."

One night, a couple of musicians heard her singing in the coatroom and invited her up to sing with them. "They were intrigued by me," she said. "If it was a trio, I'd become the fourth musician. If it was a quartet, I was the fifth. I sang against the other instruments, in a counter-count; none of the other singers were doing that." One day, a guy came in, heard her sing, and offered her a gig.

Back then all the female canaries had to wear gowns onstage. Anita didn't own a gown, so she stole one.

"I just tried it on and then left it in the dressing room. Then I came back out and tried something else on and gave that item back to the clerk. Then I went back into the dressing room for my purse, rolled the gown up real tight and stuck it under the sleeve of my coat, and walked out," she said. And that was how she managed to walk out of Gimbels with a pilfered ball gown.

I learned that that's how Anita lived her life. She was going to be a singer, and it didn't matter if she had to fuck for it, steal for it, lie for it, or shoot up for it—she was going to realize that dream. And she did.

She was a prolific artist. When she recorded her first twenty-plus albums, the sessions were live: a one-take, one-day studio recording. Whatever they recorded in the studio was what you heard on the album, warts and all. There was no time or money for retakes. Anita told me (with some pride) that she once recorded fifteen song tracks in just twelve hours.

One night she was talking to Stan Kenton, a big-deal jazz band leader that she had slept with to land a job. ("He cared more about how his hair looked than how I felt during sex—he was what I called a 'flat fuck,' but it got me the gig," she told me.)

Stan said to her, "Anita, you're not ever going to be a great singer, but you're a helluva song stylist." She wasn't sure what he meant, so she asked. "It's a singer who doesn't have the chops to sing but is so musical it doesn't matter," he said. "They can sing in front of, behind, or around the music and make you like it. Billie Holiday is one. She can't sing at all; it's all in her phrasing. So just concentrate on your phrasing. And wear a good bra."

That advice changed her life because it gave her hope. In 1941, she joined with Gene Krupa's band (a job she got her usual way) and had her first hit, "Let Me Off Uptown." For the next nine years, she was voted one of the top five jazz singers in the country by *DownBeat* magazine, alongside Peggy Lee, Ella Fitzgerald, Dinah Washington, and Billie Holiday. But then she started getting into booze and heroin and was getting arrested and serving time. The big bands wouldn't touch her after that—she was tainted and people didn't want to see a convicted felon canary (literally a "jail bird"). So, she went back to trios and slum clubs, and she had it really rough for a long time. But at least her sex life was always thriving. It was one of the things we always talked about and laughed over. Sex was the means to an end of a good, fast time for both of us. One night she said, "If I'd been born a gay man, I wouldn't have my slutty reputation, Avid-day!"

―――――・―――――

The third time I worked with Anita, we went out for what was our traditional after-show drinks-and-gossip session. She wanted to go to a bar with a good potential for picking up a guy, so gay bars were out. She needed a straight bar where she could get laid and have some free drinks. That was what she did when it came to men—she loved 'em and left 'em. She did not want a relationship. She did not want kids.

She just wanted one-nighters. Her career matched her love life: she wanted a gig for a night and sex for a night. Just as she could never do a three-hundred-performance show on Broadway ("Sing the same song the same way for three hundred nights? Not my thing."), she could never do three hundred nights with one man either; she'd have been equally bored. That's just not the way she was wired, which was very much like me.

The 70s were truly the height of sexual liberation. *Everybody* was doing it (straight, gay, confused). Everybody felt this post-hippie, pre-AIDS vibe, like "I can do anything I want and just get a shot of penicillin and then it'll be okay. I can cheat on my husband and he'll never know." The years between 1973 and 1977 were a sexual free-for-all. (Back then, I considered it a relationship if I knew somebody's name after we had sex at the bathhouse, which normally didn't happen because I just stuck it in a hole or had them lie on their stomach with their face in a pillow—wham, bam, thank you pal!)

There was even a bathhouse for straight people called Plato's Retreat on the Upper West Side of New York City, where anything could happen to anyone if they wanted it to. In some of the gay clubs in the Village or Meat-Packing District, men could walk in, get naked, and lie in a bathtub, and other men would piss on them; there was no shame (there was some odor but no shame).

Anita and I would talk about our conquests the night before, usually on the phone, and she loved hearing the details. ("Wait, *how* many fingers did you stick up his ass, Avid-day?") She couldn't stop laughing after I told her about the time I lost a fingernail up a guy's ass. This happened after the first acrylic nail salon came to Manhattan; it was located across from Bloomingdale's. I'd read about it on Page Six in the *New York Post*.

I'd been a nail biter for as long as I could remember. I always wanted a lot of things in my mouth, and my fingernails were apparently one of them. At this point, I was using my hands for sex a lot, primarily sticking them up cute guy's asses, which usually took place in various Manhattan bathhouses. As my sexual prowess grew, I wanted to have nice-looking hands with short, unbitten nails. I'd tried everything: a polish that was supposed to burn your mouth (I found it yummy), small condom-like rubbers to put over your nails (they were too easy to roll off). I even tried putting airplane glue on my nails since that was supposed to make them too hard to chew, but nope! We white trash gays had strong teeth. So, I read about this nail salon and thought, *If I have these acrylic things on my hands, then I can't bite my nails!* My nails would grow under the acrylic things and once they reached a normal length—presto! My vanity would override my desire to snack on my nails and I'd take up pretzels or something else instead. (As an aside, I did try a few sniffs of the airplane glue. I could see how some people paper-bag huffed it, but luckily, I didn't like it *that* much.)

So off I went in search of this nail joint, which turned out to be an easy find. I went in and said I want acrylic nails; the woman assumed I was a drag queen, I guess, because she started showing me these really loooong nails. "No, I want short ones, like a man has," I said. She replied they had never given a man acrylic nails before, but okay. They'd cost $300 (ouch), but they'd stay on for about six weeks. "Can you do them now?" I asked. "Sure," she said. Woo hoo!

This was the very beginning of acrylics, and they were thick—and a lot longer than I wanted them, as it turned out. The acrylics were a kind of a yellowy-frosty white; I looked like I had dipped my fingertips in buttermilk. But I figured for six weeks I could deal with it while my real nails grew in underneath. When I went to pay for them, I reached into the pocket of my 501s to grab the cash—I couldn't manipulate my fingers to hold on to the bills. This should have been a red flag, but I'd never had fake nails before, so who knew? Don't even ask how long it took me to button up my 501s.

Later that night, I'm in the Ninth Circle bar and some friends come by to say "hi." They all notice my nails and think they look disgusting, like a door had shut on them. I told them all to fuck off and we laughed, but I decided to go somewhere a little less bright. Plus, I was horny. I lurked on the West Village corners for a while, but it was slim pickin's that night, so I headed to the baths and rented my usual cubicle with the small bed. The only light in the cube was red, so no one would notice my odd, yellowly-colored fake nails.

Anyway, this really cute guy pokes his head into my cubicle and I nod. He comes in and drops his towel. He was exactly my type: nice body and a beautiful bubble butt (like two melons in a cotton sack) and a sweet grin. We start hooking up and I start playing with his ass—one finger, two fingers, three, then four. It was really hot and the whole thing took twenty minutes, which is a lot in bathhouse time. He came all over his stomach; so did I. As we were wiping off, I noticed I was missing one of the new fake nails on my left hand. Well, these things cost $300 and having nine of them was not going to look right. I started searching the bed, then the floor...and nothing. He starts wondering what I'm up to, so I think quick:

"Oh baby, you're so sexy, let's do that again," I said.

"I'm spent, but thanks for the compliment," he says. He's looking at me funny and it's obvious he's about to head out, so I had to tell the truth. Actually, I had to tell a lie, disguised as the truth.

"Uh, I left something in you," I admitted.

"You left something *in* me?"

"Yeah, just a little something..." I continued.

"What?" he asked.

(Thinking fast) "My ring!"

"Your ring? You had four fingers in me with a ring on? Fuck, okay, let me see if I can find it." (He sticks his finger up his ass, and nothing.) "There's nothing up there, and I gotta go," he says.

"It's my *wedding* ring!" I said, and I put on my saddest face. "Please let me try!"

"Jesus Christ, I'm so sorry I met you." He bends over, elbows on the bed, and tells me to go for it but to hurry up. I couldn't find it with one finger, so I went back in with two and… I got it!

I held it in my hand, with my fist closed, and he gave me a "what the fuck is wrong with you" look and took off. Soon after, I realized I had an early morning flight to pick up a tour and no way was I going with nine fingernails. So I found an open store that sold Krazy Glue, cleaned the nail up nicely, and presto—my fake nails were back on! In hindsight, that random guy at the baths was awfully nice to let me dig around his ass for my "wedding ring."

———•———

Anita absolutely *adored* stories like that. She didn't care how filthy they were. She'd fill me in on what she got up to, too. "I was with this guy," she told me, "and everything was going so well until I turned him around and saw the hair all over his back, and that was it, man. And then it was like, how do I get rid of this fucker 'cause I don't do hairy backs."

Anita had plenty of sexual conquests, and a lot of them led to pregnancies, hence her nine abortions. Sometimes she'd talk about her guilt over having them, but she knew that she couldn't raise kids. Her life was going to be on the road, rough and filled with men. Plus, she was already dealing with drug and alcohol addictions. She didn't think kids could withstand all of the things that she already was. I suspect her dysfunctional mother also made her wonder whether neglect would run in the family too.

Those were some of the saddest talks we ever had; she told me that every abortion she had was illegal. Once, she went to Frank Sinatra's mother, who was called "Hairpin Betty" because she used to do abortions in New Jersey with a hairpin. (That's how Frank got connected to the mafia. Hairpin Betty took care of all the mafia men's girlfriends.) These abortionists would go somewhere in a back room and use a coat hanger or a pin to get rid of the fetus and the women would start bleeding badly. They'd get sent to the hospital in a taxi with a cloth diaper in their panties to hold the blood. The Hairpin Bettys didn't know how to stop the girls from bleeding to death; they just knew how to get rid of the pregnancy. Anita had so many abortions that she reached the point where she tried to be careful about which hospital she went to—she didn't want to get a reputation.

Of course, she later had a reputation for many other things: lying, shoplifting, sex, alcohol, prescription drugs, and for being a heroin addict. She was a lifelong alcoholic—she'd been drinking since she was fourteen—but she got hooked on heroin because alcohol was becoming too expensive. She said a couple of people would give her bumps of heroin, just an itty-bit. Then she started snorting it. Eventually she started shooting it, just an itty-bit. It made her feel every bit as good as alcohol, but it was way cheaper (which she liked because she was always poor, living hand-to-mouth).

Anita traveled with a guy named John Poole, who was a drummer and a working heroin addict. He wasn't the one who got her on it, but he did teach her how to manage it—how to shoot it in between her toes so that no one would see the marks. She eventually got busted for heroin and spent nine months in jail. After she got out, she went right back to using, somehow surviving three overdoses. At the third overdose, she actually stopped breathing and was pronounced dead, the sheet pulled up over her head. A young doctor who was a fan of her music quickly injected her with a new amphetamine shot and it started her heart pumping again.

One summer, she was invited to sing at the 1958 Newport Jazz Festival, which she did high as a kite on junk. She had no idea someone was filming the performance. When the movie *Jazz on a Summer's Day* came out, it featured her singing "Tea for Two," which sparked a renewed interest in her career. She spent the rest of her life traveling with trios and performing at clubs. She was especially popular in Japan and Sweden.

"Avid-day, I'm popular and profitable everywhere except the United States. These American cats just don't get my kind of jazz," she'd say.

Anita was in her fifties when she finally kicked heroin for good. After her last overdose, she wanted off. John Poole had a sister who had a house on the big island of Hawaii. He suggested she go there and use his sister's place (she was out of town) to detox. He knew that withdrawing caused a lot of chills and the warm sand would help. Anita took that advice literally. A day after her arrival, she started to get the DTs and the shakes with chills, so she went to the public beach near the apartment and used her hands to dig a big hole in the sand. She was shaking so badly she could tell she was about to black out. Her goal was to make a hole deep enough and large enough that she could get in, fully cover herself with sand (except for her head), and either "get clean or die."

"Avid-day, I was hoping for the B part," she later told me. "I didn't think I had a shot at the A part, getting clean." She said two kids came over and thought she was building a sandcastle, so they helped her dig the hole. She got in and talked them into covering her up with sand. Their mother came by a little later and inquired what she was doing. Anita was so fucked up and low that she just told this woman *exactly* what she was doing.

The woman came by several times a day for the next eleven days. She fed Anita soup and some water whenever she could keep soup or water down. Anita swears she did not leave that hole for eleven days. She shit and pissed in the hole. She had her period (she thinks) in the hole. When she threw up, the woman would come by and clean her face, then bury the vomit. Anita told me she was so "in and out" of consciousness she doesn't remember all the details. On the eleventh day, the woman dug her out of the hole. Anita was boiling hot, so she went into the water to cool off; her chills had turned to sweats and jumping in the water kept her cool and clean. The woman brought her a few towels and continued to feed her as she lay on top of the sand for another ten days. This woman stuck with Anita for the entire twenty-two days it took for her to detox. She never asked Anita her name nor did Anita ask hers (that she remembered anyway). As Anita described all this, she called her "my guardian angel."

By the twenty-second day, Anita felt clean—weak, but clean—so she went to John Poole's sister's place to get her luggage. Yes, she was 'clean' but with no place and no money, and she was just hankering for a drink. John was in LA on a gig, so she borrowed money from a stranger to call him from a pay phone and he wired her $500 for a ticket back to LA. She picked the money up at Western Union, had a couple drinks at the airport, and, now clean from heroin for the first time in sixteen years, she flew back to the mainland.

"Avid-day, I bet I had ten drinks on the flight back to the West Coast, but I didn't have a desire to shoot." She told me it was her greatest success story, the one she was most proud of for herself. She never touched smack again.

Ironically, a little over a year later, she moved a packet of heroin in a nightclub as a favor for a friend in the audience, who asked her to put it on a window ledge in the ladies' room. It wasn't for Anita, who had zero desire to use it, but that's what friends do. As she was leaving the ladies' room, narcs searched the bathroom, found the heroin, and arrested her for possession. It was a setup. (Anita had had a brief affair with the woman's husband.) She did six months for that one, and it could have been longer as it was her third conviction. Turned out, the judge was a 'fan' and gave her the minimum sentence; he asked if she would sign his album covers before they led her off in cuffs. She thought that was funny, in a sick way, and signed them while laughing. As she was led out of the courtroom, photographers snapped shots of her in the hallway, still laughing. The next day, the headline in the Arts section of the *Los Angeles Times* read: "Songbird O'Day convicted a third time for heroin and finds the whole thing funny."

Anita continued to drink, smoke cigarettes, and puff on the occasional joint or swallow a black beauty (which was highball street amphetamine), until the day she died. But she never touched junk again. She didn't tell the real story about getting clean too often, either.

"I don't like to talk about it, and when I do, like now with you, I have to be drunk and tell it to someone as a cautionary tale, maybe to help someone who's an addict like me and you," she told me. "I don't like to tell it as just another part of my 'fucked up' life."

———————— • ————————

We stayed in touch up until the last years of her life. Towards the end, she was in an assisted living facility in LA because she started having a tendency to fall. Mentally, she was sharp as a tack, but she needed someone around to keep an eye on her.

When she was eighty-seven, she became so frail that it became clear she was dying. A couple of her gay friends moved her to a hospital to see if there was any way she'd get better. The doctor said she was so close to death that she should just stay there and they'd keep her comfortable. Well, Anita wanted to go back to her assisted living center, so she figured out the time of day the nurses changed shifts, took the IV out of her arm, disconnected herself from everything, somehow got herself dressed, and managed to make her way back to that assisted living center. I have no idea how. She walked in, sat down on the couch in the lobby, and told them, "I'm not going to die with a needle in my arm. I worked too hard *not* to have that." They didn't have her room open anymore, but they couldn't exactly kick her out. So they let her stay in the lobby and gave her a blanket. She sat on that couch for about thirty-six hours and that's where she died.

I sometimes think about one of our last calls, where she reiterated that our bond was a special one. "Avid-day, I wish you had been my son. We'd have had a blast. You're like the one I never had but would want, except you're gay. And that's okay, too. We both like men and their equipment, so that would have given us something a mother and son could bond over, yes?"

3.

ARE YOU A BUTCH OR A FEM?

Growing up, I didn't know any gay people (other than my closeted uncle), and the only gay person my mother knew was a guy named Sophie who did her hair every two weeks at a salon in Fell's Point. Because my mom didn't want me loitering in parks or on street corners, she determined that her hairdresser was the bridge towards finding me a boyfriend and romance, or at least sex.

Fell's Point was a trashy neighborhood on the edge of downtown Baltimore. It was here John Waters shot the scenes for some of his movies. The area was loaded with drunk sailors, weird sex shops, and Edie's Thrift Store (owned by resident psycho Edith Massey, who found fame as the Egg Lady in the Waters film *Pink Flamingos*). The epicenter of this offbeat neighborhood was Etta's Gowns, where poor Baltimore girls and women shopped for proms and weddings. (The shop was featured in Waters' original low-budget film, *Hairspray*).

Mother sent me off to meet Sophie on a Saturday afternoon. I walked two blocks past Etta's Gowns (*Plus Sizes a Specialty!*) and into the salon. I said, "Hi, I'm here to see Sophie." The receptionist replied, "Sophie, Sophie... we don't have a Sophie here." And I said, "Yes, you do, he does my mom's hair."

"Oh, THAT Sophie..." She gave me a WTF look, went in the back of the salon, and then out walks this guy. I wouldn't call him fat, but he *was* fat, and incredibly effeminate, what was called in those days "light in his loafers." (Any thoughts of sex with my first gay potential friend went right out the window.) Sophie told me he didn't do men's hair, so he couldn't help me. He gave me an even funnier look than the receptionist did and turned to walk away.

"No, wait," I said. "I'm here because I think I'm gay and my mother, you do her hair, she said to talk to you." He quickly put his hand on my shoulder and we flew out the front door where he lit a cigarette and began talking.

"How do you know you're gay?" he asked. I filled him in on how I'd always known: I enjoyed staring at boys' crotches and I'd seen a psychiatrist who'd agreed I was gay. So, my mother was sure I was gay because a doctor said so.

"And what am I supposed to do about it?" he asked. I came clean: my mother was worried because she knew I wanted to have sex, but I didn't know how to go about it, and she didn't want me hanging out in dangerous places. He thought for a minute, toying with his cigarette.

"Okay, come to my apartment tomorrow afternoon. I'll ask a couple of my friends over and we can help you figure out how you fit into 'the church of Dorothy.'" I was so naïve that I said, "There's a gay church?" He giggled. I promised to be there on Sunday afternoon.

The next afternoon, I took a bus to Sophie's apartment and knocked on the door. There he was, with two other equally effeminate gay guys, all in their twenties. (Or maybe early thirties. I was only fifteen; I couldn't accurately judge ages.) They chatted with me for a few minutes, asking why I was there and what I needed from them. I explained that my mother knew I was getting horny, and that she'd rather I have sex with someone I knew or Sophie knew. That made sense to the three of them, so they decided to take me under their very airy wings.

"So, are you a butch or a fem?" Sophie asked. I had no idea what he meant. He said, "Well, a fem is somebody who feels they're more like a woman, and a butch is somebody who feels they're more like a man."

"Oh. I don't think I'm a butch or a fem. I think I'm just me," I replied.

"Well, do you like to do guys, or do you like them to do you?"

I wasn't sure what he meant by that either, so I asked "Um, can it be both? I just want to be with another guy."

There was whispering among the group and then I was told, "Well, the first thing we need to do is find out if you're a butch or a fem, because we can't go any further with you unless we know that. So, we're going to dress you up as a fem, take you to a gay bar, and see what happens."

Soon, my face felt heavy with more makeup than Gypsy Rose Lee. I wore a brunette bouffant wig that was probably two feet high, which was typical Baltimore style in those days. They squeezed me into a tight, black cocktail dress that Sophia Loren might wear, gave me tits out to here, and put me in 'cha-cha' heels (a low heel that is easier to walk in, allegedly). They were all dressed as women and so off we trudged through Fell's Point at four-fucking-o'clock on a Sunday afternoon to a gay bar. *Everyone* was staring at us. (I didn't know if I was being stared at because everyone knew I was a guy dressed as a girl, because people thought I was actually a pretty woman on my way to a cocktail party, or maybe it was because I couldn't walk in those shoes.) I wasn't enjoying any of it, so I just concentrated on trying to walk in heels for the first time. I was sure all of this was going to lead to some magic moment where I would suddenly know who I was.

We hit a gay bar called The Point, which was dark and narrow and had a long counter bar lined with stools. There was a jukebox and a bartender, and that was about it. No dance floor, no flashy signs. Despite my young age, we had no trouble getting in. Everyone knew everyone, and Sophie and her pals told me to go sit on one of the stools at the bar and they ordered me a ginger ale. It was one of those stools that spun around, so soon enough I started spinning round like I was ten years old. "Wheeee!" Sophie ran over and told me to stop doing that immediately, then went back to her friends. A minute later, a guy came over to me. He looked a little bit like the actor Robert Goulet—obviously handsome and masculine—like he would have chopped down trees for a living had it been a hundred years ago, and he had on a flannel-checked shirt. He said, "Hi, sexy. You're really beautiful."

I'd kind of forgotten that I had dressed up like a girl, and I thought, *Wow, he called me sexy and he thinks I'm beautiful. We're off to a good start here!* And then he said, "Are you here to get laid? Because I'd like to have my way with your little pussy." I thought to myself, *That's weird.*

"I don't have a pussy; I have a penis."

"I know that."

"Well, how could you fuck something I don't have?"

"I meant the other way."

"Oh. My, uh, mouth?"

"No, the *other* other way. Do you take it up the ass?"

"I've never had sex with a guy, so I don't know what I do."

That scared him right off and he quickly walked away. A few minutes later, another guy comes up, but I somehow scared him off, too. Then another man approached, a little younger than the first two. He was dressed like a normal guy and had a cute bubble butt. (I didn't even know what a bubble butt *was* at that time, but I knew his ass turned me on.) We started talking and I shared my situation.

"This is the first time I've ever been dressed up as a girl," I told him.

"Well, how do you feel?" he asked.

"I'm really uncomfortable. I don't want to look like a girl. I just want to be me. But my friends are telling me I need to know if I'm a fem or a butch."

"I can't help you figure out what you are, but I can tell you that whoever is trying to help you is stuck in the way gay people acted ten years ago. What you need to do is find younger people to talk to, because you don't *have* to be either one."

After he walked away, Sophie and her friends came back and said, "What the fuck is wrong with you? You've just had three really attractive men, who we would all kill to have sex with, hit on you and you turned them all away!" I said, "I don't want to be a woman. I just want to be gay." Their collective reply was "Okay, you must be a butch. Come with us."

We paraded back into the sunshine to Sophie's place. They scrubbed my makeup off and examined the outfit I'd arrived in: a pair of corduroy pants and a shirt with a collar and buttons. Apparently, they needed to butch me up a little. They dressed me in a gingham shirt and took two garters (the kind brides wear at weddings to throw at guests for luck) and put them on my upper arms. With my hair now sprayed back, I looked like a member of a barbershop quartet.

Apparently, this was 'butch,' so we all paraded back to the same bar and I sat on the same stool. The first person who walked over to me was a fem, a man dressed in women's clothing.

"Hi, handsome. You look like you'd be a handful," she said.

"Well, thank you," I replied.

"How'd you like to fuck my pussy?"

"But...aren't you a guy?" I asked.

That didn't do it for her, so off she went. A few minutes later, another man dressed like a woman comes over, and there's a similar exchange where I said something wrong. That one was also gone in a flash. My trio of how-to-be-gay experts came over and said, "This is not working out. Let's go." So back we go to Sophie's apartment, where they took off the garters and the gingham shirt.

Next, they asked me if I was a top or a bottom. I didn't know what that meant. "A top means you do the other person," Sophie explained. "A bottom means they do you." I asked if there was something in the middle where you could be both, and that got them really frustrated. One of the trio even got angry and said, "David, we don't think you're fem and we don't think you're butch, but we for sure *don't* know *what* you are or how to help you. Sorry and good luck." And that was that. I caught the bus home, horny and alone, completely confused and frustrated. I felt like I had done something wrong.

Later, I understood what happened. That particular time in gay culture, in the mid-60s, was one of the most stereotypical decades in gay history. The majority of people who were gay, whether they were out or not (and most were not), thought they had to choose whether they were fem or butch. I think those stereotypes actually gave the "Sophies" and the "Robert Goulets" the confidence to *be* gay, because it meant they knew who they were; they could mirror a straight relationship where one was a man and another was a woman. If they didn't choose between being butch or fem, then it would have made them even more insecure and confused. If there was no third choice, no role model for *that* kind of gay, then you couldn't mirror the relationships you saw every day in movies, on TV, in real life. What *were* you?

The gay community had been hidden and marginalized, ridiculed and treated as deviants. For decades, everything about being gay that they read in the papers or saw on TV meant that you were a 'sissy' or a 'queer.' The stereotypical roles within the gay community might have helped some men to *not* feel like a deviant. An entire generation of gay men had resorted to role-playing (before it was called role-playing) because they saw no alternative—these stereotypes were their safety net.

This was the generation before mine, one without the luxury of underground information that started coming out via under-the-counter newsletters and a few brave articles in the *Village Voice*. A new gay culture change was being birthed just as I became old enough to want to be a man who was with another man. There *had* to be a new way to be gay—a "just be you, whatever you are, person"—but I didn't know where to find it.

Eventually I learned just to be me, the gay me with no roles or games. Sophie and her friends weren't so lucky. For their generation, it was whispers in dark alleys and mafia bars where, when the bartender switched on the blue light, it meant stop dancing, stop touching. When the police raided, undergarments were counted, and if you didn't have on at least three pieces of male clothing, you were arrested for deviant behavior and your name was printed in the newspaper. Thousands of men lost their jobs, their families, their dignity, and their lives. The suicide rate in the gay community was never as high as it was in that era. Caught = Death was as prevalent during the late 50s and early 60s as Silence = Death was in the 80s.

———•———

I didn't yet have the maturity and understanding of gay history to realize that Sophie's generation had found the only way they could continue to exist. But I was fifteen years old, I was still horny and hoping to hook up, and I had no idea how to go about getting laid, let alone how I wanted to be labeled. I didn't know who else to ask, so I told my high school guidance counselor that I was gay. For some reason, I thought she'd know a cute boy to hook me up with or offer me, duh, guidance. (Why the fuck did they call them guidance counselors anyway?) Just as in elementary school, she walked me down to the principal's office to "talk more" about it. The principal, for some inexplicable reason, called in the PE teacher, Mr. Dick.

Mr. Dick was a jerk. (Funny how that sentence could also read "Mr. Jerk was a dick.") He was your stereotypical, insecure PE teacher who probably had a little penis. (At least I hope so.) He used words like "pansy." As in "If you can't climb that rope all the way up to the top, you're a pansy!" or "If you can't do ten backward rolls, you're a faggot!" Mr. Dick came into the office and the principal explained to him that I was a homosexual. My PE teacher stood there with his hands on his hips and said, "So you're asking me what we should do with this faggot?" The principal, correcting him, said, "What we're trying to do is help David, not make him feel worse than he already does about what he is." To be clear, I didn't feel bad about what I was; I only wanted to *get laid*. But I realized that neither of them were interested in helping me find a boyfriend, so they were useless. I had been down this road many times before in three other schools. I knew the ending to yet another of these encounters.

The guidance counselor later called me into her office and said, "David, after a conversation, we've decided that probably the most important thing we can do to help you is to take you out of phys ed," she said. "We think that since there's only one big shower room, where twenty boys shower at a time, and everybody's naked and can see each other, that might not be a good place for you to be." That was fine with me since I hated gym class. I asked if I could work in the library instead.

"No, I'm not explaining it well," she said slowly. "You don't have to *do* phys ed, but you still have to show up for phys ed." There was work for me to do in the laundry room attached to the shower room.

During the next PE class, the gym teacher—being careful not to touch me in case I was gay-tagious—took me to this laundry room. It was the size of a small bedroom with three washers and dryers, a long table where you could fold towels, and shelving. There was a large rectangular window, like the kitchen pass-through you might find in older homes. Mr. Dick-Jerk asked if I knew how to use a washer and dryer, which I did. Though we were too poor to have either (except for the washer my father used to blow up our house), I would occasionally go to the nearby laundromat to wash clothes. I'd be washing and folding the towels, he hissed, and then handing them to guys through the window.

Well, it was like Mecca before me! I could see perfectly into the long shower room. *Holy fuck*, I thought, *I'm going to see every guy in this school naked. What are these teachers thinking?* I got a boner walking home from school that day just pondering it! If the gym teacher had been able to bring himself to even look at me, he would have connected the dots. But he didn't; I was a disgusting faggot not worthy of eye contact.

I started to wash and dry and fold all those towels. Good thing I'd never taken a cruise or I would have, with certainty, folded them into swans and rabbits; my body and what was left of my reputation would have been beaten to shit, for sure. My first day as laundress, the guys came in and I had a nice, fluffy, warm towel waiting for each one. (Obviously, I was good boyfriend, if not marriage material, based on my laundry skills alone.) As each guy walked up and put out their hand to get a towel, I of course looked down to check them out, a further reinforcement of my crotch-staring addiction. When the guys turned away, I'd look down again at their asses. Everyone in line could see me doing this, which never occurred to me, mesmerized as I was by the parade of cocks and asses. A couple guys would put their hand over their dicks when they caught on that I was ogling them. This reinforced something else: students are smarter than teachers. My fellow students knew *exactly* where my eyes were going.

I was the school laundress for forty-five minutes, three times a week, a gig that lasted a few months. Sometimes, when I was handing a towel over, I dropped it to see if I could catch someone bend over, but the window blocked the bottom part of my view. I knew poking my head completely out the pass-through was not a smart option, so that was a failed experiment. Finally, enough of my fellow students complained about me staring at their dicks that the guidance counselor came by one day after towel duty and told me I didn't have to go to gym class at *all* anymore. They were going to put me in the library for those periods instead (which was exactly what I fucking suggested in the first place). While my last towel day was a sad one for me, I did create a list of exactly who I was going to try to put the moves on, based on body type and, uh, a few other things. That list still exists in one of my diaries.

———————•———————

I was happy in the library; the two librarians liked me and I liked them. There was a shelf of long-playing record albums, various spoken-word theatre plays and musicals. I would grab one, take it to the back of the library office with a headset connected to the record player, and listen to the plays of Edward Albee, Oscar Wilde, Joe Orton (*Prick up your Ears* was my favorite play that year), Shakespeare, and musicals. I learned more about English, theatre, and culture from those recordings than I ever learned from any of my school classes. There was also a huge, floor-to-ceiling glass showcase in the library entrance that the librarians never knew what to do with, but I had ideas. I could start doing displays in the showcase, like the window displays in department stores. They said to go for it.

At the time, there was a Miss Baltimore County Junior High School beauty pageant set to take place in our auditorium. I got inspired. I took the bus to Etta's Gowns in Fell's Point, went inside, and explained to the manager that I wanted to borrow a prom gown to highlight in our display case. I lied and said I'd give the store credit at the bottom of the case and that someone in the beauty pageant would wear the dress. Somehow, they agreed.

Next, I needed a mannequin. I borrowed one from my (closeted) Uncle Joel who managed a G.C. Murphy store. One of my sisters supplied the wig. Then I borrowed a red wagon from the kid downstairs and dragged this mannequin in three pieces to school the next day. I dressed it up in the gown and put it in the case. The girls at school were really paying attention to it, oohing and aahing over the gown. It turned out I was a hit as a window dresser! It also turned out to be a short-lived career.

Not long after my success with the beauty pageant window, I saw a book in a local bookstore titled *Is God Dead?* The librarians weren't paying much attention to me, so I thought it would be really cool to do an *Is God Dead?* window display. I tried to get another mannequin from my (closeted) gay uncle; I thought I could dress it up as God and hang it up in the case with wire, maybe with a noose around His neck so that He was indeed dead. No dice. Uncle Joel didn't want to lend me a mannequin after I explained the concept. At the time, I didn't know there were blow-up dolls, so I used a balloon as God's head, put a white sheet over the balloon, utilized some coat hangers with crepe paper for wings, and glued cotton balls on God's balloon-head face for a beard. My mom's tinfoil-covered darning hoop served as a halo. (I figured even though He was dead, from a theatrical point of view, the guy needed a halo.) Maybe it looked more like a ghost than God, but I put some manly stage makeup on the balloon and hoped for the best. This display didn't go over as well with the school administration. The next day, I was called into the principal's office (at this point I was planning to redecorate it, I had been there so often), where the head librarian was also seated. She asked, "What were you thinking, doing an *Is God Dead?* window display?" I said, "It's a book. I'm advertising a book and you're a library, so what's the problem?"

Well, that took care of my library duty. For the rest of the school year, I sat in the cafeteria during PE using my #2 Ticonderoga pencil to sketch the crotches on my "potential boyfriends" list. The following year, the library let me back in, but with the understanding that the display case was off-limits. Thus ended my window display career.

A few years before this, I'd decided I wanted to be an actor. I'd gone downtown by myself one day after school and found a little community theatre called The Spotlighters. It held eighty people, with seats on four sides of the small square stage. The theatre entrance was in an alleyway, which I later learned was one block from a gay cruising park. The theatre had been there for fifteen years, and every month they'd change the shows, which would run four nights a week. I saw they had a performance run of *The Seven Year Itch* coming up, and I had read that play because I loved to read plays, which I'd get from the public libraries. I knew there was a part in it for a little boy, and I knew I looked younger than my ripe old age of twelve. I walked up to the woman who was in charge. Her name was Audrey Herman, and she was one of the most important people in unprofessional theatre in Baltimore at the time.

I said, "You're doing this show and I think you need a little boy for it, and I could do that." She thought I was cute, but she said, "The shows are at eight o'clock. Do you have a parent that would agree to this and drive you here and back?" I told her my mother would definitely agree to it (not adding she probably wouldn't even know about it as she would be passed out well before the end of the shows), and I'd just catch buses back and forth. Audrey didn't like the idea of my taking a bus at 10:30 p.m. but said I could play the role, which happened at the very beginning of the first act of the play, then leave before the show was finished so I could catch an earlier bus home. I had two lines: "Mom!" and "Mom, no!"

"What about the curtain call?" I asked.

"What about the curtain call?"

"Well, if I'm going to be onstage, I need to come out at the end to take a bow and for the applause." She laughed.

"Oh, you've got it bad already." She agreed that if my mother agreed to it, I could stay until the very end, to take my curtain call.

I did the run of that play and then did several more shows. My Aunt Penny gave me a hatpin to stick in my jacket lining for my late bus rides home and told me, "If any man tries to touch you, you stick him with this pin!" (I didn't tell her that I was dying for a man, any man, to touch me, and a pin was not what I had in mind to stick him back with.)

Working with The Spotlighters was where I learned about theatre life and lighting and sound, which I often ran from backstage. I never had tons of lines if I did have a stage role, but I would help take care of the tech and the props backstage, and especially if a play had food snacks as a prop; I'd shove those crackers or Triscuits or cheese cubes into my mouth when no one was looking because I was always hungry. Bus fare to and from my theatre gigs came out of the food budget, which was already nearly nonexistent. I continued to hone my skills on the technical stuff and added colored gels on the stage lights to create different atmospheres for the scenes in the plays. Plus, I already knew how to work a tape recorder from my years of speech therapy, so I was useful. My acting and tech career was short-lived, though, since eventually I grew a little bored of it. I was becoming too old to play a child, and I was too young for adult roles, so I left community theatre and went back to my other favorite hobby—looking at cute boys' crotches.

———•———

There was a guy in my grade who I found interesting. He was what you would call a "bad kid." Physically he was scrappy looking, but he had a great body. He took mechanic shop—those little grease marks on his face after that class? Major turn-on—and he didn't give a shit about learning anything. But the previous year, whenever I'd hand him a towel in gym class and looked down at his body, he didn't look away. One day during phys ed, I walked down to the track oval, sat down on the grass, and waved at him. He came over, sat next to me, and said, "I didn't think you were allowed to take this class because you're gay." (He used the word gay! Instant tent in my pants.) I told him it was true. Then I got the nerve to ask him if he maybe wanted to, I don't know, have a date or something? He thought for a second and said, "I've never dated a guy. Does anyone know you're asking me to do this? What would a date even be?" I told him he could come over to the apartment I shared with my mom who worked late and we could have a Coke—pause—or something. Then I mentioned I really liked looking through the Sears catalog; if he was interested, we could look at furniture and stuff. (I would have bought *Car Mechanics* magazine to lure him home if I had to.) Well, somehow the Sears catalog worked. He said sure and that's what we did after school that day. There we were, drinking a Coca-Cola and looking through the Sears catalog on the couch together.

We started with Mediterranean furniture—very popular in white trash Baltimore—then moved on to men's underwear. (My idea; he wanted to look at bikes.) I put my hand on his crotch and he didn't move it away. Neither of us knew what to do next, so we lay on top of my mother's bed and felt each other up. I think I maybe put my mouth on his dick and tried to get it down my throat, but with little success. I didn't know what a climax was yet, and I don't know if he did either. After about ten minutes, we stopped. We never really interacted again after that, which was fine. I'm pretty sure he wasn't gay, just bored and unafraid of me, so he decided to experiment a little bit. I later discovered that the bad-boy risk-takers made for excellent sex. I *was*, however, about to learn what a climax was. Because my big sister was going to teach me.

———————•———————

It was at this time my older sister Carol decided she was: A. a lesbian and B. going to be a stripper. I don't think she was actually a lesbian so much as an exhibitionist who loved to have her ego stroked. Lesbians found her beautiful and, since the bloom was off the rose with her marriage (she no longer found her husband "sexy"), she decided to try something new. She needed constant emotional and sexual praise, which she wasn't getting in the marriage—plus, she might also have thought it would shake people up.

Carol was always rather innovative in her approach. When I told her I didn't know what a "French kiss" was, she said, "It's when you stick your tongue in each other's mouths and suck and dance around inside with your tongue. Do you want me to show you?" I couldn't wrap my head around sticking my tongue in a girl's mouth, let alone my sister's mouth! I told her I thought the idea was gross—kissing *her*, not French kissing. She said, "Okay, what about Randy?" Randy was her husband; he was really handsome and had a huge cock (I knew this because she told me). Though she'd lost interest in him, she also was a combination of a straight-up honest person and a complete liar. The straight-up honest part surfaced as she walked over to Randy and said, "My brother doesn't know how to French kiss. I want you to teach him." In her mind, she saw absolutely nothing wrong in that; she thought of it as a lesson, like a math teacher might approach algebra with a new student. I was already laughing because the look on his face was priceless.

He stuttered and stammered and said, "You want me to tongue-kiss your *brother*?" She replied, "Well, he won't practice on me and you know he likes guys and I know he thinks you're hot, so what's the problem? It's just a kiss and he's gotta learn from somebody."

After about fifteen minutes of this back-and-forth with me sitting on the couch eating popcorn, hoping I would get to tongue-kiss him, they reached an agreement. Carol decided I would practice using my tongue to kiss Randy, but on his hand. She told me to put my lips on the top of his hand and make "figure eights" while using my tongue to lick and tickle the skin on his hand. She added, "And suck hard while you're doing it!" Randy was very much in love with my sister and knew their relationship was on the rocks. He also knew Carol was a little like Lucy Ricardo, always coming up with harebrained ideas.

Randy sat next to me and offered me his hand. I found myself, yet again, already with a hard-on; I put my lips on his hand as instructed, made figure eights, sucked and tickled with my tongue, then came up for air. My sister may have been a natural-born shit-stirrer, but she also knew how to 'read a room.' She said, "Try it again and this time breathe through your nose while you're kissing or you'll pass out before it gets good." My efforts two lessons later were better, and she asked Randy how it felt, what he thought. He said "Jesus Christ, Carol, I can't tell if he's a good kisser with him wiggling his lips and tongue around my hand—this is nuts!"

She stood up, walked over to him, and nose-to-nose said, "French kiss my brother right now or I'm packing and getting the fuck out of here." And it was clear she meant it. I was on the verge of using what was left of my lips to say, "Okay, Randy's right, this is nuts. I'm just going to go home." But before I could, Randy grabbed me with his big strong arms and planted a French kiss on me I'll never forget. It probably only lasted a minute, but it felt like an hour. His tongue explored my mouth and he sucked on my lips and made, what I thought at least, were sexy noises. I knew he could feel my hard-on pushing against his thigh, but he just kept right at it. Finally, we both came up for air. I practically swooned, weak-kneed. I had to sit down. I was in love with his mouth. I couldn't help myself, saying "One more time and I think I'll have this down pat." Well, that went over like a fart in church. By the look on his face, my lesson was not getting a redo. But what a kiss!

Carol left him a week later anyway, for a lesbian named Spike who worked in a shoe factory gluing heels onto men's oxfords and came home at night flying high on the fumes.

Carol had just turned thirty. She was beautiful and in full bloom, with a lithe body and an exhibitionist streak. She was a handful, someone who liked to do things that were considered the things you shouldn't do. She'd pushed the envelope her whole life and the idea of throwing herself into the world of stripping fit right in. Spike was delighted; she was proud that "her woman" would show off her body to men each night but come home to her.

It was during this period that I thought I had hooked me an actual boyfriend. He was a school friend who was trying to start a garage band and he wanted me in "for flavor." Bob was blond, TV teen-star beautiful, sweet, and not afraid of me. We kissed some, which is where my French kiss lesson came in handy. I thought I had him in the bag. One evening, I asked my sister if I could bring him over and use her spare bedroom to "seal the deal." She said sure, and I brought him over the next evening. She gave us each a shot of whiskey, and at only sixteen, we were both flying high already. He knew what was about to happen—that we would get naked and have sex. (I didn't know what actual sex was yet, but I hoped he did.) Worst-case scenario, we would both be naked in bed and I could at last use my hands to feel everything I had only fantasized about.

I went to the bathroom to pee and primp, and when I came back into the living room, my boyfriend Bob wasn't there and neither was my sister! I looked in the kitchen, the basement, the backyard—nothing. I went back into the living room and heard a bed upstairs, squeaking. Fuck, I knew what had happened. I went up the stairs, trying not to make any noise—not that they would have heard me anyway—and opened her bedroom door. There was Bob, screwing my sister nine ways to tomorrow, her legs wrapped around his hips. Fuck, fuck, fuck, fuck! He was *my* boyfriend! She saw me and said, with a little laugh, "Want to join in?" She meant it. It wouldn't have bothered her in the least if her little brother got naked and joined the sexfest. That's just the way she was. She didn't have filters or a moral compass; it was all just a fun game to her. And I had a lot of that, too. I quickly got over being mad and left the room. I picked up my school knapsack and walked home. She and my handsome never-to-be-boyfriend Bob had a three-day affair and then she called me and said, "Honey, you didn't miss anything. I even had to teach him how to screw!"

Carol would steal. She would say things she shouldn't, fuck people she shouldn't (uh, *hello*), lie, flirt with anyone, take her fun anywhere she could get it with no regrets. Carol had no concept of the consequences of her actions; she lived in the present moment, albeit a reckless present moment. I later learned she had a mental affliction called antisocial personality disorder—she was unable to feel remorse or guilt. She tried her best to be my friend during those years, and she did the best she could to help me. Not only did I learn how to French kiss, but I also learned how to jerk off.

 I would often go to Carol's place after school or when I hooked school, because I could say and do whatever I wanted and drink liquor. I thought it was very exotic that she was a stripper. But I never brought a boy with me again; she had the upper hand on that trick. Carol was now going by the strip-name "Devil Delicious, Satan's Slut." She had all these pretty costumes with sparkles on them in her bedroom, along with every kind of makeup and lots of wiglets. It was a gay teenage boy's treasure trove and where I discovered what was later called "gender-fuck"—a kind of cross-dressing look using both male and female clothing and makeup.

 Baltimore had a thriving market for seamstresses who made strip clothes. It was a specific art that was in high demand as there were over thirty strip clubs and theatres in the three-block area of downtown Baltimore known as 'The Block.' In a traditional strip show, the performer came out in an elaborate and tight evening gown. That's act one. The performer's sultry body movements slowly ease the gown off, usually ending with a slow zipper tease down the back of the gown. Act two, it was 'panels and bra.' Panels are pieces of gauze-like or transparent pleated fabric sewn to a kind of hip belt. These panels could be used by holding them in your hands and twirling. The fabric would make swirls around the stripper's body, almost like their body was in the center of a flower and the panels were the petals. The panels could be taken from the hips, swung around the neck, and used as wings or a gossamer-like cape. The bra didn't have much use other than be tight enough to jiggle the breasts. In act three, the panels went away and the bra came off, revealing pasties (stiff mini-cones of fabric) that covered the nipples (this was the law in most states). These were paired with a G-string. Then the stripper would go into whatever novelty acts she had to end the show and get the johns fired up.

One day, I was hooking from school at Carol's while she got ready for work. She was telling me a long story and said, "Come into the bathroom with me while I shower." This was not an unusual request; she was often naked in my presence, and it didn't occur to either of us that it might be considered odd. She took her usual ritual of a 'Baltimore Shower': with a drink and a lit cigarette in one hand, she stepped into the shower sideways and used her free hand to soap one side of her body and rinse. Then she'd move the drink and cigarette to the other hand, turn, and wash her other side. This way, she ended up clean but without having to stop drinking or smoking. It was my first time ever seeing someone multitask.

After she dried off, I would use red lipstick to apply two X's to her ass cheeks, which she would then rub in to give her stripper butt a "glow." It was then that Carol asked if I knew how to jerk off. I didn't; I wasn't even sure I knew what that was. So, she decided to teach me. (The French kiss lesson went well, so I thought *go for it, David.*)

She passed me a small plastic bag with some hand lotion in it, told me to go into the bathroom, think dirty thoughts, pull the bag up and down over my dick, then see what happened. I was very good at following instructions, so I did and soon I had my first climax. I thought it was a miracle! I came out of the bathroom, and my sister asked me if I'd climaxed. I told her I thought so—that something happened that felt *really* good and stuff came out of my cock. I asked her if she wanted to see it because it was in the plastic bag. (I thought this miracle that my body did was right up there with the immaculate conception.) She declined and just said, "Yep, you climaxed. Women can do it too, you know." Bummer! More competition. When I asked her for more info about women's orgasms and whether stuff also came out of them, she just laughed and said, "Honey, I have a feeling you'll never need to know that."

———•———

One day, Carol called me at home and said there was a nighttime gig in one of the strip clubs where she worked and that I might be good at it. It involved sound and stage lighting.

"I told the club manager about you and how you had done lights and sound for plays in schools and in a small theatre downtown. She said for you to come in and talk to her if you were interested in a job."

"But I'm underage," I said.

"Honey, in these clubs it doesn't matter," she explained. "All the politicians get paid off, plus no one would ever see you in the back doing lights and sound because these clubs are dark except onstage." She told me that all the clubs on The Block were mafia-owned; the cops were also paid off to look the other way. I asked her how much the job paid.

"It pays twenty dollars a night, thirty dollars on Friday and Saturday as there are three shows those nights. And they pay nightly, in cash. It's the same schedule as me—five nights a week."

That was a *lot* of money for me in 1966. And I wanted it. I could help my mom, we could eat better, I could buy some clothes and books and magazines, and it was show business! I could be back in show business and would make money, which would make me a professional! I was chomping at the bit to meet this manager and was determined to get the job. Little did I know that my *real* education and my *real* life was about to begin.

4.

A GAY WALKS INTO A STRIP CLUB

At sixteen years old, I got my first job in a strip club as a lighting and sound tech. All of the strip clubs on The Block in downtown Baltimore were mafia-owned, and Harry, Jerry, and Larry, my mob connections, didn't give a shit who ran the lighting and sound in their clubs, as long as the girls were well lit and looked good and the men kept buying drinks. With thirty some strip joints in a three-block area, the notoriously sleazy Block was the Mall of America for strippers and the johns who sought their services. I had never applied for a job before, so I was nervous when I interviewed with the club's owner, someone the girls called "Madam," not because of what I might see—my sister the exhibitionist had shown me everything Mother Nature gave to women and then some, and none of it excited me. (Duh, can you spell *gay*?) But I really, really wanted the money, which was a *lot*.

"Why do you think we work in a strip club, David?" Carol asked.

"Because you love to show off your body and have everyone stare at you?" I replied.

"No. We don't fuck around. We get *paid*."

My sis, always the optimist, *did* think the pay was good, not knowing that most of the girls in these clubs made more money from hustling drinks and doing uh...other things...to pull in even more cash on the side.

At my interview, Madam asked me basic questions. What did I know about lighting and sound? Would working around naked women be a problem? (Nope!) Was I reliable? Things like that. When she asked if I did drugs, I said, "Only aspirin." (I had no idea what she was asking. I was still surprisingly innocent in many ways.) She liked me and my answers and said she was looking for someone for five nights a week. The pay was $15 a night.

"Oh," I said, looking away.

"What's wrong?" she asked.

I told her my sister said I'd be making $20 a night. I gave her a little sob story.

"I figured I could take the job on top of school for twenty dollars because I really need the money to help my mother…"

Madam rolled her eyes—she was no fool—but she said fine, $20 it is. This was the first time I negotiated my salary and it worked! It wasn't the first time I lied to get something, of course, but it wasn't a bad coup for a very gay, very young teenager to start working in one of the shadiest, mafia-owned cross sections of America.

I was soon spending my nights in the dark underbelly of strip clubs, working alongside women like my sister, Carol (aka Devil Delicious, Satan's Slut), and her coworkers, all with their own amazing monikers. There was Patty Wagon, whose tagline was "I'll take you away." There was Candy Cane ("Lick this"), Candy Barr ("Eat this"), and Tempest Storm ("She blows in fast"). Pretty Pussy. Bubbles Galore was the champagne girl, who took a bubble bath in a big plexiglass champagne flute. There was Ronnie Bell and her Twin Liberty Bells. The biggest name on The Block was Blaze Starr, aka "The hottest blaze in burlesque," who was so well-known she didn't need a tagline. She was also the not-so-secret mistress of Louisiana Governor Earl K. Long.

The clubs were divided. Some strip clubs were in old vaudeville theatres that still had theatre seating. Other clubs were cheap, foul-smelling dives with little elevated platforms where the women would strip, surrounded by tables and chairs. (Pole dancing did not exist until years later, so there were no poles onstage.) If a stripper wanted to twirl, she did so with her pastie tassels or by spinning quickly on the platform or stage in outrageously high heels.

On my first night at work, I came in early to take inventory of what I had to work with. I looked at the lighting setup and realized it'd need a little rearranging. I said to Madam, "Would you mind if I refocused a lot of these lights, because it looks like they're all pointed towards the center of the stage. Don't the girls work back and forth across the platform and sometimes move around the tables?" She replied that they did.

"And don't the guys want to see the girls regardless of where they're sitting and not just if they're sitting in the middle of the room?" She agreed again.

"I know how to fix that," I said.

She arched a severely painted eyebrow at me, and her thin, scarlet lips tilted up slightly. (I would later learn this meant that she was pleased.) I was given permission to play around with all the tech, which is what I did. Some nights I'd come in before the show when the bar was open. I'd climb a ladder and focus the lights or rearrange them for better effect, moving the speakers around for a richer sound. A few weeks after I started, I found some gels (heat-resistant colored gelatin) and experimented with different colors to see how they could affect different skin tones and make the strippers look more appealing. Later I stole some new gels from my school auditorium and brought them to the club. I learned more about lighting various skin tones. This knowledge would serve me well later in my cabaret career, when I was lighting jazz greats like Ella Fitzgerald and Sarah Vaughn. I'm not sure if anyone had considered lighting different-colored skin tones before, but I definitely did it for my strippers. (*My* strippers—obviously I became very territorial very fast. I thought I was the Steven Spielberg of The Block.)

At the time I first started working in clubs, they had to have a 'cabaret license' to operate. When the singer Billie Holiday got popped in Baltimore and sent to prison, it was because she was performing in a club that had let their cabaret license expire. Her own performer cabaret license had also expired. (Some say the authorities purposefully revoked it because she sang the anti-lynching song, "Strange Fruit," to white audiences.) After that, Harry, Jerry, and Larry took the cabaret license thing very, very seriously. A cabaret license meant there had to be one musician and one comedian at the strip joint every night it was open. The comedians were not professionals but more like high school science teachers who just wanted to see some titties. They weren't funny, and they *weren't* comedians, but you needed at least five minutes' worth of material to 'be legal' so that the girls could come out and strip to recorded music. (Each girl gave me the tapes or albums with little Scotch tape marks where they wanted their songs to start.)

As the start of the eight o'clock show, these 'comedians' would jump onstage and the audience would hear some real zingers like:

"Ladies and gentlemen! Oh, I guess I mean just gentlemen! I want you to know that all our girls here are really clean! So clean, they douche with chlorophyll!"

(He'd hold out a little bottle of green mouthwash.)

"And we have a motto! Our motto is 'If your tongue is green, your girl is clean; but if your tongue is brown, you're too far down!'"

Then the drummer would play his little "ba-dum-chi!" The fake comic would tell two more awful jokes before the strippers came out, which is what everyone was there for.

But it was 1967 and the times were a-changing everywhere. Strip clubs were no exception—this was the start of the demise of the art form of 'burlesque,' as it was morphing into solo sexual acts. The original burlesque houses had real comedians with their seltzer bottles, jugglers, and dogs doing backflips. It was a legit show; some of the performers were members of AGMA, the circus union. The burlesque dancers would enter the stage wearing lavish, yet revealing evening gowns complete with elbow-length gloves and a feather boa, waving bejeweled cigarette holders, hand fans, or other costume props. Their acts were one big tease that ended in nothing but pasties and a G-string. While showing nipples was still technically illegal, the younger hippie strippers didn't care and would go 'full monty' with abandon. Some started doing wilder acts, like shooting Ping-Pong balls from their vaginas. (Ronnie Bell could even produce smoke rings from a cigar. I was so impressed! I still couldn't smoke a cigarette without coughing.)

These younger, newer girls didn't care about the art of the striptease. Many had shaved off all their pubes—very exotic! Stripping became blatantly sexual, and this angered, embarrassed, and bewildered older strippers, who considered themselves sensual performers, not porn stars. Honestly, what the younger girls did was pretty much straight porn; I saw some real down and dirty stuff. (And some oddly funny things too. One girl was also a sword swallower and another was a fire-eating stripper. It was a little hard to make these carny sideshows look sexy.) But it *was* Baltimore, so a few girls also had *very* high hair. (One girl could only play certain clubs because the height of her 'do made her taller than the drop ceiling.) Because the new girls were just getting naked, they didn't need gimmicks like the older strippers. (Unless they really were unattractive; then a gimmick could take the focus off their face.) Most were content to get naked, play with themselves, take the money and run, though a few still loved an elaborate stage act.

Blaze Starr, famous in part because of her association with politicians and organized crime, loved lavish acts and costumes. During her trademark number, she'd be on top of a bed with a smoke machine and fan underneath it. She would cut up strips of red and orange silk and tie them to the bed. Then she'd do her thing—grinding and rubbing herself on top of the bed—saying, "Oh, I'm getting hotter. I'm getting hotter!" All of this smoke would start blowing out of her bed, and she'd end with "Oh, I'm on fire! I'm a-*blaze*!" Blaze also worked with an old, toothless tiger. She'd smear honey on herself and let him lick it off, pretending to get off. Of course, she called the tiger Tony, which always made me giggle. She'd hear my muffled laughter and give me a quick wink from the stage. The customers loved the toothless tiger act, but had PETA been around then, that act definitely would have closed the very same night it opened.

One night, my high school science teacher came into the club while I was working. We saw each other, then pretended we didn't. But it gave me an idea. There was a skeleton in his classroom. (I have no idea if it was real or not.) A few days after I saw him at the club, I told him I needed to borrow the skeleton. He asked me why and I said, "You really don't want to know. I just need it." He gave me a look, and I gave him a look back that said I knew where he'd been a few nights earlier. He gave me the skeleton. I took it to the club, painted it with dayglow, and gave it to my sister Carol for the new act I'd thought up for her. She'd pretend to have sex onstage with the glow-in-the-dark skeleton, while I shined a black light on her. She put a condom on a rubber crutch-tip (the hot-dog-shaped pad that protects the armpit at the top of a crutch), filled it with lotion mixed with dayglo paint, and placed it between the skeleton's legs. At the end of her act, she'd bite off the tip of the condom and squeeze it to look like it was cumming all over her. I remembered the black-light effect from when the elementary school nurse was checking my head for lice. No one used them at the time, so I introduced black lights to the world of strip clubs. A year later? Everyone used black lights. Theatre lesson learned: Every gimmick was only good for a year before it made the rounds. Keep it fresh or get it gone. It was an invaluable insight into show business, one that I never forgot later in my career.

The women on The Block weren't paid much to strip, not even the headliners. If a headliner stripped for six nights (from 8:00 p.m. until 2:00 a.m.), she only made about $200 a week. The women who weren't headlining made even less—about $100 a week, which was not enough to live on. Instead, they made significant money at the bar (and sometimes with their hands and bodies, too). In between shows, a girl would walk into the audience, sit next to a guy, put her hand on his thigh and say, "Honey, buy me a drink." Or "You want some alone time with me? Buy me a bottle." Every time they got a customer to buy them a drink or a bottle, they'd get a colored plastic stir-stick. At the end of the night, their sticks and the different colors defined their worth: $1 to $2 for each drink, $15 for a bottle of 'champagne.' That's how they made their money. They were especially skilled at walking by a table and accidentally spilling a drink with their elbows ("Oh, handsome, I'm so sorry, let's get you another drink!") and they often worked in teams, like pickpocketing urchins from *Oliver Twist*. At the end of the night, the bartender would dole out the cash—everything was done in cash since the clubs were mafia-owned and used for money laundering. The managers and the madams knew to the dollar how much each girl made each night and how they were making it. If a girl had a slow night, they'd get a little talking-to—told to up their game or get out. Harry, Jerry, and Larry weren't mean to the girls. They looked after them, not because they were fatherly, but because they brought in money. They also made sure the women were aware of what was called 'mafia arm.'

Maybe the girls would get into a fight over something—accusing another stripper of stealing her gimmick, her music, her earrings, something. A mafia guy would come in, listen to the story, and basically be their stripper judge. ("You can't use the black light anymore" or "You can share the black light, it's not a gimmick, it's a lighting device" or "The headliner always gets her first choice of music, change yours.") If someone caused trouble after they were told not to, or if the mob thought a stripper was running her mouth about club business, they would get the mafia arm. This is when you take a person's arm and pull it up over their head, but instead of letting go, you pull it all the way behind their back until the bone that holds the collarbone is dislocated or broken. It's painful and impossible to put back together. Even if you did manage to, it didn't look right, so your stripper days were over. A couple female club managers who I worked with had mafia arm, including the one at the Two O'Clock Club, where I worked with Blaze Starr. Harry, Jerry, and Larry liked it when mafia-armed women became managers; they were a visual message to other girls not to fuck around. A picture is worth a thousand words, they say.

To make *real* money, the women who were unskilled at dancing or who weren't particularly attractive would do more than strip. Sometimes, if a john bought a bottle, they'd offer a hand job under the table. They would play with his dick with one hand and use the other to turn the bottle upside down in the ice bucket. See, the buckets had holes drilled into the bottom so that the liquor would empty onto the carpet. (This is why strip joints stunk of mildew.) They'd say things like "Oh, honey, I know you want me to finish you off, but look, this bottle is empty! Let's get another one!" A stupid trick, but it worked well—usually. Sometimes they would fuck it up. This was called 'glucking'; if you turned the bottle upside down at the wrong angle, the booze would gush out and make this *GLUCK, GLUCK, GLUCK* sound. The girls would laugh and applaud, and most of the regulars would laugh too. They knew what was up. Plenty of the johns were pros, as much as the girls were. They had their favorite clubs, their favorite girls. They knew if they wanted to get hand jobs or blow jobs, they had to go to the bar and pay for a bunch of drink sticks, and then give the sticks to the girl before they saw any action. All the tables in the clubs were covered with long, white tablecloths (the mafia also owned all the commercial laundry services), so the hand jobs or blow jobs could happen under the table. Some clubs even had a balcony upstairs where the sex stuff happened—nobody cared, everyone just turned a blind eye. Even better, a john could watch a girl ride someone on the upstairs balcony—it was like watching a porn for free—which got him fired up enough to say, "I'll have what *he's* having!"

It didn't take long for me to absolutely fall in love with this job. It was sick, twisted, lie-infused, cringeworthy—so many of the things I resonated with from an early age. I'd catch two buses and get there for the first show at 8:00 p.m., because the johns had to get off work, go home, and then get to the clubs downtown. The doors opened at 7:00 p.m., but some girls didn't get up until 5:00 p.m. The second show was at 10:00 p.m., then there'd be a mini-show at midnight (weekdays) and a full show at midnight on Saturday. The clubs were closed on Sunday due to the blue laws. Then I'd catch two buses, get off within a mile of my house, and start walking home. I'd be in bed by about 2:00 a.m., wake up for high school the next day, and do it all over again—ah, youth.

I liked the strippers. I mostly cared about playing with the lighting, but they were all really nice to me—more caring than my siblings had ever been, except Carol. They were my ad hoc family and they didn't care about me being gay. It was obvious why they'd pal up to me: I offered no threat; I wanted nothing from them.

It was Penny Cillan ("Good for What Ails You") who introduced me to the joy of hashish. Penny came up to me one night and asked, "Hey, want some hashish?" I'd never tried it before, so I said sure. I loved it. It was such a lovely, melting feeling. It was like the jazz of marijuana—smoky, slow, mellow. We smoked it on a wig pin— it was a small black sticky ball, sort of like what chewed gum might look like, and we'd light it with a plastic Bic lighter and inhale it when it started producing smoke. Close one nostril with your finger and snort the smoke right up the other one.

Soon I was smoking hash six nights a week while working at the strip clubs and still going to high school in the mornings. (Don't ask me how, and don't ask my grades.) I was making $30 a night in cash and

$40 on weekends. That was $200 a week for a high school kid—much more than a secretary made back then. I was in the money, but I didn't save a lick of it—not surprising. Had anyone ever given me a lesson in money? Was I ever even *around* anyone with money? How the fuck was I supposed to know what to *do* with it? Like love, it was a lesson I had yet to learn.

I would give my mother money to help pay for food, but she never took much. With the rest of it, I just bought whatever I wanted, whenever I wanted. I bought a pair of expensive bell bottoms, which was a big deal. If the kids in school were wearing cool clothes, I bought the same ones. And the food! I would gorge myself on butterscotch Tastykakes, which back then were the equivalent of Godiva chocolates, at least to me. It was such a luxury after being poor for so long. The rest went to bus fare or just pissing it off however I liked. Money made me feel powerful.

One thing I didn't like was watching the strippers eat butter—straight. I first noticed while at my sister's apartment. After she took her Baltimore shower (with a drink and cigarette), she went downstairs and chopped off about two ounces of butter—an eighth of a stick—put it in her mouth, chewed, and swallowed. Then she followed it with a cup of tea or a glass of hot water to get the greasy residue out of her mouth.

"What are you doing?" I asked, disgusted.

"If you eat the right amount of butter, it coats your stomach so it takes way longer for the alcohol to affect you."

So it was not unusual for the strippers to have a stick of butter sitting next to their makeup tray backstage—they'd unwrap it, bite a hunk off, chew, and swallow it. I never got used to seeing it, although I did use that trick later in life. Guess what? It works!

I teched in several clubs that were part of The Block. One was a largely untouched vaudeville theatre, with a proper stage. The orchestra section of the main floor had seating like in a movie theatre or a Broadway house. There was a bar at the back of the orchestra area and a balcony with tables and chairs for the 'taking care of business' part of the johns' visits.

This venue was named "The Gaiety Theatre"—ironic because the only thing that was gay in that theatre was me. The girls did their acts on a higher stage with more lighting than usual. I liked my Gaiety gigs; of all the clubs, the space was the closest to an actual theatre, and it even had a spotlight and an operator. OK, he was an old guy who (barely) worked the spot, which he did for free since he loved watching naked girls. It was a hobby for him, I guess. Some older men volunteer for the Salvation Army; he volunteered for strip clubs. Whenever I came up to the balcony to refocus the lights while he was manning the spotlight, I had to ask if he would please put his penis back in his pants, you know, as a courtesy. He obliged. (Had he been younger, my request would have been *very* different!)

One night after the last show, while the girls were backstage changing, I walked into the audience area and saw a guy wearing the cliché beige raincoat, still in his seat. The club had closed and everyone else was long gone. I walked over to wake him. "Mister. Mister. *Mister!*" I shook him a few times, then realized—he was dead. Fuck me sideways with a billy club, my first dead patron!

I ran backstage and told Madam we had a stiff in the house, and not the usual kind. She followed me to where he sat, gave him a few pokes with her blood red nails, and said, "Yup, he's a goner." Word quickly spread among the girls and a betting game began: Who was the stripper whose act was so 'hot' it killed this guy? While we waited for Madam to get the coroner, the girls got a pencil and paper, my sister acted as banker, and we all tried guessing what time it was when he departed for a better place.

My sister Carol guessed, "It was 10:30 p.m., when my skeleton act was on." Candy said "No, it had to be 11:15 p.m. when I shot the Ping-Pong balls at him." Ronnie Bell disagreed. "You're all full of shit; it was my cigar smoke rings at 10:45 p.m. on the nose." And so it went. I asked if I could play. Each guess was $20. The girls figured, the more people who play, the bigger the pot, so they said yes. I put in my guess and when we were all finished, we had a pot of $260. Madam was still not back, so I went to the lobby to wait. As she walked through the lobby door with the coroner, I told her, "You'd better hurry backstage, there's a problem!" Off she went, and I pulled the coroner aside.

"How'd you like to make fifty bucks?" I asked him. He asked how.

"Just tell the girls you think the time of death was 11:30 p.m." Then I handed him fifty dollars and walked him over to where the dead guy was. He looked at him for a minute, then said, "This man died at 11:30 p.m.," and he started filling out his paperwork. I collected the pot of $260 and left the theatre that night with a big grin. I had already learned *so* much by working on The Block.

———————•———————

The girls who stripped at the clubs were about 65% white and 35% black. The audience was mostly white by far, but a lot of white men had fantasies about black women, who were every bit as popular (and in some cases more popular) than the white women. Since I watched the men in the audience (looking for the handsome ones) much more than I watched the girls onstage, this was easy for me to pick up on and I had a keen eye for what excited them. The strippers had a sisterhood of sorts; they treated each other as peers and equals. They seemed to be colorblind, at a time where racism and segregation dominated plenty of news headlines. It was very interesting and way ahead of its time that way. But it wasn't always one big happy family. Sometimes my sister would say, "Don't get near Priscilla tonight, she's in a bad mood." A bad mood meant steer clear, because when a stripper was in a bad mood, it was a *bad* mood. It meant go fuck yourself, get out of my way. I saw some hair-pulling catfights from time to time—a lot of them kept razor blades in their wigs—but they never got mad at me because I made them look good onstage. I didn't just point white lights on them; I'd ask them what they wanted to look like or would help with their more elaborate acts. Much like Anita O'Day, who learned jazz by hanging at the Chicago clubs, I learned my craft by lighting strippers of all races. These skills came in handy while lighting one of the most famous Jazz singers in the world: Ella Fitzgerald.

Ella Fitzgerald was the perfect client. Later in my career, I was an experienced lighting and tech director working for record companies. I'd been hired for Ella's four shows in Las Vegas and two in LA. She was polite, showed up on time, and agreed to any sound or light check I deemed necessary. A consummate pro, one of the few I worked with who did not drink, smoke, or do drugs. She was also very, very shy when not onstage. Before that first concert together, she told me she thought she was ugly and fat, and could I please do my best to design the lights to make her look "as good as someone like me can look." That broke my heart. I wanted to do my best for someone as talented as her.

This is where my days in burlesque and stripper joints really paid off. I learned that dark skin had a tendency to absorb darker-colored lighting, which made it very hard to use overhead lights to give the performer dimension. I asked Ella if she used foundation or powder, and she showed me what she had. The foundation was a lighter shade than her skin, as was the powder. (Sadly, someone had advised her to "try to look lighter.") I said, "Ella, I'm bringing you some white baby powder, and I want you to ditch that foundation and brown powder. I want you to powder-puff some of the baby talc on your face and hands, and then wipe it off gently. It'll stay in your pores but not be noticeable and the lighting will have a little more to reflect off of."

She looked at me like I had lost my mind. She probably thought, *He wants me to do whiteface*, but she did it anyway. As primitive as the lighting was in those strip clubs, there was a vast variety of faces, bodies, and skin colors of the working girls. Black, brown, high yellow, peach-Asian, Mediterranean amber, stark white—with so many strippers of so many colors, I could have written a thesis on what worked and what didn't. For Ella specifically, I needed a lighting strategy that would light her face up, to show her varied expressions, which were an important part of her selling a song. The majority of subtle gels I used often got absorbed into darker pigments like hers.

Some of the strip clubs I worked had a spotlight; those were the best for skin tone issues, as they were much stronger than a normal stage light. I needed to use a brand-name gel (Rosco) and their specific color (#842), which was oddly marketed under the descriptive name "Whisper Blue" but in actuality brought out a little of the red tones in black skin while reflecting the natural coloring of darker performers with minimal absorption. It was effective and flattering and just what we needed.

Luckily, we had spotlights available and I gelled them to use Rosco 842. For dimension, I used ungelled white overhead lighting. The lack of color framed her black hair beautifully, giving almost a halo effect; with dimmers, I could punch up or soften this look, depending on the mood or tune. I used extra side lighting to add even more dimension to her body (these were mostly ungelled), with one or two lighting instruments using 842 gel to warm the sides of her body. Vivid colors highlighted the band behind her and as an effect on the flooring around her. Ella was not going to look like she had on clown makeup on my watch!

When we did the light and sound check for that first performance, Ella, like so many performers, said she could "feel" that the lighting was complementary. After the first show, when the inevitable parade of well-wishers and fellow performers came backstage to congratulate her, many of them commented on "How well she looked." That was music to my ears; they didn't say "You were so well lit," they said she looked "Healthy and fine." That's what she wanted and what I was able to deliver.

The next afternoon, before the second performance, Ella very politely asked me if I would mind writing down the colors I used on her and their placement. "I don't know what you did last night, but I don't remember ever getting that amount of compliments on how I looked. Honey, you know your stuff, so thank you!" she said. I was so pleased I could deliver that to her, to a woman who had been told nearly all her life she was ugly and fat. With her three-octave range and genuinely expressive face, how could anyone see anything *but* beauty on the stage when Ella Fitzgerald was singing? All they had to do was listen. That night, back in my hotel, I gave a silent "thank you" to my stripper training and all the women I lit who allowed me the generosity of experimentation with their skin tones.

I later heard some stories about Ella from another celebrity singer I worked with. How, in her childhood, she had an abused family life, moved away from home, ran numbers as a young teen for the mob, and tried to make money playing dice, something she had a knack for. She also served as lookout for a whorehouse in Harlem and briefly ended up in a juvenile detention center (which in those days was worse than now, especially for black folks). I heard she liked the occasional joint and would have smoked more, except it did no favors for her throat and voice, which she had problems with from the beginning.

She was truly the most bashful person I ever worked with, and she was so insecure about her looks. I told her the second night that she looked very handsome onstage. I didn't use the word pretty because I knew she was not that, and she was a very smart cookie. But she had a great stage persona and it saddened me she couldn't enjoy it. She would look to the floor when I said things like that—it was sweet, but it came from insecurity, not from being demure. Ella told me that when she was getting started, a famous big-band leader said to her manager, "You're not puttin' *that* on my bandstand." That was at the beginning of her career and she still remembered it, it still hurt her. I teared up at that story.

I asked her if it was true The Macombo Club refused to book her because of her skin color. (The Macombo had no issue with hiring black musicians, only singers.) Ella said yes, but "Marilyn put a stop to that." She meant Marilyn Monroe. Turns out, they had a yearslong friendship (I think it was more a mentorship), mostly by phone. Marilyn called the owner of the club and said, in her soft whisper of a voice, "You book Ella and I will be at the front table for every show—think of the publicity I will bring and the crowds that will come." It was Marilyn who shattered that ceiling. Ella performed the one-week gig, with Marilyn at every sold-out show. Ella implied that she tried her best to "help Marilyn out" later in their friendship, but that the drugs and alcohol won.

The manager of The Macombo was a terrible bigot and a racist. He was the brother (or uncle) of a mafioso, or else he would have been long gone from that club for being so repugnant, but the mafia *always* looked after their own. (They weren't racist themselves—they only cared about one color, and that was green.)

———————•———————

It turns out that I didn't just master the art of lighting while working with the strippers on The Block; I became skilled with sound, too. I helped the girls get creative with their music. If a stripper was an expert at spinning her tassels, I'd tell her I could splice the tape and make a musical phrase longer, make it happen three times instead of just once, and they loved things like that. I was sad to see the burlesque-style shows give way to down and dirty stripping. Real burlesque was a sight to see and my sound and lighting tricks made the acts even better.

Once the club I worked at was short a stripper—someone had called in sick or been murdered or something. The woman who usually sold the tickets at the door had to fill in. She'd once been a really well-known stripper, but she was probably fifty at this point, which was far too old to strip. But she came out that night and did an act I can still picture. You didn't see her pull down her zipper, and you didn't know how she did it, but suddenly she was gownless. It was amazing. She simply twirled and then was in nothing but pasties and a G-string. It was so erotic that she got a standing ovation. Burlesque gowns were fascinating; while they looked normal to an audience, they were usually complicated in construction. The goal of the gown was twofold: a woman had to get out of it in a sexy and seamless manner, and it had to show off a stripper's best advantages while it was on. Strippers with exceptional busts usually wore gowns with low necklines that showed them off; those with lush buttocks required hidden seams to focus attention on that detail. Short girls, or those a little on the plump side, tricked the eye by elongating their bodies with vertical stripes or rows of sequins, leading the audience's eyes to look up and down, not side to side. And all of the backs of the gowns needed to look normal but would be held together in a seamless way (no buttons, no hooks) that allowed for easy disrobing. In the early days, this was done with snaps; later it was with Velcro, although the A-list strippers didn't like Velcro because it made a very unsexy noise when it was pulled apart. So snaps were preferred. (There is even a song made famous by Elaine Stritch, about getting out of an elaborate burlesque stage gown, titled "Snap.")

The interior of a proper stage gown looked like the LA freeway— a series of figure-eight and crossing seams and bones (thin pieces of whalebone that shaped the fabric and was also flexible). The actress Marlene Dietrich was known for gowns that it was said could "stand up on their own." There were also sewn-in pieces of rubber or foam, to add curves where needed. The average stripper gown, properly constructed and with rhinestones, sequins, and all the other trimmings, weighed twenty-five pounds.

The gowns were handmade by specialized seamstresses, and it was not unusual for a stripper to spend well over $2,000 for a bespoke gown. (By today's standards, that would be nearly $10,000.) A lavish feather boa was de rigueur, the perfect hand prop. Worn around the shoulders, dragged behind as the stripper prance-walked the stage, pulled behind the gown to draw the eye to the ass, and, depending on the split up the front of the gown, sawed back and forth between the legs. The earrings were almost always rhinestones, dangling long and heavy. At the height of burlesque, a girl could guesstimate how long someone had been in 'the business' by the stretch of their earlobes, like counting the rings of a tree trunk to guess its age. Pasties were handmade to fit the varying width of each performer's nipples and they were not cheap. They were made by horse-gluing tiny shreds of muslin to create a pointy foundation that fit over the tip of the nipple; then a piece of shimmering fabric was glued over that foundation. Some strippers sewed on tassels, and if they knew their stuff, they could make the tassels spin to the left, to the right. The *real* pros could get one going in each direction! For that kind of movement, you also had to have really good breast control, which was always a highlight for the johns in the audience.

When I realized the art of burlesque was dead, if not dying, it was the first signal that I didn't want to do this forever. Plus, I was starting to get bored with the equipment. I wanted to go bigger and better, and I figured that this was too small-time for me. (After all, I was seventeen now!) I was also exhausted. Catching those two buses every night in the cold was tiring, and I was sick of worrying about the cops. While it's true that most of them were bribed with cash and didn't hassle the clubs too much, you also didn't want to fuck around with them—they still wielded power.

One night I was working the lights and sound at the very back of the club, when I noticed a cop. He was tall, good-looking, and in a uniform—three checks on my gay sex wish list. I watched him walk over to Madam and whisper something in her ear. She came over to me, looking apologetic.

"David, sweetheart, that cop wants you to blow him."

I asked her what she meant.

"That cop said he wants you to blow him, you know, suck his dick, and he's a cop and could take our license if you don't."

I was confused. How was this even going to go down? She explained that I would crawl under a table covered by a long tablecloth. The cop would come over to the table, sit down, and unzip himself. I'd give him a blow job and he'd leave. "Everybody is happy and all is well," she summarized.

Hey, a guy in a uniform wants a blow job! I'd been dreaming of *getting* a blow job for such a long fucking time, at least I could give one and see what all the fuss was about! I hadn't had sex yet or ever given a blow job. I was a simple gay teenage virgin. So this would be my first.

I agreed, got under the table, and waited for him to sit down. Once he got there and unzipped, I saw what turned out to be the biggest cock I would ever see in my life. He was freakishly hung—it had to be eleven inches long, was incredibly thick, and was curved, like a banana.

I panicked (not easy to do under a table)—*I can't even get my mouth around that. How am I going to give him a blow job?* He started getting antsy, nudged me with his foot, and said, "Come on, I don't have all night."

Maybe I can just lick it like a lollipop? It didn't take a minute of licking it before the guy climaxed all over my shirt. Then he said, "Get up, you little perv. You are such a pansy, you don't even know how to give a blow job." He pushed me with his foot so hard that I fell backwards onto the floor, then he left.

Madam came rushing over to see if I was okay.

"Sweetheart, don't worry. Nobody can fit that big dick in their mouth. He comes in asking for men but they're rarely here, so he'll take a woman. But he saw you tonight and he wanted you. We had no choice but to give you to him. Are you okay? Do you want some ice? Do you want to go home early?" They were so kind to me, considering my first real sexual experience was coerced—and wasn't even fun! (Okay, maybe just a *tiny* bit fun.)

It wouldn't be the last time a cop demanded me to blow him. About two weeks later, I was waiting for my bus when a police car pulled up with two cops in it. They asked what I was doing; I explained that I worked in one of the clubs and was waiting for the last bus home. They told me to hop in the car and, stupid me, I thought they were going to give me a ride home. Instead, they pulled into an alley and demanded blow jobs! Nobody had given *me* a blow job yet, but I was getting the hang of what to do, so I gave them both blow jobs. (It would have been kind of hot if one watched the other, but they took turns in the back seat.) I knew this was bullshit. While a part of me got off on anything having to do with a penis, another part of me was angry that these cops thought they could just push us gay guys around like we were sex toys. For the first time, I was angry about a sex act.

It was not long after that when, taking the bus home, I passed by a magazine shop, the kind that sold male physique mags. Many closeted men bought them, pretending to read the stories about weight lifting. I went in and bought one, and that's when I found a poorly printed newsletter on the floor. "The Gay Activists Alliance and Gay Liberation Front Manifesto" was stapled together and sold for twenty-five cents. I picked it up to read on the bus. When I went to pay at the front counter, the clerk gave me a look that told me everything he thought about this 'faggot' in front of him, and I gave him the exact same look back, the little shit. As I was getting braver, I was starting to get pissed off. I read the manifesto while sitting in the center of the bus; I could see people around me taking in the headline and slowly moving away. But I didn't care.

I read about a place in New York City called the Firehouse, a safe place where The Gay Activist Alliance and Gay Liberation Front held their meetings. They were a small but growing movement in the city. (This was still two years from the Stonewall riots in 1969.) The more I read about vice squads, mafia-bar owners, and gangs beating up queers, the angrier I got at how bad it was for us gay men. *This is just wrong.* Cops shouldn't be able to use us, demean us, call us names. We deserve better than this.

I decided to go to New York and visit the Firehouse. I needed to share my frustrations, to vent about my experiences, to do something, anything to change the circumstances I lived in. I was ready to leave the world of strip clubs behind and start making the world a better place for people like me.

5.

WELCOME TO THE FIREHOUSE

My first experience hitchhiking was not the sexual escapade I imagined it would be. I'd given enough on-demand blow jobs to cops in alleys, and I was frustrated that I didn't fit the top/bottom/butch/fem stereotype. It was time to go to New York City to visit the Firehouse. In my mind, the Firehouse was like Aladdin's Cave of Wonders—filled with handsome and horny genies. I decided to hitchhike instead of taking Amtrak.

I had it in my head that, I don't know, a hot young guy with a cute bubble butt would pick me up. Maybe he'd let me fuck him or would blow me while we were on our fun little road trip. Plus, this was the 60s, where everybody in the hippie movement was starting to hitchhike everywhere. Hitchhiking then wasn't like it is today—it was mostly safe and often fun.

I'd only left Baltimore once in my life until then. When I was really young, we visited my mother's mother in West Virginia. We took a sleeper train to get there. I woke up early, before my mom, and saw a bright red light filling the sky. I thought the world was on fire or a nuclear bomb had gone off, so I started crying. A woman sitting nearby asked me what was wrong, and when I said I was scared of the fire in the sky, she asked, "Honey, have you never seen a sunrise before?" Apparently not.

In order to hitchhike, I first had to take a public bus to an area near the interstate going north. I'd told my mother what I was doing, and she didn't seem at all concerned. She just told me to be careful. I was seventeen, working at a strip club, officially pronounced gay by a psychiatrist, and I continued to stare incessantly at men's crotches, so in her mind, I was practically a grown man.

I decided to dress 'gay' for the trip; this meant wearing Levi's 501s. They had five round metal rivet-like buttons at the crotch, which at that time was considered very suggestive, especially when you left the bottom two unbuttoned. (I learned the number of buttons left closed and opened was gay code for what you were into, much the way colored bandanas stuffed in your rear pocket was a sexual tip-off.) It was May, so it wasn't too cold. I wore a (tight) sweater, no jacket, and carried the same kind of bag I used for school, with my diary tucked inside.

I made it to the highway, stuck out my thumb, and was picked up by an old man who talked to me about the Bible. He was nice, in a grandfatherly way, but he wasn't exactly who I hoped to catch a ride with. He drove me about halfway, somewhere in New Jersey. My second ride was a guy who *did* seem interested in me sexually—and was a looker—but I'd never been cruised before. We sort of talked about the weather and what New York was like, looked at each other sideways, and then he dropped me downtown near the West Side Highway. So that was also a bust. My first hitchhiking experience got me a Bible lesson and blue balls.

It was my first time in New York City, but coming from the Holland Tunnel I didn't see the cityscape—that panorama of tall buildings printed on the postcards—so it didn't look all that exciting. Not knowing what to do next, I started walking east, because west was the river. I found a subway station and walked up to the token booth. The lady sitting inside looked like she didn't give a shit about anything and was being held captive in that tiny glass box. I asked her for a subway map and directions to Houston Street, and she turned out to be kind. Asking where I was going, she explained that I could easily walk the seven blocks to get to where I needed to go. And so I started making my way to the Firehouse. I strolled up Broadway (what would be SoHo today), past factory buildings and idling box trucks. As I got close to the Firehouse, I kept walking. It looked closed, and I lacked the courage to knock on that door. I wandered the area and stopped for my very first cup of coffee because I thought that's what you do in New York. (It was disgusting—I loaded it with so many creams and sugars it tasted like a milkshake.) As I roamed the neighborhood, I thought, *There's really not a whole lot to New York; it's just factories.* At one point I looked north and saw the Chrysler Building. Then the Empire State Building. I knew from photos what they were, and I realized, "Oh I get it, I'm in a warehouse area." We had those in Baltimore, too. I'd later learn to love the area just beyond that, the Meat Packing District on the Hudson River—with so many giant trucks on the street, it was the perfect place for anonymous sex. (Although a lot of people also ended up getting pickpocketed, beaten, or murdered there.)

Around six o'clock, I returned to the Firehouse at 99 Wooster. My knees wobbled with fear, but I knocked on the door and a nice guy, maybe in his early twenties, opened it. I could see inside, and I realized this space had been a real firehouse. I guess the city decided they didn't need one in that area anymore and leased it out to The Gay Activists Alliance and The Gay Liberation Front, who were sharing the space. He looked kindly at me, and not knowing what else to do, I laid it all out for him.

"Hi, my name is David and I think I'm gay but I don't know if I'm a butch or a fem and so I hitchhiked here all the way from Baltimore because I think I need to meet with other gay people and find out who I am and I'd read all about this place in a pamphlet one time when I was on the bus and that's why I'm here." I'm unsure how I got all that out in one breath, but it was, on reflection, a good indicator that my breath control would come in handy for various sexual acts to come.

He looked me up and down. (I was seventeen and handsome, and since I didn't wear underwear, every gay man looked me up and down.)

"You're eighteen, right?"

"No, I'm seventeen."

"You mean you're eighteen, right?" he said.

"No, I'm seventeen!"

He tried one last time. "You *are* eighteen." Shakes his head up and down. "Right?"

I finally caught on.

"Oh, uh, yes, I'm definitely eighteen."

"Great, come on in!"

He told me to make myself comfortable and pointed to the coffee machine (no thanks) and the water fountain. There were lots of folding chairs and several beat-up couches with stuffing spilling onto the floor and, I think, no windows—or, if there were windows, they were painted black for security reasons. Handsome door guy assured me that people would come over and talk to me. He probably thought, *At your age, you are such dick-bait that there will be a line of people hoping to talk to you.* He was cute and welcoming, and I felt instantly at ease, so I sat down on one of the beat-up couches. Sure enough, it didn't take two minutes before a guy came over to talk to me. He was older, and I could see 'Yummy, a new one!' in his eyes, but that wasn't why I was there. I thought to myself, *How did the strippers get rid of someone they weren't interested in?* Well, they just stood up and walked away. So I did the same, pretending I had to go to the bathroom. Then a second man came over and sat down. He looked about five years older than me and was *very* hot. He asked why he hadn't seen me before, and like the poor guy at the door, I poured out my whole story. He quietly listened, really listened, and I was so relieved to talk to another gay person, one who didn't get angry at me because

I didn't know if I was fem or butch. He told me there were plenty of people just like me—not butch, not fem, not top or bottom—but something called "versatile." *He* was versatile.

"Depending on who I'm with and the way they turn me on, they can have the front of me or the back of me, or we'll decide together to do something or not. Sex is a negotiation, but not in a business sense. It's an emotional negotiation." Such sweet music to my ears.

I took out my diary and started jotting down notes, which he quickly told me not to do. He explained that people would get nervous and think they were being interviewed or that I was a very young, undercover member of the vice squad. "A lot of people here don't even use their real names," he said. (I'd later learn that plenty of the men at the Firehouse weren't out yet, although some of them were married, conveniently, to lesbians.) I learned the difference between The Gay Activists Alliance (GAA) and The Gay Liberation Front (GLF), both of which shared the space. "The GAA is older, more mature men that are trying to change the laws. The GLF is younger, angrier, and more interested in breaking down the laws, and the walls, rather than changing them." I decided to attend both meetings and learn as much as I could.

The first meeting was the GAA. On the agenda that night was how to find a way to buy the Firehouse, because the city needed a permanent "safe house" for gay people. The speaker explained that too many gay youth (some as young as thirteen) were kicked out of their homes and needed a place to stay while they searched for gay-friendly foster homes. Uncloseted gay people couldn't foster children—it was illegal to be gay. Single gay people couldn't either—only a 'straight,' married couple, a man and a woman, could foster a child. The activists kept a list of gay men and lesbians who were married to each other, mainly for business reasons because they couldn't be out at work. A lot of those couples became foster parents to gay youth; so many of those kids were so badly abused by their birth parents. ("You're diseased. We hate you. You're sick. We can't look at you. Get out. Read the Bible!") I was extremely moved, and shocked, by his speech. It had never occurred to me that parents could be that upset about one of their kids being gay. That sure wasn't my experience and it opened my eyes.

The GLF meeting came next, and it was a much angrier gathering about how to stop the mafia from raiding our bars, how we had to fight back. "How many of you in this room want to fight back with Molotov cocktails? Or should we lie down in the streets and block traffic? Or how about you go to your place of work and tell them you're gay, and if they dare fire you we'll help you find a gay lawyer and sue for discrimination!" (My new hotty friend whispered, "There aren't any anti-discrimination laws. Every law discriminates against us.") A lot of the GAA people thought the GLF people were crazy, dangerous, a threat to decision makers and to the greater cause, and vice versa. But I liked the GLF meeting more because I *wanted* to break the laws. That seemed faster and more fun. I didn't grasp that *changing* the laws was actually more important. It was those archaic laws already in place that allowed the cops or the vice squads to raid the bars and to keep 'deviant' names on file in the city records, which were often shared with the newspapers. The mafia owned most of the gay bars along the East and West Coasts, but they couldn't control the vice squads like they could control the cops. If the vice squad guys didn't bust a certain number of bars or bathhouses a month, they wouldn't get their bonuses or whatever, so the mafia just turned a blind eye to it and would get a heads-up if one were to take place. The same thing used to happen in the strip clubs in Baltimore too—about every six months, the vice squad would make a raid and around thirty men would get marched out to the paddy wagon, and the strippers showing their nipples or vaginas would too. The girls didn't even run when these raids happened—they knew the drill. One night in a holding cell, and they could be back at work the next day. The mafia sprang them; they needed those girls, their assets, to be back at work the next night.

After the two meetings, because it was Friday (there was dancing on Friday and Saturday nights), someone put on music, the chairs were pushed back, and the dancing started. It wasn't rowdy; it was just a safe space for gay men to dance and let loose. There wasn't any alcohol because it wasn't allowed at the Firehouse. I should note that there were *only* men here. The Firehouse did not attract lesbians or make much effort to do so. They were different tribes at the time. I remember one time after I moved to NYC, my sister came to have her breasts injected with silicone (no implants in those days), and she wanted to go to a lesbian bar, so we went to the door of a well-known joint in the West Village, the Henrietta Hudson. We entered and the door woman put her arm out to block me. My sister said, "I'm a lesbian and my brother is gay; we want to have a drink together and catch up." They refused to let *me* in. But you have to realize chauvinism was also still rampant in the (gay and straight) male community. While the women—both straight and gay—were burning their bras and fighting for equal rights, us gay men mostly cared about getting our dicks sucked. In fact, it wasn't until AIDS that gays and lesbians finally rallied together for the greater cause and realized it was better to work as one.

When the music was turned off after about two hours, my new friend (in my eyes he was already my forever boyfriend) asked me where I was going to go next. I had no plan, and I told him I was probably just going to go out on the streets and hope that someone would pick me up, because I didn't bring enough money for a hotel. He told me that was too dangerous…and that he lived nearby.

"Why don't you walk back to my place, and I'll fix us something to eat because I'm hungry. We can watch TV and my couch is very comfortable; you're welcome to sleep there. Ugly things can happen on the streets to kids like you." I practically jumped in his arms! We went back to his place and ate scrambled eggs on toast, and then when it was time for bed, he looked at me and said, "Am I putting a pillow and blanket on the couch, or do you want to come to bed with me?"

Halle-fucking-lujah! I was *dying* to go to bed with him! I'd been walking all the way to his place with a tent in my 501s and I told him as much, and he smiled and went into the bathroom. Suddenly, I freaked out. I didn't know what to do next. Was I supposed to get naked? Lie on top of the bed with my clothes on? Strip my shirt off? I was so confused, but then he came out of the bathroom completely naked and with a raging hard-on. *Oh, okay,* I thought. *That's how this works—balls to the wind!* We started kissing, and soon he started giving me a blow job. It was something I'd dreamed about, but I froze. It didn't feel the way I thought it would, and it wasn't doing much for me. He stopped and asked me if I liked it, and I told him I wasn't sure. I think he realized then that I didn't have any experience, and he was so gentle about it. He asked me about my gay fantasies and assured me I didn't have to be embarrassed, that he was like me. "The first time I had sex I was a nervous wreck, but don't be nervous. There isn't anything wrong or bad about this."

I told him I thought I would, uh, rather blow him, I guess, and then he asked if I wanted to fuck him. Eyes up! I very much did. He introduced me to real lube—no hand lotion—and then I lost my virginity inside the man who was surely the love of my life. It was beyond great. I was on fire. I loved it. I was so excited that I climaxed in about two minutes, and then he did too (probably just out of solidarity), then he said, "Let's get a little bit of sleep and we can do that again in the morning." And we cuddled. I'd never cuddled with a man before and it was so much more intimate than the sex. I watched him while he slept, listening to the rhythm of his breathing and matching my breath to his. He was so handsome, and his eyelashes were so long. I circled his nipple with one of my fingers, and he purred. I'd finally had sex with a guy, and it felt so comfortable, so right, that I wanted to do it again and again. I woke him at about 3:00 a.m. and asked, "Can we have sex again, please?" He laughed and said sure, and then we did it again. After breakfast, he showed me around New York. He took me to Midtown and Times Square; *Funny Girl* was on a marquee on Broadway (but with Lainie Kazan, not Barbara Streisand, a decent substitute). We went to Macy's, walked by the Empire State Building, and chatted about his life. I assumed he was a hairdresser or had some other 'gay' occupation, so I was stunned when he told me he worked as an investor on Wall Street.

"Do they know you're gay at work?" I asked. He said no, they'd never asked but if they did he'd tell them the truth. "I'm not ashamed of who I am," he said. "If they can't handle it, that's on them, not me." Oh that was music to my ears—we were so meant to be! I was already mentally redecorating his apartment.

We went back to the Firehouse together later that evening. It was Saturday and crowded, and we moved apart for a while. I wanted to attend another meeting and he needed to do something else. A couple of other men came up and tried to talk to me, but I had no interest. I was already hopelessly in love with *my* man from the night before! I decided he was going to be my husband or maybe my wife, or maybe we could take turns. Together forever! A few minutes later, he came over to where I was, holding hands with *another man*. He introduced me to his boyfriend and said, "We're in an open relationship." He asked if I knew what that meant, and I assumed it was a three-way, and they wanted me to go home with them, so I said "Okay." "David," he said, laughing. "That's not the right answer to my question." Turned out, they both just wanted to make sure I had a safe place to stay that night and said I could sleep on their couch if I needed to, but he made it clear that I would be *sleeping* on the couch. Keeping my heartbreak and jealousy in check, I decided to search out one of the other cute men who had approached me earlier. I found the best of the bunch and explained that I needed a place to stay the night. He was *very* interested in that piece of news.

"Why don't we leave right now," he said and then pulled me towards the door. "You've been to enough meetings, and I can show you better things than a meeting can." I realized immediately that I had a new forever boyfriend. We hopped on the subway and went to his place in Brooklyn Heights, a pretty apartment with great views of the city. The minute we walked in the door he started tearing my clothes off. He was much more aggressive than my now ex-boyfriend; he wanted me right that minute. He was also loud—the kind of guy who loves to make noise during sex, and I realized that was a definite turn-on for me and another first. We both got naked, and it was all very sexual, until we got to his bed and he turned me over like he wanted to fuck me. I got nervous—I told him I wasn't sure I was going to like it, and he said, "You'll never know unless you try!" That made sense so I thought, *he's right. Maybe I will like it?* So he did what he did, and it didn't really hurt and there wasn't anything *wrong* with it, but when he turned me over so he could see my face, he saw that I wasn't hard. He could tell I wasn't particularly enjoying it.

"You're not a bottom, are you?" he asked.

"Well, this is the first time I've tried it, but whenever I have fantasies about sex, it is about me fucking a guy," I said.

"Okay. Well, how about we do *that*," he said, turning over and shaking his pretty ass at me. So it was a very successful, albeit noisy, happy ending. The next morning, after more sex, we grabbed breakfast, and he told me how to get to the Firehouse. Standing outside his apartment, he pointed me in the direction of the subway entrance, so I thanked him and went in for a hug and a goodbye kiss. He backed away fast.

"Not in public," he said. "I'm not out. I come from a very religious family, and if word ever got out that their only son was gay, I wouldn't have a family anymore. And my family means everything to me." I was shocked. I'd never met anyone who'd cared about their family before.

Back at the Firehouse, I realized I needed practice cruising. I saw a guy I'd talked to the day before and decided to cruise him. I'd been watching how to do it (when my two ex-forever boyfriends weren't looking), and it appeared to be done mostly with the eyes—a looking up and down motion, followed by a little smile and a lowering of the eyelids. I practiced, and *my* eyes turned a lot of other heads that night! I wondered if I was being a slut, but thought, *Fuck it, this is the first time I've ever been able to be myself and be gay and have sex, and I love it.* I walked up to my backup choice from last night and said, "If it's okay with you, I'd love to go home with you after this meeting." Eyes up, eyes down, lashes flickering. That was more than okay with him, and soon we were at his place on the Upper East Side.

"I'm a bottom, is that okay with you?" he asked. I almost laughed—he had the butt of my dreams so I replied, "Perfect, I'm a top and I can't wait to plow you until you're sore!" (I think my former-forever-boyfriend's dirty talk rubbed off on me). We had amazing sex, then went to the movies. I was so full of happiness and sexual fulfillment—I loved the feeling of no longer being alone. (I also learned to stop making everyone my 'forever' anything.) While cuddling that night with my very cute 'right-now' guy, I tried to piece together the difference between fun, casual sex and more intimate relationships.

The next morning, my *not* forever-boyfriend, my trick (I learned that word on Friday night), told me to take the #1 train towards the Holland Tunnel, where I'd be able to hitchhike back to Baltimore. I didn't have my thumb out for more than a minute when a guy in an eighteen-wheeler picked me up. We weren't even through the tunnel before his hands were all over me. He wasn't great looking, and I'd just had sex about nine times in forty-eight hours, so the last thing I wanted was to have sex again. I blew him just to get it over with—much like I'd done for the cops back in Baltimore. He offered to pull over at a truck stop and do the same to me, but I decided to get out and find a better ride. Soon, a woman pulled over. She said I looked too young to hitchhike and she could take me all the way home since she was heading in that direction. I hopped in.

"You're gay, aren't you?" she asked immediately. I told her I was.

"Well, then I'm driving you to your front door, because my son is eighteen and gay. I wouldn't want him risking his safety by hitchhiking. You're handsome and young and could really get into trouble." I worried she might lecture me, but she was remarkable and supportive. This older woman was the vice president of marketing for Sarah Lee, which I thought was amazing, and we talked about all of their products, including why I liked Tastykakes better than Sarah Lee's. I wrote down my address, and she said she would send me a bunch of Sarah Lee products after she dropped me off. Two weeks later, I got a big box of almost every Sarah Lee product ever made—cheesecakes, pound cakes, cinnamon rolls, the works. Enclosed in the box was a sweet note telling me to take good care of myself, and if I was ever in San Francisco, to look up her son. She thought we'd make a cute couple. My mother saw the box and asked, "What'd you have to do to get all *that*?" I just smiled.

My weekend trip to the Firehouse was such a success! I had (lots of) sex, learned to cruise, and got free Sarah Lee cakes! More importantly, I knew who I was. For the first time, I realized I could just be myself—no roles necessary—and it did so much for my self-worth; and it gave me focus. I suddenly felt a responsibility to help other people like me. There were a lot of young guys coming out with no one to talk to but the 'Sophies' of the world, and her well-meaning generation was a time warp of stereotypes. Maybe, just maybe, I could help *my* generation figure out who they were but with fewer speed bumps. I was jazzed up by the gay activists and the gay libbers and I *knew* what I was supposed to do. I had the mimeographed booklet and the pamphlets from the meetings and could use those to do something for my community while I could. I knew that the minute I graduated high school, I would leave Baltimore for good. I was moving to New York City, back to the Firehouse, and to a career in lighting and sound. Until then, I would start The Baltimore Gay Liberation Front.

At the end of a Gay Liberation Front meeting at the Firehouse, people would stand and say something, ask a question, or just share a thought (much like they do in AA meetings). When it was my turn, I stood up and said, "In Baltimore, we don't have anything like this. What do you think I should do?" Two or three guys said, "Start one." I talked with one of them after the meeting to ask how I would even go about that. He said that I first needed to understand what gay liberation was and to understand that gay history was our foundation. The second thing was to distribute information, to get people on the same page, because there was strength in numbers. There was something called "The Complete Gay Liberation Manifesto," a more comprehensive document than the one I bought in Baltimore for twenty-five cents. He gave it to me and told me to set up a meeting space and then go to the gay bars and hand out copies; the people who agreed with what they read would come to the meeting. "You don't just want to host a meeting with a bunch of gay men cruising each other," he explained. (I did in fact want that too, now that I had learned *how* to cruise, but that was beside the point.)

The Tuesday after I returned to Baltimore from the Firehouse, I thought about where I could host a meeting near the gay bars, which were all downtown. The only place I could think of was the YMCA, which had a huge ballroom. I wasn't sure how much traction I'd get with the Young Men's Christian Association, but I tried anyway. I walked in and approached the woman at the front desk near the executive office.

"Hello. I'm interested in renting out the big ballroom you have here for a Gay Liberation Front meeting, but I don't have any money to rent it. Is there any way the YMCA will give it to me for free?" I smiled politely.

She just stared, then got up and slowly walked into another room. She returned with an older man, about forty, wearing a suit. I thought, *fuck, it's the same old pattern—I tell someone I'm gay, and then they go and get the principal or the gym teacher or whoever it is to come and have a little talk with me.*

The man asked me what I was there for, and I told him I wanted to start a Gay Liberation Front.

"Please step into my office," he said. Once I was seated, he asked me again to tell him what I was there for. I decided to tell the whole story.

"I went to New York last week to a place called the Firehouse and attended several Gay Alliance Activist meetings and Gay Liberation Front meetings and I'm gay and I've known that since I was seven years old and we're getting pushed around here in Baltimore by the police and I've even had to give a few blow jobs in cop cars while waiting for the bus and if you read this manifesto it will explain what The GLF is trying to do and I think Baltimore needs one because we gays shouldn't be pushed around anymore." I took a breath, finally. He slowly nodded and asked me my age. I told him the truth.

"You're only seventeen? You're so young. What is motivating you to do this?" he asked.

"Well, *somebody* has to do it. And I don't think age has anything to do with wanting to fix things that are wrong."

The man's eyes welled up with tears.

"Well, of course, you're right, somebody does have to do this," he said, then stood up and left the room. When he returned, I could see he'd been crying. It then dawned on me that this man was gay.

"Okay, David, two weeks from this Sunday from six to nine o'clock, I can give you the ballroom and about a hundred folding chairs. You can give our address, but just don't make it sound like the YMCA has anything to do with starting a gay liberation front."

Victory! Now I just needed to distribute the manifesto outside the gay bars with the invitation to the first meeting. There was only one problem. Xerox machines and copy stores weren't around then, and no one was going to print this manifesto. Good thing I was still in high school!

———•———

I had an English teacher who also taught drama. His name was Harry Adams. He'd taken a liking to me because I was pretty good at drama since I'd been in some real theatre and read a lot of plays. I'm sure he knew I was gay from my crotch-staring addiction. He was an effeminate man, what one of my brothers would call "light in the loafers." He always crossed his legs when he sat on the edge of his desk, and he actually *wore* loafers and white socks. No one ever outwardly said he was gay, and everyone enjoyed his classes and just let him be. I went to his classroom after school that day. I needed to ask him something.

"What is it, David?"

"Well, I'm pretty sure you're gay and I want to start a gay liberation front but I need someone with access to a mimeograph machine to make one hundred copies of this manifesto that I can hand out to people outside of gay bars." Like the YMCA director, he was quiet for a minute.

"David, are you asking me if I'm gay?"

"No, I'm pretty sure you're gay."

He shut his door and sat me down. "David, if this gets out in school I will lose my job. I'm planning to retire in two years and if I lose this job, I won't get my pension. So I need to stay closeted to protect my retirement years." He seemed relieved to be able to tell someone. Then added, "Yes, I am gay and I have a longtime boyfriend. We don't live together but he's my partner. Anyway, I will help you but I have to be really careful about how I do that." He looked at the manifesto. Then he said, with a little smile and a wiggle of his eyebrows, "If I'd known I was going to have this conversation with a student, I would have retired early. I don't know if you make me feel old, scared, or happy. I do know I'm proud of you."

Then, in typical Harry Adams English teacher mode he said, "Oh dear, some things are misspelled, and this could be better spaced. I'm going to fix this, because what it says, what it represents—it's important that it looks right." (He murmured to himself, "And because *it is right.*") "Then I'll run off about two hundred copies for you. Because I think a lot more people are going to throw it away than you expect. And you should take somebody with you, because you'll need to be careful. Bring a girl—that will be less threatening. Oh, I'll add the meeting place details on the back." As they say, not all heroes wear capes. Harry Adams will never know just how close he came to being kissed by his student that day.

I brought my best girlfriend Deborah into the fold. She knew I was gay, but that didn't prevent her from having a crush on me. She knew I worked at strip clubs, and even though she was a 'good girl' who got straight As, in her head she had a secret life, one where she wasn't such a good girl. She told me her fantasies, and I told her mine. I think my weird and unusual life appealed to her. I explained that I needed her help, and she asked to read the manifesto. When she was done, she said, "This is really important stuff. I'll help. But what's our plan if we get beat up?" I hadn't thought about that. I replied, "Uh, Band-Aids and Ben-Gay?" As verified many times over through the course of my life, sometimes you have to jump in the pool at the deep end and hope for the best. We smiled at each other and joined pinkies.

It was Friday night (I called in sick to work), so we went to the biggest gay bar in downtown Baltimore. We stood out front and passed out The Gay Liberation Front Manifesto to the patrons. Some pamphlets were thrown on the ground immediately; some men read the headline, "Gay Liberation Front Meeting," folded it up, and put it in their pocket. Soon enough, two big goons came over to where we were standing and told us to leave. They were clearly bouncers hired by the mafia, who owned the bars. The goons followed us a few blocks to make sure we were gone, which really freaked me out, but not Deborah. She was fired up. "We've given out almost half of them; where's the next bar?" she asked, raring to go. We continued at two other clubs, leaving when the bouncers would inevitably chase us away. Finally, our hands were empty—we had given out all two hundred of the flyers. I couldn't believe it! A week later, we'd have our very first Gay Liberation Front meeting. Surely some of those men would be there?

That week I was so nervous I could hardly sleep—I kept worrying nobody would show up. When Sunday rolled around, I got to the YMCA at 6:00 p.m., and the director helped me set up all the chairs. Then he wished me luck with my meetings.

"You're not staying?" I asked.

"David, I can't stay," he said. "I'm not out."

I was still shocked when people were stuck in the closet. I didn't understand that other people had been raised differently. I was born gay, knew it from the time I started forming thoughts, and it never seemed like a big deal to me. If someone called me a fag or a pansy, it didn't hurt; it rolled right off my back because I never hid who I was or cared what people thought of it. I was lucky—I guess I was just wired that way. So many other people seemed shocked that I was out, loud and proud from my preteen years onwards. The people *I* shocked? They had different fears and responsibilities, to their families, to their religions, to their jobs. I lived a life completely undisciplined. I didn't have parents who took me to church or taught me lessons in morality. If I'd had normal parents and told them I was gay at seven years old, it would have been a different ball game—I'd have been taken to church and to priests and psychiatrists. The only time I went to church was when my mother decided I needed to be baptized when I was thirteen. (My Baptist minister was young, handsome, and hot, to my eyes at least, so I took my underwear off before I put on the white ankle-length, thin cotton robe. When he ducked me under the water, which was a kind of small swimming pool for complete submersion for our 'practice baptism,' I came up with a serious hard-on underneath the wet robe that he totally stared at. I thought hopefully he was going to ask for a date. He later called my mom and said that he would be unable to do my baptism. Coward!)

'Loving' parents ended up driving their kids deep into the closet more than anything else except religion, so in a way, I was actually lucky that I didn't have loving parents. No one cared about me enough to suppress me! The director at the YMCA didn't have to explain anything else about being closeted. I was starting to recognize closeted men, and all of them, from what I could tell, were miserable. He gave me a hopeful look over his shoulder and a smile and left. That's when the gay men began walking into the ballroom.

And what a crowd it was! It was so different from the Firehouse, where men dressed in Levi 501s and tight shirts, looking to talk about liberation and then get laid at the end of the night.

Instead, it was a diverse crowd of people, mostly in their twenties and thirties; they looked like responsible businessmen with jobs and wore casual clothes. It was thrilling to see so many people in the room. These men were here because they were tired of being oppressed. Some came because they were afraid of the cops and vice squads. Some, like me, had been forced to give cops blow jobs. When we ran out of chairs, people sat cross-legged on the floor. It was a Noah's Ark of gay people and their stories—lives lived in so many different ways, but all of us together for this one night, unified! *This is beyond what I dreamed, what I thought it could be!*

But wait! Why are they all staring at *me*? Ah, right. Jesus fucking Christ on a stick, this was *my* show. I didn't know what to do. I felt like a ten-year-old, on the edge of panic. Taking a deep breath, I thought back to the Firehouse. I decided to tell my story of going there, how I had hoped to find other like-minded gay men like myself. I shared how much I'd learned from the Firehouse meetings; that as a community, we could help each other. We knew the alleyways where the cops took people for blow jobs; we could wait in those alleys on weekends, ready with whistles and flashlights to shine on them! Ready to make some noise, ready for change! We could take on the corrupt bars that watered down our drinks and looked the other way when the vice squad loaded us in paddy wagons and printed our names in the paper. I was good at talking, and all of that attention appealed to a part of me who wanted to be an actor. I got people excited, *me*! Soon, everyone began chatting about how there were other ways to live—how we could be both gay and free. Someone stood up and asked when the next meeting was, and I explained that I needed help organizing it. I was, after all, still in high school with a job that went late most nights. But I'd try to get the same ballroom the following Sunday.

After the successful meeting, I called the YMCA director a few times to book the space again. Finally, he called me back and asked me to meet him in front of the building later that day. When I got there, he wasn't wearing his suit. He told me he'd heard the meeting went well, but he wasn't going to be able to let me have the ballroom again.

"I've been fired," he said. I was so taken aback that I didn't grasp what he was saying. "What?!" I asked him why. He thought for a moment, as though searching within himself for an answer.

"David, I knew when I was giving you that ballroom, it would be the end of my career with the YMCA. But I was so impressed that you wanted to do this, that a seventeen-year-old young man had the courage to do this—it inspired me. *You* inspired me, a man twenty years your elder. I realized as a closeted man, it's time for me to come out and maybe do something to help this community too."

I asked if I could hug him. He looked around at the people on the street and finally said, "Sure." We had the greatest, longest hug, and I knew this was the biggest step around his hidden sexuality that he'd ever taken, hugging another man in public. I was so proud of him, I could have popped. I didn't know the phrase at the time, but it would have been "A trip around the world begins with one step." Giving me that ballroom, taking my hug—those were his very first steps.

I saw him once, a few months later, on another trip I'd taken to New York to visit the Firehouse via Amtrak. He was at the train station, headed to New York too. We recognized each other, and he seemed nervous. I walked over and gave him a hug, which he timidly accepted. "I can't find work in Baltimore, but it doesn't matter. New York is where I need to be." He smiled at me and walked away. I still wonder about him. I like to imagine he spent the rest of his days living happily, going to the bathhouses, having boyfriends and lovers, and finally living free. He thought I was brave, and it wasn't until I matured some years later, that I realized who the *really* brave man was in that encounter. And it wasn't me.

One of the more vocal men who'd been at the first GLF Baltimore meeting had given me his number. I called and explained that we couldn't go back to the YMCA.

"David, we know you're underage and we love what you're doing, but you really can't be standing in front of those bars handing out papers," he said. "The police will find out you're underage, and they could send you to foster care or juvenile detention." We both knew I had the best intentions, but that I wasn't the one to lead this good fight, so the grown-up gays took over. I was relieved because I didn't know what else I could do with a group of two hundred men who wanted to advocate for change. I was going to graduate high school in two months, and I was ready to move to New York.

The day I graduated, I had my bags packed before my mom, stripper sister, and I even went to the ceremony. My mother had bought me a suitcase and even helped me pack—she'd been waiting twenty-eight years for this day! After I graduated in my cap and gown, I took the afternoon train to New York City with $100 in my pocket and no idea what would happen to me once I got there. I made my way to the Firehouse, but it had closed. So guess where I stayed? The 23rd Street

YMCA. I had steaming-hot gay sex there that night. And I made sure I was loud!

6.

A FOURSOME ON JANE STREET

I read in the *Village Voice* that the McBurney YMCA, which was on the West Side next door to the Chelsea Hotel, offered small rooms with shared bathrooms and showers for $40 a week. Hello! It sounded like the perfect destination for me and my eleven pieces of clothing. (Yes, I counted them. There were eleven—no need for underwear.) I'd live at the Y! The thought of shared showers already made me a little nostalgic for my junior high days, and even though this was before the Village People sang about the party-like atmosphere at this specific YMCA, it seemed obvious that I would not feel out of place there. I called to make a reservation, and the response was laughter and a man hanging up. It turned out it was an "Only if there's a room available" residency—the Waldorf, it was not.

After my train arrived, I walked from Penn Station in Midtown to the West 23rd Street Y, suitcase in hand, a blank diary packed. It was only a ten-block walk down 7th Avenue, and once I got there, the check-in was done with minimal fuss or paperwork. However, you did have to be eighteen to register. I would not turn eighteen until September, but Ronnie Bell (my stripper pal and frequent hashish supplier) and the stripper girls made a fake driver's license for me as a going-away present. ("Sugar, you're gonna need to prove you're eighteen to get anywhere in New York, so the girls and I have a little present for you.") The desk guy was so old that he looked like he'd been dipped in brine and pickled. He glanced at my ID, had me sign a paper, took my $40 cash for a seven-night stay, and gave me a sheet of paper with the rules:

*Renters only!

*No visitors allowed in the rooms!

*No sexual encounters in the rooms or in any area!

*Cigarettes allowed, no pipes or cigars!

*No drugs, no alcohol!

*The Reception Desk will not take messages for any of the guests!

I signed on the dotted line and was given a room on the fourth floor. The elevator was broken; I was told later, after my first prohibited sexual encounter by 'Bubble Butt #1,' that the elevator had not worked in nine months. This guy had been at the Chelsea Y for nearly two years. "It's cheaper than the bathhouses, there's more action, and location, location, location!" I was given a card to flash in the lobby and a room key on an elastic band, and I found my way to Room 423. Inside was a single bed with one pillow, a lamp, an overhead light, a nightstand, a wash basin with exposed piping screwed to the wall, a hand towel, and a small closet with two coat hangers and a top shelf. A laminated sign over the wash basin said, "Hand towels changed every three days at the front desk." I folded my eleven pieces of clothing neatly on the shelf and explored my new digs. The shower rooms were on every other floor; a large communal bathroom was on each floor. To shower, you grabbed a towel from the pile on a table at the tiled entrance, and after showering, a sign said to put the used towel in the basket. (A bold sign read, "DO NOT TAKE SHOWER TOWELS TO YOUR ROOM!") I guess that explained why a good number of men were walking around the halls and stairwells naked—they must not have packed a robe or swimsuit.

I was very gritty after my two-hour train ride, and I needed a shower immediately. (Okay, I was clean, just horny.) Back in my room, I disrobed, walked naked to the shower room, turned the water lever (there were twelve shower heads in each area and no dividers), and wet myself down before realizing there was no soap. An older guy was watching me; he smiled and threw me his bar. Not being good at sports, I missed the throw; it landed on the ground, so I bent over to pick it up. Then it occurred to me he missed on purpose, and I had to laugh—I had just fallen for one of the oldest tricks in the gay-book. He laughed too and we shouted our names to each other. Then he mouthed, "First day?" and I nodded yes. He said, "Meet me by the sinks when you're finished," and walked out with his towel around his waist. I came out, also wearing a towel, and returned his soap. Eddie knew he didn't have a chance with me, but he was sweet enough to give me a rundown of how things worked around here.

"If you want some ass, throw your towel in the basket and walk around as though you're headed back to your room," he explained. "If you don't want sex, wear your towel. Buy a bar of soap or you'll have scabies within the week. If you have sex in your room, take the sheet off so you have less chance of getting crabs from whoever you're fucking. If you go to the food counter in the lobby, order mayo on the side for your sandwich, palm the mayo to take back to your room for lube. Buy a pair of flip-flops on 14th street so you don't get athlete's foot, and get yourself a new pillow and a lock for your suitcase. Keep your valuables in there, always locked. Just trust me."

I thanked him. As he was leaving with a towel around his waist he called, over his shoulder, "happy hunting." I slowly walked back to my room, naked (I had to follow the rules, right?) and within five minutes had hooked up with a guy around my age who didn't mince words (about the only thing he didn't mince). "Fuck me," was his introduction. And without another word spoken he followed me to my room, I pulled off the bedsheet, he lay on his stomach and wiggled his ass, and I used spit in lieu of lube and while I fucked him I thought, *This place is gonna work for me just fine.* When it was over, he kissed my forehead and walked out. I never saw him again. No names, no foreplay, no tender moments, just 100% animal sex. It was my first time having sex that way, and I liked it. I suppose it appealed to the efficient part of my personality.

I used the basin in my room and the hand towel to wash up, dressed, and headed to 14th Street to pick up some supplies. After buying a pillow, washcloth, towel, soap, shampoo, and shower shoes, I headed back up 7th Avenue and passed a blacked-out window that said "Sex Shop." As I entered, I thought to myself, *This is a day of firsts! I am a grown-up, I'm free, I can do what I want!* I felt so liberated. I suppose my eyes looked as big as a kid's in the proverbial candy store as I walked the aisles, an old, very fat man sitting on a stool next to the register watching me. When I walked through the dildo aisle he said, "Hey kid, it's okay to pick 'em up." Wow! Everywhere I looked there was something I wanted, no, I needed! About $40 later, I had a dildo, lube, porn magazines, poppers, and a battery-powered vibrator. Oh, and a cock ring, which the clerk was nice enough to explain to me what it was and how to put it on. (I thought it was a rubber wrist bracelet and chose a big one to get it over my hand—I realized after he explained to me what it was for that I needed to, uh, size-down, and why he was giving me the fish-eye at checkout before I knew what the fuck it was!) Walking back to my new home, I thought *Jesus, New York is expensive. I'd better get a job fast!*

A few days later, I met a sexy young guy on the street in front of the Y and used my newly practiced 'eye-cruising' technique on him. He walked over and said, "What are you into?" Feeling very 'I'm a New Yorker now,' I replied, "You." We both smiled and he said it had to be at my place. Fuck! The Y rules were no visitors. I told him I was living at the Y and the rules and he said, "Have you got five bucks?" I said yes and he said, "Put it in your hand and give it to the guy at the lobby desk." I did, and without even looking up, the lobby man just used his hand to wave us towards the "Residents Only" stairwell. At the end of our sex encounter the guy hit me up for twenty bucks.

"Steve..." he said.

"David," I corrected.

"Dave, I'm hungry and that twenty dollars would really help me out." Right. My months around strippers didn't teach me nothing—I knew that he was trying to con me for a handout.

"If you're hungry, there's a counter in the lobby and I'll buy you a sandwich," I told him. He countered, as I thought he would.

"Uh, I don't have time to eat right now but give me the twenty dollars and I'll eat later."

"Sorry. Bye bye."

Place to live, check. Room supplies, check. Sex toys, check. How to handle a hustler, check. Finding a job was next on my list. While walking the streets, I was approached a few times by older men who thought I was a hustler and offered me money for a quickie in an alley. I didn't want that—I'd seen too much go wrong in the strip clubs, and I was having so much sex at the Y that I wasn't even sure I had the stamina in me to be a gay hustler for old guys. (Also, the Y had a scale and I was up to 150 pounds! I could barely see my rib cage!) I wanted a job that moved me around, kept me on my feet. I was sitting in PennyFeathers, a twenty-four-hour diner, having a cup of coffee, which I had learned to enjoy. It was the cheapest thing on any menu and you could sit and nurse a coffee for a long time, usually getting a free refill if you flirted. The guy behind the counter was cute, and we were flirting a little when a heavy woman, maybe in her early fifties, walked over and said to him:

"Phil, John just called in sick, again. I need you to work a double."

"No way, Angela, I'm not working a double and especially not the graveyard shift!"

"Please do it as a favor to me, please!" I could see she was desperate, so I said, "I'll do it!" Angela looked at me.

"Have you ever worked in a restaurant?"

I dusted off the same story I'd told Madam at the strip club, with a few new additions about moving to NYC: I was staying at the Y, was dependable, had kept a job working nights while going to high school, and that I was reliable and not on drugs. Angela smiled.

"Phil, please, will you stay a few hours and train him? If you can get him up to speed, I'll fire John and you'll have a reliable relief guy."

"Shit. Okay, I'll train him, but only for four hours and he has to promise to blow me." I was beyond shocked he said that in front of his boss! But I really wanted the job—I liked the place and the people who came in; it was good cruising and I could start immediately. I agreed to the blow job.

"I'll blow you in the bathroom room right now if you'll stay and train me!"

"Deal!"

Angela started laughing. "Now, boys, you need to take this outside."

I thought she meant I should blow him in the alley next to the restaurant, so I said, "Okay, let's go to the alley, right now."

"David, that's just an expression of speech. I don't really want you two to take it outside."

"So I should blow him here then?"

Phil stepped in. "Angela, the bathroom has a lock and you know it's not the first time somebody got a blow job in here, come on."

"Oh, all right, but don't leave a mess."

Phil looked at me and smiled, walked from behind the counter, and stood by the bathroom door. It occurred to me that the restaurant had about twenty people sitting at the tables, listening to every word of this exchange. But I wanted the job. So I walked over to Phil, and as

I did, the patrons started laughing and clapping! It didn't take long before I had an apron on and was learning how to write on an order pad. My first job in the Big Apple!

I was a natural behind the counter. I had a good personality, was a great flirt, had a sharp memory, and was well liked by the rest of the team. The graveyard shift was tough to fill, and if an employee didn't show up, it affected other team members on each side of the shift. I was used to late-night work, and after the first couple of nights, I became fascinated with the variety of people, many of them drunk, who staggered in after the bars closed. Drag queens, leather guys, bartenders, other waiters, hustlers, horny closeted men—it was right up my alley. I was making seriously good tips because I looked great, gave off a 'horny' vibe (well, I was always horny), remembered people's names and their orders, and I showed up! I fit in like a rubber glove on a fist.

A month after working at PennyFeathers and living at the Y, I knew I needed better living arrangements. I was exhausted from the amount of sex I was having in my room. I couldn't seem to control myself—if I saw it and liked it, I tried to get it and usually did. Sex was becoming about conquest and not physical feel-good times. Later, I realized that given my addictive personality, sex was yet another addiction. I knew it was time to get out of there.

My fate changed one night as I was working behind my counter. (It did kind of become *my* counter—I reorganized everything to make it more efficient, plus I called regulars by name. Also, the two lesbians and the gender-fuck guy who worked in the kitchen liked me, and they didn't like anybody!) Angela told me people would call or come in and ask if I was working, and she even offered to move me to the busier late lunch/early dinner shift based on my personality. I thanked her but said no.

"You really like the graveyard shift, don't you? Is it because it's when the weirdest ones come in?"

"Yup, one hundred percent. It's like living in an Andy Warhol movie." So I stayed put. Around 3:00 a.m. one night, a remarkably handsome guy came in, I mean runway model beautiful, and with an ass that instantly spoke to me. He sat at the counter and I, now a pro at a lot of things, immediately came on to him. My gaydar told me he was a bottom, and I suggested we hook up after my shift. He asked me an odd question.

"Is your dick ten inches or longer?"

Very matter of fact, like asking someone what size 501s they wore.

"No, but I don't get any complaints. I'm kinda close, and don't forget I do have ten fingers, and I know how to use them!" I figured that would seal the deal.

"Sorry, no tenny, no get any."

I don't know why but I started laughing. It seemed so surreal, so silly, to be discussing cock size and fingers at 3:00 a.m. in a Village diner. It *was* laughable. He started laughing too. The ever-present Angela walked over and asked what we were laughing at.

"I don't have as many inches as he's looking for, and he won't count my fingers!"

She started giggling as well and said, "If he can't count, don't let him near the register!" So all three of us just cracked each other up for a minute. Then I took his order and we started talking. His name was Bryce. He told me when he found a ten-incher, he knew how to hang on to him, and I asked how. With a sly smile, he said, "Look at me. You wanted it, everybody wants it. That only a few get it makes those few want it more." Now I knew I was really good-looking, but had it been a male model competition, I would have taken Mr. Congeniality while he got the grand prize. He was that beautiful.

We chatted while he ate, and he asked me where I was living. I told him at the Chelsea Y but I was looking for an apartment share in the Village. It turned out he was looking for a fourth roommate to share his studio (one room) apartment on Jane Street. Each roommate slept on a piece of foam against one of the four walls and everything else was shared space—the bathroom, the pullman kitchen, the one closet. I said, "So it's a four-way?" He gave me that fabulous grin again and said, "Darling, a four-way is just two bored couples." We both cracked up again and I realized Bryce could be a friend. We had the same sense of humor, and I felt comfortable around him.

I had Thursday night off, and he suggested I meet his other two roomies at The Ninth Circle. I didn't know what that was, and he explained it was *the* bar in the West Village, filled with celebrities, hustlers, drag queens, anybody and everybody. When we all met, it was obvious within five minutes that we were great fun together, and clicked as a team. I moved in the next day. The rent was $180 a month, each. That price was even better than I had hoped for—only a week's tips—so I agreed without even looking at the apartment.

The next day Bryce took me to 12th Street, where there was an industrial foam store, and I bought a thick piece cut in a single-bed size; we rolled it up with a cord and headed towards the apartment. En route, we passed a moving warehouse, and Bryce told me to buy a large packing blanket. "It's way cheaper than a blanket at Macy's," he said. One more stop at a bedding shop and I had my pillow. We dropped it all off in the apartment, which was small but clean and seemed perfectly okay to me considering all four of us worked late nights. In fact, the place looked luxurious after my time at the Y—wood floors, a full kitchen, a bathtub and shower combo, plus a pretty corner window overlooking brownstones and with a view of the sky. The building had a small elevator, but it was faster to walk up the four flights. My ribs were showing again, I was back down to 140 pounds, and I wanted to stay that way, so the stairs were a plus.

The four of us grew close over the next decade. While we all went separate ways as we got older, we still kept in touch. We were so tight in those early days that the bartenders at The Ninth Circle, which had become our hangout, nicknamed us "The Four Musketeers."

Three months after landing in New York City, I had a job I liked, a place to live I liked, roommates I liked. So why did I feel so alone? New York seemed like it had already stopped talking to me. It was getting cold, all of the color the summer brought was gone, and the city looked grey. I grew bored with the good things I had going; they weren't good enough. I paid six months' rent in advance and told my roommates I was going back to Baltimore, "just for a little while," and to keep my wall, my foam, and my packing blanket for me because I'd be back come spring. I didn't even bother taking my suitcase—I just packed a few things in a Bloomingdale's shopping bag, went to Penn Station, and caught an Amtrak train to go back to my roots. Little did I know I was about to meet a photographer and begin a life of crime.

———————•———————

Oh lord, was I handsome when I was nineteen. I knew it and was totally convinced that *everybody* wanted me. I turned heads on the streets and in the sheets. When I returned to Baltimore after my short stint in New York, I met a handsome photographer named Michael. He could only use one arm, for reasons I never thought to ask.

Michael lived in a huge brownstone in a neighborhood called Bolton Hill just outside the center of Baltimore. It was once a wealthy and beautiful area with wide streets and mansion-like turn-of-the-century brick homes, but with inner-city Baltimore down on its luck, the buildings began to crumble. Wealthy people moved out, replaced by renters of dubious backgrounds and squatters. The brownstones were carved into apartments and rented at low rates by slumlords who bought the homes in the hopes that one day the neighborhood would be on the upswing again. Michael was hired by a slumlord to be the caretaker of an empty brownstone so that it wasn't broken into or further damaged, and he lived in the basement apartment since it was connected to the backyard and offered pretty views from the rear windows.

He was a pretty view, too—think Robert Redford mixed with Cary Grant. He straddled the line between looking like the All-American stud and an English gentleman, half rugged, half foppish. I was invited to his apartment by a friend of mine in the theatre community. Michael was having a hashish party with the hopes of selling some to his friends and the friends of their friends. While trying to make a living as a photographer, his secondary income was as a drug dealer, but just the soft stuff. Michael was not afraid to use his looks to get what he wanted, when he wanted, which was usually from equally beautiful young women who were looking for good sex with no strings attached. As the party began, I got very high on hash and flirted openly and outrageously with Michael. He thought it was funny and said so several times. "David, you are so wasting your time, I'm only into women."

I smiled.

"We'll see about that." We both laughed. By the end of the night, we had determined that Michael was lonely living alone in such a huge brownstone. A thought popped into my hash-clouded head.

"Well, why don't you let me stay here because I'm just floating around." He agreed, and we decided I'd bring my Bloomingdale's shopping bag over the next day. Moving in, for me, was easy, a one-handed job. Michael said, "Choose any apartment you like, and that can be where you live." There were five units, not counting his. I chose the third floor one-bedroom with huge windows overlooking the street, which had a meridian running down the middle with lovely, mature trees. The tops of the front windows had intricate stained glass work and the oak floors, though no longer shiny, were nonetheless striking.

Michael found me a futon and a lamp, and my one-bedroom apartment was furnished. I spent the majority of my time in his place anyway. We soon developed a pattern: we'd wake up, I'd come down the common stairway in as little clothing as possible (always with my eye on the prize), and go into his place where we would make coffee and smoke a joint to take the edge off a day that hadn't yet begun. Then we'd talk, or read, or walk about the neighborhood, feeling stoned and happy. I'd put my attempt to seduce Michael on hold for a while, knowing it was going to require his trust, which I could only earn over time. I was completely obsessed with wanting to fuck him, which I knew would need to begin with a blow job. (I always found those boring, but sometimes necessary—like knocking on a door to get in.) Having never experienced love, I thought what I was feeling for him *was* love. I guess I hadn't determined the difference between love and lust—yet.

A couple months went by with Michael selling hash and pot. Meanwhile, I'd begun to sell hot dogs from the only metal stand with wheels in Baltimore—yes, a hot dog cart. It was owned by an eccentric guy who wanted to create a wiener empire in the same way they existed in Manhattan. I would walk six blocks to his large garage and stock my hot dog stand with the supplies he ordered, then push it about a mile to the center of the city. By that time, the hot water had cooked the wieners and I was ready for business. (Ironically, those were the months I had decided to be a vegetarian, so I never ate one of the hot dogs I was selling.) Many people in the Baltimore city center had never seen a hot dog stand and were intrigued by it (and to be honest, maybe a few were intrigued by *my* tube steak, proudly displayed in my 501s, sans underwear, as usual). It was a mostly lunchtime business with men and women in legal offices, banks, governmental buildings and insurance agencies, looking for a fast, cheap lunch. I did a good business, and after lunchtime I pushed my cart the mile back to this guy's garage, cleaned it up, and counted the money with him; he took 70% and I took 30%, which averaged around $40 a day for me. The cart was in business Monday through Friday as downtown Baltimore was dead during weekends. I didn't start until 10:00 a.m. and was back to my crash pad by 4:00 p.m.—hippie hours!

At night, friends would come over and we would hang out in Michael's apartment listening to albums, smoking hash, and sharing our dreams. It was at that time I found an autobiography of Isadora Duncan titled *My Life* in the public library. I was enchanted by her colorful and eccentric lifestyle. ("I can only drink champagne, darling, water is so watery!") Isadora performed a free-form dance in bare feet, wearing gauzy fabric, listening to the classics and emoting with her body. I thought, *I can do that!* Hell, I *was* doing that—emoting with my body, though it was called cruising. At night, in my third-floor apartment, I would drape a sheet around my shoulders and dance to imaginary music like Isadora. It was obvious my new career should be teaching and dancing the Isadora technique to children! (Did I mention I was often very, very stoned?) I was bored with coming home smelling like hot dogs and I was bored with looking at Michael every night, wanting to fuck him and not getting him. Michael had a Volkswagen van and had talked about driving it to Mexico and hanging out with his camera in the various cities and towns. One night I said to him, "Why don't I come with you to Mexico, and while you are taking photos of the locals, I can teach the children Isadora Duncan dance technique!" He thought about it for a minute and said, "That might be cool." That got my hopes up (and more)!

———•———

A few weekends before this grand idea, I'd been on a call with my mother.

"Oh David, I'm so nervous that I'm going to be robbed," she said. I asked why. She explained that every Friday she'd take the paychecks of the guys who worked in her office to the bank, cash them, put the cash in her purse, and walk back to the office. Then the guys would get their paychecks in cash and wouldn't have to go to the bank.

"When I come out of the bank, I'm in the lobby of a big office building and there's a long corridor that I have to walk down to get outside and there's hardly anybody in that corridor and I'm always thinking, 'What would happen if somebody just grabbed my purse with all that money in it and ran?' Nobody would even see it probably." It crossed my mind that maybe she was trying to tell me something, but then I thought, *Nah*.

But it did get my hashish-lubricated wheels spinning. Michael and I would certainly need money for this Mexico trip during which I was *surely* going to charm him enough that he'd let me fuck him. We'd need cash for gas, sleeping bags, food, and all the other things that would require using the van as a mobile home tootling through Mexico. It was also not lost on me that the sleeping arrangements would be the two of us in sleeping bags, in the back of the van, an approximate six-by-ten-feet space. All I could think of was Michael and me, in the middle of nowhere. I'd get a little liquor in him, and he'd let me do what I wanted to him. In my mind it was that simple.

I told Michael about my mother carrying cash in her purse every Friday and her telling me she thought it was about $5,000. I looked at Michael. Michael looked at me. We were both thinking the same thing. I said it first.

"We're going to rob her, aren't we?"

"Yup." He was a man of few words.

"How are you going to do it?" I said softly.

"Me? I'm not going to do it! *You* have to do it!"

"Michael, I can't rob my own mother."

"Why not?" he asked.

"Well, for one, don't you think she might recognize me?"

"Oh. I hadn't thought of that," he said.

"Yeah, well, think about it."

"I know, what if we disguised you so she wouldn't recognize you?" he suggested.

"What if we disguised *you*, and then she wouldn't recognize me for sure, because it wouldn't fucking *be* me!" We went back and forth like this for a while, while passing the hash pipe.

"David, you don't drive and I do, so I have to be the getaway car guy and you have to be the robber. What are we going to do otherwise, rob her and catch the bus?"

I said, "Well, what about a cab?" but he stared me down.

With that out of the way, we discussed what kind of disguise I could wear. As we were mulling it over, a local actress and friend of mine, Sandy McDonald, came to visit. She was rather well-known in the inner city for wearing five or six platinum wigs, one on top of the other, an outrageous amount of makeup, and a consistent hooker-like wardrobe. (She wasn't a hooker—she worked days for BellSouth, the regional phone company—and acted in local theatre at night.) She got every role she wanted, based on looks alone. Big hair, big breasts, big makeup, and the ability to memorize lines, kinda. She couldn't act her way out of a paper bag, but the audience rarely cared because they were too busy staring at how bizarre she was. She was literally a feast for the eyes, and very, very Baltimore.

Sandy had a big crush on Michael, so she came by a lot. She would park her VW Beetle in the alley next to the back door of his apartment; when it was time for her to drive home, always stoned out of her mind, she had it in her head she could only drive backwards. Which is exactly what she did, giggling, for as far as we could see and hear her, because we always went into the backyard to watch her drive backwards down the alleyway. Was it just for dramatic effect, or did she drive backwards all the way to the suburb of Towson eight miles away? Who knows? Baltimore *was* a very strange town.

When she came to visit that night, Michael and I both realized that Sandy was a walking costume resource. If I borrowed a couple of her platinum wigs, a trench coat, a scarf and earrings, and added some drugstore makeup and a pair of flat women's shoes, I would look like a girl. My mother would never recognize me in a million years, right? So that became the plan. We didn't overthink it. (To be fair, it is really hard to overthink things when you are buzzed out of your mind on hash.)

The Friday before the heist, we staked out the area. Michael parked his VW van in front of the door that my mother would have to exit after walking down the corridor to leave the bank. I hid inside the corridor to scope out where to stand so as not to draw attention to myself (even though I was a teenage boy dressed to the nines in female hooker clothes and make-up). When she came out of the bank door and into the corridor, I could grab her purse and run like hell to the getaway car. What could go wrong?

That fateful Friday morning, I donned the wigs, the makeup, and the trench coat and was ready to roll. Michael, the getaway man, drove me to the office door as planned. I knew my mother would complete this transaction around 10:00 a.m. So we waited in the van and watched my mother open the door and go inside. Then I waited five minutes and went into the corridor, standing close to a stairwell up to the second floor. I hoped I would just kind of *blend in* and not draw attention to myself, despite the fact that I looked like a gay teenage hooker in drag. My heart pounded like I had a drum accompaniment. Sure enough, the corridor was empty. My mother walked through the door with her purse. I walked up to her and said, in my most girlish voice, "Give me your purse!" She just looked at me.

"Give me your purse!" I demanded again.

"Oh David, what the hell are you doing?" she said.

"Mom! I'm robbing you!"

"David, oh David, oh David. What the fuck."

I didn't know what to do, so I grabbed her purse and ran to the door, pushed through, jumped into the getaway van, and off we went. The reality of what had taken place hadn't fully set in. Back at the apartment, I rummaged through her purse, and sure enough there was about $5,000. And a container of Valium, her ID, and some makeup. I immediately took two Valium to calm my nerves and then Michael and I smoked a joint and congratulated each other on a robbery well done.

Between the two Valium and the joint, I was feeling floaty so I decided to lie down on the couch and have a little nap. As I was settling in, the phone rang. I answered it, and it was… my mother.

"David, I was robbed! On my way back from the bank by a big man with a beard who took my purse, and thank God he didn't hurt me. I've been questioned by the police, and they are looking for a tall bearded guy, but they don't think they'll have much success finding him. I am so nervous. I'm going to come over to where you and Michael live after work and maybe you two can calm me down. I'll expect you to be there to help me get over the trauma of all this." Click, the phone went dead.

Oh shit! For the rest of the afternoon, I was on pins and needles and thinking, *Jesus, what have I done?* Michael was less concerned but he wasn't exactly looking forward to her visit either. At 6:00 p.m., there was a knock on the door. When I answered, my mother came barreling in loaded for bear.

"You son of a bitch! Jesus H. Christ, what's wrong with you?"

"Hi, Mom," I said sheepishly.

Mom demanded a drink. Michael said we had some brandy.

"Good, bring me some with ice in some water. I can't decide if I'm turning you in or putting you over my knee. Both of you. Do you have any idea how what you've done has affected my nerves? And David, did you really think that with a wig on top your head, the same color as your hair, and in a raincoat I wasn't going to recognize you? I have to say I didn't realize you were so stupid."

"Mom, I'm sorry. I'm really sorry. I thought about it all afternoon and I'm so sorry. Michael and I needed money to go to Mexico so he could take pictures and I could teach Isadora Duncan dance technique and we didn't know how else to get it and we didn't really think you would recognize me and, and, and, and…" I rambled on while she drank her brandy and water and stared at me like I had lost my mind. Michael, my handsome snake in the grass, spoke up.

"Mrs. Vass, this was all his idea."

"What the fuck, Michael?" I exploded. "Who was the getaway driver? Mom, you know I don't drive so it wasn't me."

My mom said, "I don't care who came up with it. I only know who did it and it was both of you. How dare you!" Then, after a pause, out popped a little laugh.

"Mom, you're laughing. You can't be that upset," I said.

"David, I'm not laughing because it's funny. I'm laughing because it's…" She paused again and looked at Michael, then looked at me. She started laughing harder and said, "Well, in a way, it *is* funny." Then I started laughing, and then Michael started laughing. There we were, all three of us unable not to laugh. But then things got serious again as my mother turned to us both.

"The bank says you got $5,430. You say you are using it for a trip to Mexico. Here's what we're going to do. You're going to give me half of that money." I was stunned.

"Mom, you want a cut of the robbery money?" I asked.

"Yes, I do, David," she replied.

Michael, always practical, said, "How about one-third?"

"What do you think this is, a negotiation?" Somehow she agreed to take one-third of the loot. And then, looking me right in the eye, she said, "David. One day, probably soon, you're going to get in real trouble, because if you continue living your life the way you've been living it, trouble will find you. One day or one night I'm going to get a phone call, and it's going to be from the police and you're going to be in jail for breaking the law. And so what I'm doing with my share of the money is I'm putting it in the bank. When I get that call, and I know I'll get it, I'll have a little money to try and help you with bail or a lawyer.

And if you could do me one favor, and I know you're not religious, and neither am I, it would be to get on your knees tonight and pray that you come to your senses and learn right from wrong."

She stood up and asked for her purse. She looked through it, checking her Valium was in it first and then her ID. She looked at Michael and she looked at me.

"What happened today is between the three of us and never leaves this room as long as I'm alive." She didn't hug me, we didn't kiss; she turned her back and walked out the door. Two years later, when I was living on the West Coast, I had to call her after I'd been arrested for possession of marijuana in Orange County on my way to Disneyland with a cute guy. She bailed me out. Guess where the bail money came from?

Michael and I made it to Mexico. We spent two days driving south, dropping LSD as we wove down the narrow bridges on US 1 to Key West. After a brief visit there, we drove for another two days to the Mexican border and landed in some dinky town. I made my move on Michael that night in the back of the van, and he politely but firmly declined, moving his sleeping bag to the roof of the VW. He slept there the next two nights, not really talking to me much during the day. I finally realized I was never going to win the 'fuck the straight man' game, so I asked him for airfare back to Baltimore, which he gladly gave me. He even drove me to the airport. That's how sorry he was to see me go.

Turns out, Michael was only an amuse-bouche to my love for photographers. When I returned to New York City, I met one of the most famous men working in couture fashion. And guess what? He sure as fuck didn't want to sleep on the roof when I put the moves on him.

7.

FIRST LOVE, WORST LOVE

As spring sprung in New York City, so did I. I returned to my paid-for crash pad on Jane Street, but it turned out my foam pad had been "sublet" by my dear fellow musketeers (aka those double-dipping fuck-alls). I had nowhere to sleep. It somehow didn't kill our friendship, but I found myself on the streets again, which ended up a lot more fun than it sounds. I was living out of a shopping bag with literally one dime in my pocket (the price of a phone call in case I needed to call someone) and was having a blast. This was how I preferred to live. It was 1970, prime hippie years, and I felt freer without possessions and money. I wasn't a street person or a hustler—I simply walked the West Village, found guys I wanted to have sex with, then asked if I could stay overnight, post-fuck. It wasn't unusual during that time and within my age group not to have roots or an apartment.

I had two slightly older gay friends who had given me their numbers and assured me I could crash on their couches when needed. Occasionally I'd go to their places to catch up on food and a shower—maybe wash my 501s and socks in their sink in exchange for a quick BJ. One afternoon while I was mindlessly walking down Christopher Street, hoping someone would buy me a drink and burger at Julius (NYC's oldest gay bar), a very chic young woman walked up to me. Turns out she was scouting some long-hairs to be part of a fashion shoot.

"I work for a famous fashion photographer," she explained. "He is looking for three hippies to be part of a photo shoot for a *Harper's*

Bazaar spread. The shoot is this Sunday at noon and will take about three hours. The pay is one hundred dollars cash, and the only instruction is that you wear exactly what you have on now"—my 501s, duh, and a pink collarless 'poor boy' shirt—"and don't cut your hair between now and then. Would you be interested?"

Would I? Be paid $100 for three hours of doing nothing? Yes, I was very interested!

She gave me the address, and I was excited thinking about what I was sure would be the birth of my extremely successful male modeling career. Two days later, I found myself at a large photo studio at 100 5th Avenue, a massive loft space. Walking in, I saw a humongous table crammed full of food—fruits and cakes and all the cheese imaginable, along with wine and soft drinks. I was as skinny as Karen Carpenter but proceeded to chow down all while thinking, *How much of this food can I fit in my pockets when I leave?* There were two professional female models and one other hippie guy. He wasn't bad looking; his hair was longer than mine, and he was also a blond. A third guy never showed—the scout assumed one of us would flake and the photographer only needed two hippies in the shoot. After we got settled, the photographer came out from an adjoining loft room, looked us both over, and introduced himself.

"Hi, I'm Bill King."

He was around five feet, nine inches tall (oh how I loved it when they were shorter than me!), very cute, with longish chestnut brown hair and a great smile. When he turned around, I spied my downfall—he had a bubble butt! I didn't know it yet, but I'd soon learn he was the most influential fashion photographer of the time, someone who shot covers for *Harper's Bazaar* and other high-end fashion magazines and couture fashion advertisements. His eyes locked with mine and my gaydar picked up immediately; he was interested in me, and I already knew what I wanted as payment. Fuck the $100, I wanted him. And it didn't look like it would be very hard to get.

For the actual shoot, the studio had two industrial-size fans on the floor, loads of bright white lighting, a floor-to-ceiling white paper background, and a woman with a spritz bottle full of glycerin. A stylist approached and wrapped six different narrow, tie-dyed, gauze scarves around my neck (*I wonder how many of these I can stuff in my pocket when I leave?*), sprayed my shoulder-length, straight blond hair with something, and brushed it through. Then she smiled and told me I looked great, which helped with my nerves. The other guy received a similar treatment. The female models entered the room wearing the kind of super couture outfits you might see in *Harper's* or *Vogue*. Bill positioned us on the white paper floor with the two girls in the center, a hippie on either side. His instructions were simple: "When I say start, everybody jump up in the air repeatedly, like you are on a trampoline, and make lots of motion with your arms—swing them around, over your head—whatever you want so long as all your body parts are moving. Just keep jumping until I say stop. Oh, don't be afraid to knock into each other a little if you want. Don't push, but if a part of you touches a part of the model midair, that would be delicious. And look happy!"

The fans came on and suddenly we were in a wind tunnel, everyone's hair and scarves blowing all over the place. "Go!" shouted Bill. I jumped as high as I could (but not as high as I was), bending my knees under me a few times. I intentionally started having my ass or hips hit the side of whatever model was near me and they got into it. I was laughing and shouting to the two females, "Hey, we're playing hit the hip-pies!" The three of us were having a ball! (The other hippie guy didn't grasp the concept; he just looked stoned.) The woman sprayed us all with glycerin again, and we were given a glass of water to drink. Bill told the other guy to move further to the side and back "to give the pictures more dimension." (Uh-huh—Bill wanted the guy out of the shots.) When the shoot was done and people were leaving, Bill pointed at me with a shy smile.

"What's your name again?"

"David. Thanks for having me, that was so cool. Really fun."

"Wanna smoke a joint?"

"Sure!"

We smoked a joint as his studio cleared out, and we were left alone. Bill asked if I'd like to make another hundred bucks. My mind immediately went to his dick in my mouth.

"Um, why? How? Probably."

"I'd like you to do some solo shots with me—they would be nudes for a book I'm working on."

"I'm not interested in the hundred dollars."

"I can't pay more, sorry," he said, giving me a fuck-you look.

"That's not what I meant. I mean, you don't have to pay me at all if you also get naked for the shoot. And then let me fuck you." Bold move, but it worked because that's exactly what happened. Our rhythms matched perfectly and with the kind of chemistry lacking in my twenty-minute encounters. We engaged in serious tongue-kissing (not usual for my 'fuck 'em and leave 'em' routine.) He suggested dinner, and I pulled my one thin dime out of my pocket, held it in my hand, and gave him my best grin.

"Oh, don't worry, I'm paying," he said... and giggled.

After dinner, we went back to his apartment and I stayed the night. I made a little money, ate a hearty dinner, had great sex, and now lay in a warm bed with more sex. Perfect! Bill lived on the eighth floor of a 1930s brick-red condo building on the corner of Bleeker Street and Waverly Place; it had a doorman and a deco elevator and there was a little park across from the entrance. He lived in a large studio with dark-wood floors, a pullman kitchen, and an all-white bathroom—tiles, towels, tub, everything all white. (Made me think he was a Virgo. Turned out, he was.) We had more sex, cuddle-slept through the night, and connected with lots of kissing and sweet caresses. The next morning, he asked if I wanted to see him again and I said, "You bet. How about tonight when you come back from your photo studio?"

He asked where I lived. "If you let me stay here a few days, then I live here a few days." He thought that was funny and agreed right away, telling me to help myself to anything in the kitchen; he'd be home around 4:00 p.m. and we'd have dinner again. I lay in his giant bed watching TV and realized I *liked* this guy. I hadn't felt that in a long while, maybe ever.

For several days he seemed happy with the arrangement, and I was too. We had so many tender moments, which was also new to me. *What is happening?* I wondered. *I'm having feelings I've never had before.*

A few days later, on Saturday morning, Bill gave me a kiss and went to work. I lay naked in his bed with a box of chocolates, eating bonbons and watching TV, wondering if Bill and I were going to develop into something real, when I heard the door unlock. I thought maybe he had come home early for lunch. I smiled, thinking, *I'm falling for this guy!* But instead of my sexy new boyfriend, a stoutly woman around sixty years old walked in with a big bundle. When she saw me, she froze.

"Who the hell are you?"

I thought she was maybe his cleaning lady, so I replied, "Who the hell are *you*?"

"I'm Bill's mother. What the hell are you doing in his bed?"

"I'm his lover, and I'm staying with him," I replied, with a huff and a little shake on the bed, which I knew would make my dick jiggle.

"*What*? You need to get up right now—put your clothes on and get out!"

"I don't think so. Bill and I are having a thing and we're both enjoying it and I am staying so get over it." I turned the TV volume up.

"*Arghhhh!*" She dropped the laundry and ran out.

That exchange didn't, uh, go well. Bill had left me his studio number but with strict instructions not to call unless there was an emergency. I decided this was probably one of those times since she was his mother, so I rolled a joint and called him.

"Hi, so...your mother?...was just here and I think I freaked her out. Oh, looks like she brought your laundry."

"Wait, what? Oh my God, *what*? I'll be there in fifteen minutes." Click.

It hit me. His mother didn't know he was gay! I had just outed him! *Shit, shit, shit!* I thought of all the scenarios of what could happen next, and they all led to Bill kicking my ass out. I really liked this guy, and not just for the fancy digs or the good food. I was developing feelings for him, and I wanted to see where this would go. This was new emotional territory for me.

When Bill arrived, I had gotten my dick hard, thinking it might be a good distraction strategy. He stopped in his tracks and stared at me, still naked in bed, with the candy box and scattered, crumpled brown wrappings and a bundle of his laundry on the floor. He stood there with his mouth hanging open. For some reason, maybe the way he looked, maybe because I was stoned, I saw the humor in the whole thing and couldn't help it, I started laughing—I laughed so hard I almost peed myself and my dick deflated. He looked so adorable right then, albeit aghast. After a few seconds, he started laughing too. He laughed his way over to the bed, I tore off his clothes, and we had lunch sex. Afterwards, I said, "I'm sorry if I've caused you trouble with your mom. It never occurred to me she didn't know you were gay, but I understand if you want me to leave." Instead of kicking me out, he gave me that smile, crinkled his eyes, and told me to stay for as long as I liked. He was happy to come home to me, he said, and was developing feelings for me, too. We were on the same page (although he said it first), and it was music to my ears!

We had an intimate, emotional, funny, sex-positive time for several weeks, and then I started to give serious thought to what was happening to me. I was falling in love with Bill, but he was a powerful, successful man, making tons of money, with a huge reputation, and admired by the fashion industry—he was fashion's 'It' boy of the year. What did I have to offer him? Good sex? He could get that from an array of the crazy-handsome male models he shot. Why was he still even interested in me? My sense of self-worth was so broken that I couldn't wrap my head around Bill liking me just for being me.

Bill took over from Richard Avedon to shoot the *What Becomes a Legend Most* photo campaign for the fur industry. During our time together, he shot Liza Minelli, Peggy Lee, and Lena Horne—famous women that, ironically, I too would later work with. At the time, I felt like that same white trash boy from Baltimore—nothing to offer, no sense of entitlement, literally one thin dime, and a shopping bag that housed my entire wardrobe. I freaked out that evening and blurted out I was going to leave the next day to hitchhike to the West Coast, to Hollywood. His face fell and he asked why. I was too embarrassed to say that I didn't think I was worthy of him, that he'd made a mistake about me, that I was so embarrassed that my addictions included lying and worse, so I just said the easiest thing that popped into my head, that I didn't like to stay in any one place for very long. The way he looked, the sadness that generated from him as he started to cry—it terrified me and I couldn't think straight. That one minute of my just spitting out untrue shit talk and the sadness in his reaction—I didn't know what was happening.

"But I am starting to fall in love with you and I thought you were feeling the same way," Bill whispered. Oh God, I wanted so badly to say, "I *am*, I'm falling in love with you too!" It wouldn't come out of my mouth! I tried to move my body to take him in my arms, lick the tears streaming down his face, hold him as tightly as I could. To say I loved him and all of the other emotions I was feeling. But I couldn't—I was frozen in place, verbally and physically….. Overriding all of that was a heavier, all-encompassing thought, a dark, heavy mind-cloud—that I did not deserve him. He could do so much better than settling for me.

I lay on the bed crying, then decided I needed to get out *right then*, because if I spent another minute staring into those brown eyes I would have spilled my real feelings, and that scared me. I had to close down. So I filled my shopping bag with my few pieces of clothing, the book I was reading, and my diary, said goodbye and bolted, fast-walking to the door. His final words to me were "At least let me give you airfare to LA, I'm scared something might happen to you hitching and call please David call because I..." I never heard the end of that sentence, because I slammed the door and ran down those eight flights of stairs before I could change my mind, before I ran back and collapsed in his arms, holding him all night and whispering "I love you, I love you, I've never loved *anyone* before, I love you, I don't know how to do it but I love you..."

Bill King died in the first wave of the AIDS genocide. I followed his career by checking out fashion magazines through the years. I saw he moved from *Harper's* to *Vogue*, and on occasion I would read something about him on Page Six. When I learned of his death, I wondered if he might still be alive had I stayed and had the confidence of my worth to embrace our relationship; allowed it to blossom and grow into love and security for us both. By leaving that night, had I effectively killed him? I was haunted by the possibility for many, many years. Maybe we wouldn't have lasted another six months or even six weeks, but maybe we could have lived happily ever after. Maybe I ran away from my prince. I'll never know, thanks to my shitty self-esteem and deep-rooted belief that I was unlovable.

———•———

I left New York for the second time, taking my thumb and my shopping bag west, first to LA, through San Francisco, and then to Portland. My nomadic, homo-hobo self just hitched around, looking for nothing, feeling nothing, shell-shocked from my feelings for Bill and accepting everything that happened on the road. Nothing mattered. I worked my way up the coast for no particular reason, arriving in Portland, Oregon. The place called to me on some visual level and I decided to stay put a while. I met a young woman, Nancy, who was renting a Victorian house for cheap—it was run-down but with the usual architectural accents: stained glass windows, chain pull toilets, gouged wood floors, a front wraparound porch. It sat on a corner lot, worn but beautiful. Nancy was my age, and she offered me a room for free. She didn't like being the only one in the big house (for safety reasons) and appeared lonely, with sad, vacant eyes. Nancy explained that she had just finished shock treatments because her parents thought she was 'a loony-tune,' and didn't know what to do next. She wasn't interested in me sexually; she needed someone to talk to, and I was a good listener. (She didn't quite get that I was so stoned I usually couldn't do anything but listen!)

Soon we fell into a rhythm. At night, I went to a local gay bar called The Family Zoo while Nancy worked as a waitress at The Spaghetti Factory. She would bring back tasty midnight dinners smuggled out under her apron. One evening I walked into the bar and saw a guy who was about my height and attractive in an unusual way; his expressive face was slightly 'off.' He was a little taller than me, which normally was not a turn-on, but he made eyes at me, cruising me in an amateurish but rather sweet way. After a quick conversation, we drove to his place in the heart of downtown Portland. His name was Pieter, and he had a garage and a car and a fancy apartment—*holy shit, he must be rich. I'd hit pay dirt with a bubble butt!* He was Australian, in the U.S. on a college visa, with a big, uncut cock; he turned out to be a very eager and demanding bottom. We started dating, and after talking to Nancy, we offered Pieter a room in the house. It was a great deal for all of us— we saved money on rent and I got all the free sex I wanted while Nancy had an additional pair of ears for her tales of woe. We were eighteen and nineteen, Pieter and I, and thought we were a genuine serious couple, so when he decided he wanted to move to NYC to study at Pratt in Brooklyn (a university for fine arts), it was decided I would go with him. I wanted to see if this relationship could turn into the same kind of love I'd felt for Bill King. I'd also learned that he had a $4,000 monthly allowance, compliments of his crazy-wealthy Australian father. His dad was so rich that he'd been asked by the leading political party Down Under to run for prime minister but had turned it down because there wasn't "enough money in it."

Pieter wasn't out to his dad, and a few months after we got together, I talked him into writing his father and explaining he was gay and in a living-together relationship with me, and that he was very much in love—the whole nine yards. He did, after I literally put the pen in his hand and the paper on his desk, and his father's response came back, two weeks later, air mail: "I will have my secretary research homosexuality and get back to you with my opinion and any potential actions that may need to be taken."

Pieter and I had only been living together for three months when the FBI knocked on the door one night around 11:00 p.m. while he was visiting his family in Australia. Fuck me standing up on a trampoline, the Feds finally tracked me down for refusing to acknowledge my Vietnam War draft letter the year before, which was a serious offense. Back then, every young man, on turning eighteen, had four weeks to go to the post office and register for the draft and shortly thereafter received a letter with the location of your draft board and a date and time to show up. A potential draftee was then asked a series of questions: Were you able and willing to serve, what were your religious convictions, were you willing to kill for your country, etc. Then about two weeks later, you received your number. A number was chosen once a month on national TV, after the news, in one of those air-blowing machines like it was bingo or the lottery—only there were no winners. If the number called was 195, 95-195 were drafted, and so on. Sometimes the number was 682 or 373. You never knew, you just sort of held your breath and waited. Well, most did—not me.

Of course, there was some 'funny stuff' within the system. Young men with connections could be exempted for weird reasons, like they were the only living son or had to stay in college because the degree being obtained could help war efforts. It was a shell game, and Blacks were 14% less likely to be exempt than Whites. You could also claim exemption if you were a homosexual or for certain religious reasons. But I never answered my letter, and I never showed up to my draft board hearing—I just ignored it altogether. Because I was publicly out *and* a very vocal and visible member of the anti-war movement and the gay community. All I needed to do was go before the board, put my hand on a Bible, and confirm that I was a homosexual, but something about that didn't sit right with me. Plenty of straight men pretended they were gay in order to get out of the war (others fled to Canada), but at the time, I was so focused on proving that us gay folks could do everything that straight folks could do that it seemed ridiculous that homosexuals couldn't fight this horrible and pointless war if they wanted to. I felt like I would be letting down my own ideals if I'd just used the gay card to get out of the draft. I was even willing to go to prison over it—if they ever managed to find my country-roaming ass, that is. They did.

―――――•―――――

When the knock came near midnight, I answered the door naked and covered in an ointment used to kill a nasty case of scabies (which I caught while cheating on Pieter, which I did often). The two FBI men were dressed in black suits and skinny ties (always a serious turn-on to me) and announced they were there to take me in. I explained about the scabies and suggested waiting until morning to arrest me, once I was sure they were all dead, "'cause they can jump pretty far." They exchanged horrified looks, backed off, and agreed to sit in their car outside the house overnight.

Just after sunrise, after I showered and put clothes on, I walked to their car. They put me in handcuffs and drove me to the Joint Base Lewis-McChord on the outskirts of Portland. One agent was *seriously* cute, with ice-blue eyes. He sat in the back of the police car with me while I joked, "Oh no, I think I just saw a scabie jump on you!" He'd just laugh and give me a glimpse of those baby blues. *This guy could be had!* My thoughts should have been focused on going to prison, but that was already a done and dusted conclusion. So instead, I thought about fucking the FBI agent, trying to get my dick hard so it would show through my 501s. It worked! I pointed at the outline in my crotch and raised my eyebrows at him; he laughed, and I did the same. I whispered, "Wanna touch it?"

We were having fun then playing "I spy with my little eye," but the brutish jerk in the front who was driving gave us both dagger-eyes via the rearview mirror. Spoilsport! At the induction center on the base, I was given a physical, which included an eye exam, body check, an agility and aerobics test, and a talk with the center's psychologist. He asked me if I was gay. *Come on.*

"I'm sure you already have a folio on both my gay and anti-war activities and know that I refused to cooperate with the draft board, so why are you asking me questions you already have answers to?" I was being sarcastic, but I should have known from his crew cut and the *huge* picture of Richard Nixon on his wall that he had no sense of humor. He dove right into his standard operating procedure questions:

Him: "Would you kill an enemy for your country?"

Me: "I don't believe in murder."

Him: "Have you ever had sex with a man? How many?"

Me: "Do you have a calculator handy?"

Him: "Are you a supporter of the Vietnam War?"

Me: "No, uh, hello!"

Him: "Do you have religious reasons to be considered for wanting an exemption from the draft?" (This one only worked if you could prove you had been a Quaker for many years.)

Me: "I'm not a Quaker, I'm a queer. Don't you know that already?"

When he was finished with the Q&A, he said, "I find no reason why you can't fight for your country, like thousands of other young men that are mature enough to understand their patriotic duty to flag and family."

I was livid. "These thousands of young men are not being inducted because they *want* to out of some patriotic pride, but because their draft lottery number was called and they had to enlist or else go to prison, you dumbwit, so your reasoning is full of shit." I knew I was going to prison, so I saw no reason not to speak my truth. I added, "And we gay men can fight every bit as well as straight men, so being gay is no reason to give someone a psychological discharge, which is why I'm sitting here right now. I don't want out of the military because I'm gay, I want out because I have a conscience and prefer not to napalm babies on Wednesdays. And I'm not putting up with your homophobic bullshit."

He glared.

"I am approving you as psychologically unable to serve your country due to your homosexuality, but you are now in the hands of the federal government for the felony offense of evading the draft, which is considered treason. And I would just like to say I hope they throw the book at you, because I wouldn't sleep well at night knowing a fag was what stood between my wife and family being safe in the USA and a Communist takeover."

Oh brother. I found it funny in a sick, sad way. I laughed, which was my go-to reflex when confronted with hateful situations. I stared right into his dead grey eyes, winked, flicked my tongue, and blew him a kiss. *Asshole.* Then I wished him a "Napalm New Year," before he buzzed a guard to take me back to the FBI agents, who walked me into the military court, which was in the same compound. The blue-eyed FBI agent, my not-so-secret man crush, offered me a cigarette, which I took. We chatted a bit as we walked and I couldn't stop staring into those amazing eyes and using every cruise technique I knew for one last quickie, pre-prison. He asked how I got scabies. I told him that I had sex with men, because I was *so* good at it—especially at giving quick blow jobs to straight FBI men. He laughed but didn't keep up his eye contact with me. I mentioned the free health clinic for hippies, gays, and 'heads' (slang for pot smokers) and promised there wasn't anything he and I could do and they couldn't get rid of with either a pill, an ointment, or a needle in your ass. We both started laughing while the other FBI goon-guy eyed us both with disdain.

I was scoping out where the nearest men's room was (I hadn't quite abandoned my primary mission, which was my first FBI agent blow job), when a hateful-looking man wearing a black robe entered the courtroom.

There is no jury in military court. In mere minutes, I was pronounced guilty of draft evasion, labeled a "proven qualified fugitive," and sentenced to nine to eighteen months in a minimum-security penitentiary. The judge banged his gavel and said, "Next!" And that was it.

The FBI agents took me to a small side room and turned me over to the sergeant at arms and blue eyes said, "I'm sorry they're putting you away. When I took this job, I thought I was going to arrest criminals, not political prisoners. Good luck to you." Never one to give up, I said, "Hey, give me your phone number and when I get out, maybe we can have a drink!" He laughed yet again but didn't give me his number. Really, there was no scenario in which I wouldn't try to fuck a straight guy.

———————•———————

I loved prison! It was a low-security, farm-like facility in Napa Valley, surrounded by gorgeous views and vineyards, with near perfect weather every single day. My first twenty-four hours was entry paperwork and uniform selection: two pairs of underwear, two tee shirts, two sweatshirts, a pair of Levi's jeans (not 501s but not bad), a baseball cap, an orange jacket (I looked good in orange), and low-top Converse sneakers. I knew I wouldn't be using the underwear, even in prison. When I saw who my fellow inmates were, I thought, *This place looks like a fucking gay bar, only in daylight!* Tee shirts and jeans as mandatory uniforms on young men? Come on!

The prison had three large buildings: a cafeteria bunker, the grounds maintenance building, and the building dormitory where the majority of the guys bunked in rooms. Each room held eight men; there was a small section at the end of a long hall with small cells; each cell had two beds. These cells were reserved for gay guys and other 'potential trouble' prisoners. None of these spaces had bars or doors.

I was assigned a small room, where I met my cellmate, Derek. He was in his early thirties, and also gay, but sadly not my type (too hairy, no ass) nor was I his. But we became cell buddies. He asked if I would mind the bottom bunk (which was meant to be his) as he preferred the high bunk. I said no problem and settled in. I had a decent pillow, a wool blanket, soft sheets, and a little sink with hand towels. Okay, it could have used some wall art, and the toilets and showers were down the hall, but overall, it wasn't that dissimilar to the Chelsea Y—except for the lack of outside windows. (The top bunk was preferred by many inmates because it was harder for the guards, called custodians, to see you jerk off. But I didn't care if someone saw me jerk off. It was a 'free-love world.')

My sentence was commuted after five months, but those life-changing months were filled with *great* sex and life lessons. In prison, I was the king of good old-fashioned man-on-man sex. There were 220 of us in the dormitory building, and the showers held forty at a time—showers holding large groups of men seemed a recurring theme in my life. I showered on even days, and Group #2 showered on odd days. It was just like the Chelsea Y and I immediately felt at home. Most of the men were young political prisoners, and most of them were straight. The majority of gay men cooperated with their draft boards and were discharged with a 5-E, which didn't land you in prison like my 'draft evasion' did. (Luckily, after I was released early, my criminal record was expunged, thanks to free legal help offered by The Society of Friends, aka the Quakers. So I was able to find work without a black mark on background checks. I also kept my right to vote.)

I had a routine in the shower room around who I would entice. First, I'd carefully examine each butt to see which ones I liked. Then I memorized the owner's face. (The face was secondary—if they were ugly, I'd turn them on their stomach. Problem solved.) During dinner, which was open seating in the cafeteria, I'd find my way to nice-butt's table and chat and crack jokes, talking about how much I *loved* sex and how frustrating it must be for the poor straight guys but how wonderful it was for me, what an opportunity it was to see how the 'other team' lived. I always threw in "I feel it is my patriotic duty to blow or fuck any man here, for so long as I am here." It always got a laugh and allowed me to see which men might consider what I was not so subtly offering. I also made a point to befriend other horny gay guys so that we could, on occasion, switch our shower days with each other to widen our potential sex partners. I made a deal with my gay roomie Derek that I would make myself scarce if he needed me to, if he'd do the same for me. He didn't actively try to recruit sex partners, so I rarely had to 'get gone' for an hour or so. During my last month he was getting a little annoyed at how often he needed to get scarce, so for his birthday I recruited an older, hairy guy for him as a b'day surprise (three packs of cigarettes was all it took). Derek was delighted! But prison wasn't just enjoyable because of the massive amount of sex and genuinely intelligent conversations with my fellow detainees; the entertainment was fucking incredible.

On weekends, entertainers who were part of the anti-war movement came up from San Francisco to perform shows for us. We housed some famous political prisoners, like Daniel Berrigan from the Presidio Mutiny (he and his brother were both very well-known priests active in the anti-war movement) and Tom Lewis, a well-known Vietnam War protester and speaker. We'd nicknamed our prison "The Napa Inn." It had a decent sound system that could be moved outdoors for concerts on the grass or used in the cafeteria for indoor fun. Performers were allowed to mingle with the prisoners for an hour after concerts and vice versa. My favorite shows were Judy Collins, Mama Cass, Pete Seeger, Joan Baez, and Mimi Farina (Joan's sister). One night, I talked to Joan about teching for strippers while in high school. She suggested I get involved in the music business as a lighting and sound man when I got out. She even offered to introduce me to Bill Graham, the biggest producer of music shows in the Bay Area and the owner of The Fillmore West Theatre. Holy shit, did that plant a seed!

Hollywood anti-war execs also provided entertainment to us in jail, sending in first-run movies, often the same films playing in theatres across the country. We even had a popcorn machine. Crafts included watercolor classes, pottery (with a manual pottery wheel), and a Berkeley professor who would come up to teach us poetry. (We called him "Mr. Haiku.") We gay detainees even had ad hoc chats as needed to compare notes around our sexual conquests, which straight guys were an 'easy turnover.' (There was this one 'gay-for-pay' straight guy who had a huge member and would let you suck it in exchange for cigarettes.) I wasn't really into blow jobs, I was more of a top, and this is where I learned that many straight guys liked to be fucked. And I mean many! I guess they thought it was exotic since it was obviously something their women couldn't do. Well, maybe with a dildo or some fingers, but I knew from experience that nothing beat the real thing! Sorry, girls.

Our days were spent reading and growing vegetables for our cafeteria meals; you could grow just about anything in that rich soil and with the temperate weather, which, yes, included pot. The custodians just turned their heads when we smoked, or they rolled one up and smoked with us. All of us became a family, albeit a quirky one, but there was respect all around. I quickly learned how to grow veggies, especially tomatoes, but the pot growers were a more exclusive group. They were friendly but didn't want trainees. I learned a few years later, when that facility was closed, torn down, and replaced by a winery and vineyard, that some of the custodians and the pot-growing detainees had a deal, and a lot of that excellent primo prison weed was sold on the outside, with a split between the guards and the inmates.

After my conversation with Joan Baez, I started thinking. *What do I want to do with my life?* I still smoked pot, but there was no more liquor, pills, or mushrooms to distract me. Why did I have this constant desire to have sex? Was it the temporary combination of conquest and intimacy? Emotional intimacy was not a part of my life growing up, so I craved it any way I could get it, even if it was only through twenty-minute hookups. I was ready to make some changes when I got out of prison and used my time to think it through.

I would go back to New York with my partner Pieter and get serious about a career in lights and sound. I wanted to start making some money—no more living out of a shopping bag.

After I was arrested by the FBI, Pieter promised to "wait for me." Despite each of us promising to remain monogamous in our relationship, we both fucked our brains out while I was in prison. I got out just in time for our move to New York City. I flew to New York to find us an apartment since I already knew the turf and Pieter had never been. Pratt is in Brooklyn; I checked out Brooklyn Heights, but it was too expensive. The next neighborhood was an up-and-coming area named Cobble Hill, which is where I found our place. His rich dad picked up the rental costs, we moved in, and Pieter studied art at Pratt while I looked for work. I insisted on paying my half of the expenses (not easy for me), and he let me. Meanwhile, he bought a brand-new VW Beetle with daddy's money while I was slinging hash off the books in a Brooklyn diner. It kind of pissed me off. Our relationship soured soon after starting our East Coast life together. He became less interested in sex, refusing to give me blow jobs, which had already been a rarity from the beginning. (I wasn't really keen on them, but it was an option I felt should be available on nights when my dick was sore from fucking him.) He told me the head of my cock looked blue(!), and it turned him off. A couple months later, the relationship got even rockier. Suddenly my dick wasn't big enough to satisfy him—weird, as there were no complaints before or from the hundreds of other men I'd been with. One night, I'd had it. I was so incensed with his criticisms of my cock, I pulled a broom out of the hall closet and waved the handle in his face, yelling "So I'm not big enough for you, am I? How about this up your fat ass?!"

He actually looked... interested. Um, okay? I lubed up the end of the wooden broom handle and I rammed it so far up his Aussie ass I'm surprised it didn't come out of his mouth. *And he liked it!* That made me even angrier. I slapped his ass hard several times and he moaned— a sound I'd never heard from him before. A lightbulb went off in my head: Pieter wanted it *rough*. Okay, I could do that, no problem. So, I bought a few dildoes, a butt plug, and some bondage gear to use on him.

One night as I was working him over with my new toys, his welted ass decided we should move to Manhattan. He could drive his new VW to and from classes at Pratt. *Maybe a change of scenery would do us good,* I thought.

One lucky day later, I landed us a one bedroom apartment at 24 Washington Square North, opposite Washington Square Park, on the top floor of a posh brownstone (three apartments, each a full floor walk-through). The apartment had an amazing bedroom, plus a den, two working fireplaces, and a four-hundred-square-foot outdoor terrace overlooking Midtown, with views of the Empire State Building and the Chrysler Building. It was a breathtaking view. Once again, his rich daddy signed the lease. It was a combination of my smarts and getting on my knees for the ugly realtor that got us the lease. We moved in, but he still had minimal interest in sex. My attempt to reinvigorate our sex life with belts, poppers, handcuffs, and toys was DOA. I was too young and immature still to realize the relationship had run out of steam.

I started working at a very famous nightclub—Reno Sweeney—on West 13th Street in the West Village, doing lighting and sound. I didn't get home until 1:00 a.m., Pieter would leave for Pratt at 8:00 a.m. and return home around 5:00 p.m., so we only had three hours a day to spend together. Two months later, I was walking around our living room, coffee cup in hand, bending to light the fireplace, when I saw a wallet tucked in our huge, shaggy flokati rug. I opened it and sure enough, it wasn't Pieter's. The driver's license said the wallet was the property of a guy named Toby, an attractive someone I might have seen at a local gay bar. I called the phone number on his ID card and, using my best Australian accent, said, "G'day, mate, I had a good time last night, but your wallet fell out of your pants, and I have it here." Toby said, "Oh, I hadn't noticed. I'll come by for it now if it's okay. Maybe we can do it again, that was one amazing *blow job* you gave me." I was barely able to grunt out "Sure." Then I grabbed a shower, because revenge sex is a dish best served clean.

When Toby rang the door, I buzzed him in and he walked up the stairs. I opened the door. This guy had serious good looks and a body to match. Upon seeing me, he looked confused and said, "Umm, is Pieter here?" I was in my 501s, mostly unbuttoned and with a semi-hard-on and no shirt. In my lowest, sexiest voice I said, "No, but I'm here, and I'm happy to substitute for him." Well, there you go—seconds later, we're naked.

Afterwards, I shared that Pieter and I were supposed to be monogamous, but I'd found his wallet and decided to have revenge sex. I asked Toby if I could hold on to his number because I'd had a seriously hot time. He looked at me with puppy-dog eyes and a sweet upward turn of lips and said, "Please call, please!" I was delighted.

When Pieter came home that afternoon, he ignored me as usual and went straight to the fridge, saying, "I'm making a snack." I replied, "Not that you asked, but I already had a snack, and it was delicious—a blow job from your new friend Toby. By the way, his ass was way tighter than yours. I read there's an exercise for that, you might want to check it out." He froze, processing what I'd said and staring at me with a confused look on his face. I should have been upset he 'cheated,' but instead I felt free. Suddenly, it all came together—our relationship was over.

I told him I'd found Toby's wallet and invited him over to fuck, and Pieter got enraged. He pulled my arm behind my back, hard; he was stronger than me. He dragged me to the front door, opened it, shoved me through the short hallway, and tried to push me down the long flight of steep stairs. I grabbed the stairwell railing and held on for dear life, kicking him in the shin. It startled him, and he let my arm go for a second. I used that moment to bolt down the three flights of stairs. I heard him screaming as I ran: "Get out, don't come back, you don't live here anymore, fuck you, I'll kill you!" and other hateful things. I *would* come back, but the following morning, checking first for his car on the street; if it was gone, I'd grab my clothes and a few things. Then I had a great idea! I called Toby from a pay phone on the corner and asked if he wanted to see a show at Reno Sweeney that night, and we could re-create our fun from earlier in the day. He readily agreed.

I organized a little table for him with a glass of champagne while he watched Odetta perform her set. As we left the club, Philip, the maître'd, walked over and whispered in my ear, "Someone whose name sounded like Peter called four times and said to tell you he was sorry, he forgives you, and to come home." I didn't call him back. I'd just liberated myself from a man who was verbally and physically abusive, who made me feel ugly, who was demeaning. I wanted to get over feeling that lack of self-worth I'd been carrying all my life. That was not going to happen with him; there was no reason to return.

I knew then that I didn't really fall in love with Pieter. I fell in love with the *idea* of love. Ending the relationship brought relief, but it also brought sadness. *Would I ever experience real love?* Maybe I should give up on trying to find love and go back to one-night-stands, something I was very good at and something I was secure with. So I fell into my comfort cocoon of 'conquest and split' that both unsettled and freed me. I was a fucked-up mess yet again.

Shortly after we broke up, things finally started to turn around for me. My time with Pieter at least brought me back to New York, and I would soon be working with the biggest celebrities of the day at one of the most famous nightclubs in the world. *And* I'd discovered the wonderful world of bathhouses!

8.

LIGHTS, CAMERAS, AND SO MUCH ACTION

In the early 70s, I met Ted Hook at a party through a mutual Broadway dancer friend. He was the nightlife impresario who'd had the idea to have Saturday night performances at The Continental Baths, a gay bathhouse located in a 40,000-square-foot basement space underneath the Ansonia Hotel on 74th Street. These weekly shows were at 8:00 p.m. and began with the Divine Miss M herself, Bette Midler, whose career was on the verge of taking off, and the shows were starting to draw in big crowds. Ted asked if I would interview to be a freelance lighting and sound manager for the Saturday performances. The interview went well—as soon as he heard I'd worked with strippers, he signed me up. "Perfect!" he replied. Ted smiled and asked if I had any lighting gels in my tech belongings. I didn't but said I could easily get some in the lighting district on West 44th Street. I asked him why he needed them.

"I'm going to the Everard Baths tonight, and I like to put a piece of very flattering gel over the little light in my cubicle—I'm of that age— and I lost the one I was using." The Everard, (or "Ever-Hard" Baths, as we gays called it) was a dirtier version of The Continental Baths and was located in what is now named Chelsea; it was dirtier both in deeds done and in cleanliness. I looked Ted over. He was in his late forties, which as far as bathhouse bait goes *was* past his prime. So I trotted over to 44th Street, picked up my favorite Rosco 842 gel (which I knew would even out his blotchy complexion), and we organized a meeting place for the 'exchange.' It was an odd thing to do on a street corner at 5:00 p.m. in Midtown—handing over a piece of gel, a pair of scissors, and a roll of Scotch tape, all bundled in a brown paper bag, like some sort of late-afternoon drug deal. I had a little chuckle over it on the subway home.

Ironically, I was already a loyal customer at The Continental Baths. It was where men wearing nothing but towels would cruise each other for random hookups. It had about six hundred gym lockers for belongings and three hundred private cubicles with doors on them for rent and a giant swimming pool as its main attraction. (Actually, the random sexual encounters with anonymous men were the *main* attraction.) The steam room and sauna (aka the orgy rooms) were the icing on this erotic cake.

Then, on Saturday nights, straight people of both sexes would come to the Baths fully clothed and sit on damp folding chairs to watch performances by Bette and her pianist, Barry Manilow. This weekly event would later be described by nightlife historians as one of the most unique and fabulous see-and-be-seen 'happenings' of the 70s, colored as a fun experience for all. However, for the *actual* customers of the Baths, the reality was just the opposite. In the early 70s, plenty of gay men were still closeted or somewhere in between out and closeted. We came to bathhouses for sex—all kinds of sex—not to hear someone sing. When those first Saturday night gigs started with a relatively unknown Bette Midler, they were tolerated by the regular clientele because Bette was special. She had a gay, rowdy sense of humor (even though she 'borrowed' as many of risqué Sophie Tucker's comedy routines as she could find), interlaced with retro versions of 30s songs by the Andrews Sisters. But by around the third month of these events, the Baths became crowded with a fully clothed straight crowd who reveled in a night of 'slumming it.' They stared at us gays like we were animals in a zoo, and our acceptance soon turned to anger. It was always clear to those 'in the know' that the Saturday night bath shows were just a gimmick, and one at the expense of the gay community.

Performing at The Continental Baths was sort of like performing in a dumpster, though it was truly the most famous dumpster in Manhattan for about two years. As the new technical director, I had little to work with. There was no stage or curtain, no sophisticated lighting or sound. Yet somehow the space in front of the swimming pool magically turned into a supposedly 'chic' New York City cabaret stage from 9:00 p.m. until midnight once a week. Every performer with a manager wanted a slot at the Baths—it was the hottest fad in town while it lasted. (Emphasis on *fad*.) Still, it wasn't exactly a great place to perform. From a technical point of view, the sound system was beyond primitive. It only had the ability to handle four microphones; each mic had a slider on the board that controlled the volume, but there was only one reverb for *all* the mics. A piano sat to the side of the pool (when it wasn't showtime, exhibitionists often fucked on the piano top). It could never be kept in tune because of the humidity. I mean, *you* try to get a piano tuner to come to a gay bathhouse and see how far you get. (Hello, Acme Piano Tuning? Do you happen to have a tuner who wouldn't mind working on a moist, old baby grand next to a swimming pool in a gay bathhouse surrounded by naked men blowing each other... Hello? Hello?)

It was decent money, I got to work with some of the better-known performers, and I also was able to ogle the headliners who came for the shows. Some of the better-known celebs who I saw on the Saturday night folding chairs were Bob Fosse, Gwen Verdon, Alfred Hitchcock, Mick Jagger, Rudolf Nureyev, Valentino, Andy Warhol, Rita Moreno, Halston, Liza Minelli, Princess Margaret, Carol Channing, and so many others. It wasn't unusual for paparazzi to hang outside the entrance door to snap those with famous faces paying their way in. Originally, this audience came to see Bette, whose career soon grew bigger than the bathhouse. Barry Manilow played a few more solo shows after she left, once while wearing nothing but a towel even though he wasn't officially 'out.' (Actually, Barry was fairly out until he signed his first record contract. Then he went back in the closet and fast!) Other performers included Cab Calloway, Lesley Gore, Manhattan Transfer, Ellen Greene, Melba Moore, Lady Dawn Hampton, Melissa Manchester, Jane Olivor, Sarah Vaughn, and plenty of other smaller names that later fell by the wayside.

As I said, the regular patrons were *not* thrilled at having their prime hunting grounds taken over by clothed straights during prime-time Saturday nights. These audiences were overwhelmingly rude—staring and whispering to each other—and seemed to be there only for the privilege of saying, "I was at the Baths on Saturday night, darling, and you'll never believe what they do there and who I saw..." (It would have been nice if the NYC intelligentsia spent less time caring about being seen in a trendy spot and more time working towards the legalization of gay rights, but woulda, coulda, shoulda.)

When the straights weren't around, members of my tribe usually rented the cubicles with doors that closed, while others paid less for a locker in the hopes that someone with a small room would invite them in. Otherwise they could get or give a blow job or fuck in the shower room, the steam room, the orgy room, the swimming pool, or even at the small on-site café that sold food. (I once watched a guy give another guy a blow job while the blowee ate a tuna fish sandwich on a stool and belched his appreciation.) One night after the Saturday show was over, I was in a towel getting some action, and I opened my room door to let out a cute guy, and as he exited, he *literally* ran into a fully clothed Alfred Hitchcock, who had been at that night's show. I headed towards the little café to grab a Coke, and that's where I stumbled into Liz Smith, the celebrity gossip columnist for the *New York Post*, who wanted to ask me a few questions. While I had been out since I was seven years old and had no issues with my sexuality, I was *very* annoyed that a gossip columnist was prowling the hallways looking for a story when the people she wanted to interview were just looking for an anonymous fuck. To her credit, Liz became a staunch supporter of gay rights shortly thereafter and came out herself before most of the other 'well-knowns.' But lines were crossed as a result of these Saturday night shows, so a lot of men started going to the Everard Baths on 28th Street. This hurt the Continental's financial bottom line so much that they eventually stopped hosting live performances. The general manager, a man named Steve Ostrow, lost his lease on the space in 1976. He went on to other things (including Australia, since he owed the mafia money), and the new leaseholders changed the name, reopening as "Plato's Retreat," a bathhouse concept for the straight community. And it was *hugely* popular. I didn't miss those Saturday night gigs because by then I'd become technical director of the trendiest, hottest, and most popular (legitimate) cabaret nightclub in Manhattan: Reno Sweeney.

The timing of getting hired at Reno's was interesting. I was on my way to interview for The Continental Baths gig with Ted Hook, when I met another new friend, Lewis Friedman, the owner of Reno Sweeney. I literally bumped into him while walking up 7th Avenue in the West Village. Lewis was a *very* short man (I'm guessing around five feet two), and I simply didn't *see* him coming as my eyes were on another man's cute butt as he walked by. When Lewis and I collided, he yelled, "Why don't you watch where the fuck you're going!" I very rudely replied, "Why don't you grow four inches so I can see you!" I immediately realized that was a horrible response. He stormed by me, so I turned around to catch up to him, tapped him on the shoulder, and apologized.

"I'm sorry. I'm on my way to an interview for the tech director job at The Continental Baths for their Saturday night shows and I was just deep in, uh, thought. My mind was completely absorbed with what I was going to say to get the gig."

Lewis responded graciously and introduced himself.

"I'm the owner of Reno Sweeney and I'm actually looking for a part-time tech guy. The club is on West 13th Street if you don't know it. Stop by in the evening sometime this week and we can talk."

Fast-forward to the next day. I'd aced the interview for the Continental bathhouse gig and was flying high off that, so I decided to stop in Reno's that night to talk with Lewis. Based on the way he eyed me, I was fairly sure my getting the job was contingent on whether or not I'd fuck him. I'd reached a point in my life where I almost expected to have to put-out in order to land a job or a nice apartment, so I just came out with it. "Okay, I see it in your eyes. I'll fuck you. In fact, I'll pick you up and fuck you while you straddle my hips and, baby, I'll bang your ass good while I carry you around, because that's always been a fantasy of mine and you're just the right size."

I thought this was a surefire way to seal the deal, but instead it pissed him off. He said, "My club doesn't have a casting couch, sweetheart, and if it did, you wouldn't be on it because you're not my type!" (Whoops.) Suddenly desperate for this job, I dropped to my knees so that I was closer to his height and joked, "Let's discuss this man to man, eyeball to eyeball." I knew it was either going to crack him up or get my ass kicked out the door. Luckily, he started laughing, and I was in again. I also got the gig, doing tech three nights a week.

Reno Sweeney was at the corner of 13th Street between 6th and 7th Avenues. It held 120 people and was the type of venue that celebrities played when they were either on their way up or on their way down. (And, at that point, also those who were losing their battles with alcohol, pills, coke, or heroin.) Occasionally a record company would rent it out for a gig or record release party—Manhattan Transfer had their first record-release gig there. When the Harlettes divorced themselves from singing backup with Bette Midler and changed their name to "Formerly the Harlettes" (Bette wouldn't allow them to use "The Harlettes" anymore and threatened to sue), they had their release party at Reno's.

Club owner Lewis Friedman was an extremely savvy fellow. He saw my abilities and finesse with lighting and sound, and within two months he took me from a three-night-a-week contract to full-time tech director. A week after my promotion, he invited me to go to the baths with him. (Remember his "We don't have a casting couch, sweetheart" speech?) It wasn't unusual for a couple of friends to go together and compare notes later, but sure enough, his little legs *were* around my hips and I *did* walk around the Everard hallways fucking him while carrying him—we were neither of us shy. I knew it was bound to happen, and this is something that's always been the key to my successes. And it was kinda fun—those little guys usually have *great* asses. Lewis sure did!

The lights at Reno Sweeney were old incandescents from the 60s. They had been purchased secondhand from clubs and theatres before being torn down or closed for lack of business. (This was before LEDs and preset boards. I had to manually adjust the lights with dials and sliders for every effect or change; likewise, the sound was mixed by hand on a six-channel board.) The club was in the double-wide basement of two brownstones and had a very low ceiling. This made the use of a spotlight impossible, so all the various lighting units needed to be stationary and attached to the ceiling and the wall sides. It was a beast of a club to create magic in, but I figured out a way based on the dives I'd worked in during my Baltimore strip club days. As technical director, I was responsible for the lighting and sound design for each performer and the nightly running of both shows. I was also the person who would meet and greet the talent upon arrival. We'd discuss their act, cues, the order of their songs, and what kind of 'feel' they wanted for each tune and their overall presentation. Then I'd do a sound check to better understand how to mix their voices. I'd have them stand onstage while I tried out various gel colors on their skin to maximize a good look for them. It was a small, tight place and the lighting was critical—there was no distance between the performer and the audience. On this stage, you could count Doris Day's freckles! After they left the tech check, I'd get busy refocusing lights and creating an ambiance that worked for them. I'd also make sure they had what they wanted backstage—in some cases, their contracts had a 'rider,' a document attached to the contract that stated their requirements. Some of these riders were outrageous and certainly not within the budget of Reno's. I'd sit with each performer and cross out what *wasn't* going to happen. (Fresh flowers in the dressing room each night, piano tuning daily, a bottle of Dom Perignon per performance, and on it went.) Luckily I had an even temperament, a sense of humor, and a winning personality as I red-lined requests that might have been appropriate for Carnegie Hall but not for a small club, however popular and trendy. I rarely had an issue, but when I *did*, it was critical for me to stay the 'good cop.' So I'd call Lewis (and later, the new owner, Jim Maxey) and have *him* play bad cop with the performer's manager. I kept my hands clean so I could get good shows out of what were often 'difficult' personalities, which is how I became friendly with many of them. The performers did two shows a night and they needed someone to talk to in between sets, and plenty needed a drink after their shows (and some in between). I was easygoing, I made them look and sound great, and I loved to regale them with salacious stories of my gay sex life (or if they were gay, I would help them, um, relax between sets, even though I sometimes had to close my eyes and use my imagination), so I was usually who they went for drinks with. Soon I became widely known within the industry for being able to handle *very* difficult people, which led to Columbia Records eventually hiring me away from the nightclub circuit; they had plenty of 'difficult' talent, aka junkies, boozers, cokeheads, and quaalude or Black Beauty poppers that needed handling.

I was absolutely enamored with the Reno job! Instead of lighting strippers, I was working closely with some of the biggest names in showbiz. One early memorable performer I worked with was Diane Keaton. She'd already achieved great success as an actress in Woody Allen films, but she was also playing around with a nightclub act since she loved to sing. She had a great voice and wonderful phrasing.

One of my favorite nights to tech was Mondays, when Reno Sweeney hosted their "Monday Talent" nights. Singers and celebs of note were booked for twenty-minute spots and then they had to leave the stage, with a ten-minute interlude to set up for the next mini-performance. An impressive level of performers sang on Mondays and included some real A-listers: Melissa Manchester, Cissy Houston, Chita Rivera, Tommy Tune, Redd Fox, Meatloaf, Sarah Vaughn, Nancy Wilson, and such. Many of the 'already famous' performers used Monday Talent nights as an opportunity to try out a little new material before adding it to their full show. Monday nights were always packed!

The audiences were even more star-studded: John Lennon, David Bowie, Mick Jagger, Ethel Merman, Andy Warhol, Billy Joel. It wasn't an easy gig to tech, because some of the singers didn't understand or respect the strict twenty-minute limit. It then became my job to cut off their mic while they were still onstage. First I'd flash the stage lights once, then again one minute before cutting them off cold, at which point I'd bring up the house lights while killing the stage lights. I'd speak into the mic: "Ladies and gentleman, as I'm sure you know, all of the performers you enjoy at Reno Sweeney Paradise Room Talent Nights are told they have a twenty-minute maximum; if we don't adhere to that policy, the other performers and their musicians who are waiting are unfairly detained, and some have later gigs elsewhere. Let's thank [whoever dimwit I had just cut off] one more time, and this is an excellent moment to wave your waiter over for a drink order. Thank you!"

Some of the performers I cut off threw a shit-fit. Carly Simon had a female 'friend' she was pushing, and she tried to rip me a new one when I cut her never-to-be-heard-again protégé off after her time was up. But as usual, I prevailed. I used a backstage mic to introduce the performers, so when Carly was yelling at me, nose-to-nose—a quick flip of a switch and all 120 audience members heard her call me a "motherfucker, a little cunt, a power-hungry fag." Once she heard everyone laughing, that nasty-ass shrew was out of my face in a flash. I hear she's mellowed…

Most of the various pianists or musicians 'got it,' and they often helped clear the stage, moving their amps and music charts; they had other gigs to play as well. Diane Keaton was always good about the time limit. She'd stand backstage and, just before her set began, she'd ask me to hold her purse. Then she'd sing three songs and fast-walk, head-down, out of the club. She never remembered her purse. Diane had serious stage jitters; all she could think of after her set was to bolt out of there via the kitchen. I would run after her, purse in hand, and catch her just as she hit 7th Avenue to hail a cab. It got to be 'our thing.' She was shy and kind, an overall sweetie pie. She was also the first singer I heard perform that iconic pop tune "Goody, Goody" in a dirge tempo as a ballad, and it was amazingly effective. I knew she wanted to explore her musical side, but her sudden movie fame ate that dream. I don't think she ever had a chance to explore it seriously. 'Hollywood called' as they say. She would have been a formidable singer if her career track hadn't led her in a different direction.

Cissy Houston was another one of my favorite performers at Reno's. Cissy had 'chops' to die for—she could sing anything, any way you wanted her to. She was a backup singer for Elvis for years and recorded a lot of studio album backup singing. Her dream was to make her own gospel album—a dream that came true for her later in her life after her daughter's success. She lived in New York City for a while, then New Jersey, and would do various gigs around town, at different clubs, in between touring as a backup singer with nearly everybody, and I mean everybody—this lady was a workaholic and always in great demand. I loved talking to her, even though she would never dish like I wanted her to. I told her I'd do anything but go straight if she shared some Elvis stories, but she remained closed-mouthed about him. She did tell me, "At first I thought he was a joke. He wasn't a joke," but I never quite figured out if she meant his talent or his career. But she did watch him slowly kill himself with drugs while backing for him in Vegas, just as she later watched her own daughter Whitney overdose.

Whitney was often part of Cissy's act. I first met her when she was just fourteen years old. She'd come to the club to do two songs as part of Cissy's set. Cissy was a proud mama and knew Whitney had 'that voice.' When I first met teenage Whitney, she sported a super dyke haircut, wore leather pants and a leather jacket, and was with her girlfriend. The two made goo-goo eyes at each other while backstage or at a side table in the back—ah, young love! Whitney definitely had a butch vibe during her growth from girl to woman. She gave the impression that she could lift your car and change the tire with just one arm. It was so strange to later see her on TV when her pop career was blowing up, wearing so much makeup and long hair extensions, stunningly dressed and dancing with the grace of Michael Jackson.

One night in between her sets, Cissy and I were talking backstage when she turned to me and asked, "Do you think my Whitney might be gay?" *Might be?!* She assumed that, as a gay man, I would be able to shed some insight. I really liked Cissy, but it wasn't my place to discuss her teenage daughter's sexuality—plus, it was so fucking obvious. So I said, "Why don't you ask her?" I should have said, "You give me the dish on your time with Elvis, and I'll give you my opinions on whether your Whit's a lesbian," but I stupidly didn't think of it at the time.

———•———

Some of the performers I worked with had all of the talent in the world but, for whatever reason, never found the fame they so deserved. Ellen Greene was one of those people. She was later nominated for a Tony, a Drama Desk, and a Laurence Olivier (she would have won a Tony with certainty for *Little Shop of Horrors* but it played Off-Broadway so it was exempt). There are plenty of older theatre gays who adore her, but ask a young person today and they'd probably say, "Who the hell is Ellen Greene?" Ellen was one of my first gigs at Reno's.

She was so open, had no attitude, and was quirky; we got on great from the start. Ellen was also a perfectionist about lighting, and I loved to work with her because she could find any light on any stage at any time, and I mean *any* light—you never had to tell her to hit her mark. She just organically moved into the lights as they came on and dimmed off and could even feel the angle of the lighting and 'play' it for dramatic effect. She had a kind of lighting-radar—she just knew where to be, could find the most dramatic place to be—something most performers simply don't have a feel for.

Greg was a Broadway stage manager and a dear friend of Ellen's. He had tons of extra lights (OK, so he 'borrowed' them from the Broadway shows he stage managed) to use for her set at Reno's. He and I ran cables like crazy along the ceiling and hung an additional twelve lights for her three-week club run. It was a tough gig in the tech sense but with fantastic results. As Greg stood on a ladder hanging cables, my face was level with his beautiful ass feeding him the cords (and fantasizing about feeding him something else). Greg was extremely cute with a capital C and of course had my downfall, an amazing butt. He made a point of wiggling it at me several times the first day we met; I would rest my head on his ass when we were both on the ladder and mumble, "I'm so tired..." I suggested that we discuss Ellen's, uh, cues at his place on the West Side after our first meeting. We fucked all night long—and for the rest of the month. I adored him in a completely sexual way—he was just so agreeable!

When Ellen showed up for our first tech run-through, Greg and I were sitting at a table waiting for her, looking through cue cards and trying to take our eyes off each other. She took one look at us and said, "You two are fucking, aren't you?" I couldn't contain my grin, and Greg gave the sweetest little giggle. She said, "I'm happy for you, but it better not fuck up my show!" Then we all laughed, and we assured her that the shows would look and sound great, or as Greg put it, "Ellen, you know two dicks working for you are better than one!"

Ellen's show was selling out. Fast. Ahmet Ertegun, the founder of Atlantic Records, and a bunch of other music execs showed up for her opening night. Ellen was thrilled. "They're thinking about offering me a recording contract!" she told me. (That album did get made but sadly was never released. I heard it on the down-low a few times and it was brilliant, as Ellen always was. Anybody that still has a brain in what's left of the music industry should find that tape and release the album—it is not too late.) Around that time, Ellen was also in previews for a zany Broadway show called *Rachael Lilly Rosenbloom and Don't You Ever Forget It!* It was written originally for Bette Midler, who passed on it, so Ellen took the lead. When it opened, Ellen got rave reviews, but the show, not so much. It closed opening week.

After her Reno gigs, Ellen found herself playing Audrey in the run of *Little Shop of Horrors* Off-Broadway, at the Orpheum Theatre in the East Village. It became a mega-hit and ran for years, primarily because of her. When the movie version of *Little Shop* was to be made, the producers told Frank Oz, the director, that they wanted Cyndi Lauper for the role. Frank fought them like crazy—he was dead set on having Ellen recreate *her* role. Around that time, Ellen appeared on *The Tonight Show* and sang "Suddenly Seymour" with everything she had in her. She brought the house down, and host Johnny Carson stood from his desk to clap, which was rare. She bantered with him (they had an electric chemistry), finishing each other's sentences, and he couldn't keep his eyes off her breasts, which if she'd pushed them up any higher would have been on either side of her ears. Shortly after, Ellen won the casting battle for the film of *Little Shop*; she was Audrey in the movie, opposite Rick Moranis, who played Seymour. She was not nominated for an Oscar that year, which to this day is one of the Academy's most head-scratching mistakes. She truly should have gotten so much more attention, and work, for her massive talent.

Ellen was good friends with the Australian singer Peter Allen. As much as I thought Peter was a fantastic songwriter and pianist, I couldn't stand him as a person. We just never got along—his swanning and rolling around on top of the piano annoyed me to no end. In a 3,000-seat venue, *maybe* it worked, but in a cabaret, it just came off as silly and self-aggrandizing. It also fucked up how I could mic the piano, an important part of his act; his keyboard work was excellent, but his vocal efforts were mediocre, and that's on a *good* night! Someone who *could* sing his songs to perfection was Ellen. After Peter died of AIDS in 1992, Ellen worked her ass off to produce and perform a tribute evening to him at The Bottom Line, a black-box few-hundred seater showroom in NYC. She sang most of Peter's songs, as only she could— better than Peter, better than any other singer. (Again, that should have been an album that didn't materialize.) If I could have one magical show business wish, it would be that Ellen's career took off the way it should have. Even though I was front and center to so much happening behind the scenes in the music industry, it's still a business I'll never understand.

———————— • ————————

As much as I loved working with the celebs, I sometimes preferred the oddball cabaret queens even more. One of my favorite performers was Holly Woodlawn, a Warhol superstar best known for her astounding performance in Andy's movie *Trash*. George Cukor, the uber-famous Hollywood director, submitted the paperwork to nominate her for a best supporting actress Oscar for her performance. There was quite a controversy, as Holly was transitioning from man to woman. (She ran out of money during the process, so she was legally a 'man' her whole life.) The Cukor nomination generated a lot of press, but the Academy didn't approve it so she mostly did Off-Broadway stuff and had a nightclub act, with novelty songs like "Air-brushed" and other play-on-words-tunes. Her act was fun and she was a natural comedienne. She couldn't really sing or keep pitch, so she mostly improvised onstage and nearly always pulled it off. We palled around together a lot after her shows, and she introduced me to her other Warhol friends like Candy Darling and Jackie Curtis. (I did their clubs bookings too, when they could afford me and were sober enough to show up for their gigs.) One night after her show, Holly introduced me to Joe Dallesandro, her male costar in *Trash*, who was drop-dead handsome in a menacing kind of way. I had seen his tight ass in the movie (and his big dick) sans pants, so I approached him to see if he wanted to get together. He was all for it, and we went to a bar for a drink, but then he told me how much he cost and that I could only blow him. Eh? I was every bit the looker he was in those days and with similar equipment, and I sure as hell didn't need to pay for it, so I said no dice. He lowered his price and I said no again. He then told me to go fuck myself for wasting his time. I told him if I could fuck myself I wouldn't need *him*! Lesson learned—when trying to hook up with handsome male Warhol stars during their fifteen minutes of fame, ask their price first!

———•———

In the late summer in 1978, a producer friend of mine named Jerry invited me to the Hamptons to have a look at Grey Gardens, the house made famous in the Maysles Brothers' cult movie. I figured there was a reason behind this invitation, but who could resist? During the drive to the Hamptons, Jerry explained that he'd contracted "Little" Edie Beale (her mother, "Big" Edith Beale, had recently died) into signing a contract for a one-woman act that he would cobble together. His concept was that she would sing (a lifelong dream of hers) and also participate in a long Q&A session with the audience. Jerry asked if I would be the technical director and also the offstage mic voice asking Little Edie the Q&A questions. The performances were to be at Reno Sweeney, a run in January. During this period, I was sometimes teching Reno's and sometimes on the road with record company acts, but I said yes immediately as *Grey Gardens* was one of my favorite movies.

We arrived at the house, which had been cleared out and cleaned up—no cat shit, no raccoons, no piles of clothes and papers, as when the interior of the house had been filmed. But the walls weren't painted, the floors weren't refinished (there were holes in them), and some of the rooms sported wallpaper peeling off the walls.

Big Edie was the sister of John Bouvier, Jackie Kennedy's father. So Little Edie was first cousin to Jackie and Big Edie was her aunt. In the early 70s, before *Grey Gardens* came out, a *New York Times* reporter visited Big Edie and Little Edie and found them living in squalor and, frankly, with an obvious degree of shared mental illness. After the article was published, Jackie was embarrassed and planned to move the Edies' into an assisted living facility, completely renovate the house, and put it up for sale. This came as a relief to the Edies' uber-wealthy neighbors, who considered the sagging structure and its large overgrown yard an eyesore that decreased the value of their Hamptons mansions.

Unbeknownst to Jackie, the Maysles brothers had already arranged to shoot their documentary of the eccentric women. They began filming a week after the *Times* article came out and Jackie didn't have a chance to put her plan into action. When the movie was released in 1975, the world saw how her close relatives lived in poverty and filth. (To the point where their electricity or water was frequently turned off and local authorities continually threatened to condemn the place.) It was *not* good publicity for one of the wealthiest women in the world to allow her relatives to live this way. She stepped in ASAP to renovate, which is why Little Edie was no longer living at Grey Gardens during our house tour.

I met Little Edie several months later, in mid-December of 1977. Jerry had tucked her away somewhere, and he was doing everything in his power to keep her entertained indoors, since she could rarely remember where she was or even how to unlock doors (I kept good notes in my Dairy of the various odd things she said to me). During the rehearsals for the run, she asked me if there were any of those things called "locks" where she was performing, because "I just don't understand how to do those, I've never needed one."

He wanted me to meet Edie to figure out how to light her and to listen to her 'sing' so I'd know what to do for her shows. He also wanted me to help determine the questions to ask in the Q&A part of the act, since some of the questions would be pre-written, i.e., planted. (Other questions would be spontaneous and come from the audience members.) After I arrived, it took me maybe two minutes before I realized she was a total nutcase. She *was* funny—her confusion hid a lot of wit and humor—but she so obviously had mental health issues. She was also physically *very* sturdy, with a big bone structure. I remember thinking, *Holy fuck, she's a female lumberjack!*

Edie wore a red dress with red slacks underneath, with a red piece of fabric wrapped around her head. (There was a plastic poinsettia pinned to it, since we were coming up on Christmas.) My first thought was, *I cannot be part of exploiting this sixty-something mentally challenged woman. It just wouldn't be right.* My second thought was *Fuck that...I've gotten drugs for performers, taken needles out of their arms, pushed them onstage and off, and looked the other way when they were rebellious on many levels. So who the fuck am I to say no to working with someone just because they have mental issues? I just need to light her, sound her, get her on and off the stage, make sure she doesn't break any bones, and get the money.* So I stayed at wherever it was we met to see what she sounded like. Plus, Jerry was so excited about Edie's stage debut it rubbed off on me. He knew there was going to be a crowd, and he knew I could handle the Q&A segment because my mic voice was good.

She started to sing for me. Her favorite song was "Tea for Two," but she constantly forgot the lyrics. To her credit, when she forgot a line of the song, she just made up words to stick in. She had no sense of pitch, and the various notes she did hit were bewildering, but she was completely sincere and obviously living her dream. Little Edie was sweet, and I was fascinated by her. I decided to focus on the part of helping her live her dream and ignore the rest. After all, anyone who had seen *Grey Gardens* (and why else would they come to an Edie Beale show?) knew they weren't coming to listen to her outstanding vocals. While I talked with her, she fell over the couch once, tripped over an imaginary something once, and went to sit down but missed the chair and landed on the floor. Three face-plants within forty-five minutes. It didn't occur to me, yet, to think what this clumsiness might mean when she was onstage. I was just so impressed that she bounced right up and we weren't calling an ambulance to treat a broken hip—this woman was indestructible!

When opening night for the show rolled around, Edie came in to Reno Sweeney for a sound check and a look at the lighting I'd designed. We decided we would go over a few of the planted questions she was to answer. Jerry assured me she had memorized all her responses. He brought her in around 2:00 p.m. and she wore the same outfit from the day we met—red everything. It's not a great color to light, especially in a small nightclub, but she was insistent. ("It's my lucky color!") Reno's had no spotlight since the ceiling was too low, and the stage was in an 'apron' shape, with a baby grand piano on the left and two iconic artificial palm trees sandwiching each side of the stage. The height of the platform stage was twenty-eight inches, and there was a pull-out 'runway' that could be used for shows, but I was already worried her ass was gonna fall off the platform, never mind adding a runway. When Edie walked in, she looked really confused by everything she saw. "How can the audience sit on the chairs when they're all on top of the tables?" Oh dear God. I put my arm around her shoulder to help her feel comfortable. A dishwasher set the chairs down around the tables so that Edie would understand that this was a nightclub, that the chairs would indeed be on the floor. Then I began to walk her through things.

"Edie, hi, it's David, and this is your stage! The pianist will be over here, and you can see it isn't very large and there is no spotlight. So it's really important that you stay in the center of the stage for lighting reasons. This is your mic. It will stay center stage on that mic stand, and I'll have it turned on for you so all you need to do when you get onstage is walk to the center and talk and sing directly into the mic—no need to take it out of the stand and hold it with your hands, and no need to move. *Ever.*" She seemed so in awe of everything. Then she started tearing up.

"I've waited so many years for this," she said as a tear rolled down her cheek. Then a smile lit her face. "But how do I get up on the stage?"

"You step up onto it. It's just over two feet high so, uh, I'll tell you what, we'll have someone walk you through the audience aisle and help you onstage for each show."

"Good. I've been practicing and I think I'm ready. But where's the audience?"

Jerry and I looked at each other.

"Edie, this is a sound and light check—it's just a rehearsal. There is no audience until tonight."

"Well, I can't wait. I heard they give a performer energy."

I nodded. "Yup, they sure do, especially when they can see and hear you. Which is why it is *so* important to stay center stage and just talk and sing into the mic and not move around the stage. Really." I was determined to help her not fall flat on her face in front of 120 people. She didn't deserve that to happen. We decided to 'practice,' as she called it, so I helped her up on the stage. She walked right across it, past the mic stand, and fell off the other side and onto a table. I ran over.

"Edie, are you all right?"

"Oh I'm fine. I fall all the time. Mother told me it was because I have a cross-eye!" she said with a laugh. I gently placed her center stage in front of the mic and made a mental note to remind the person escorting her to the stage that they needed to take her to that *exact* spot. Then I noticed she had on cha-cha heels (the kind usually worn by preteens before they can manage real high heels). Those seemed like they could exacerbate the klutz problem.

"Edie, you're tall already. Maybe we should lose the heels and go with flats?"

"I don't want to lose them. I like them. Also, where would I lose them?"

"Okay, we'll talk about it later. Let's just take those shoes off for now and you can rehearse in your bare feet." I held her while she slipped off the shoes and I put them on a table where she could see them, then told her I was going to turn on the lights and for her to stand right where she was. I walked fifteen feet to the area by the bar with its saloon-like swinging doors and where the lighting and sound equipment was. I got on the backstage mic to talk to her.

"Okay Edie, I'm going to turn on the lights."

I brought the lights up slowly to 100%—all of them, because I already figured out that any attempt to do lighting cues, blackouts, fades, etc. was out of the question. Edie was impressed.

"These are so beautiful!" She stared up at the lights while walking over to the piano—where she hit it hard and fell down. Again.

"Ouch!" She laughed, but I was panicking.

"Edie, remember my telling you not to move, to just stand in the center and speak into the mic? Let's do that, okay?"

She walked back to center stage, went past the mic stand, to the other side of the stage and fell off it once more, this time into a different table.

"Oh dear, it's hard to see up there with all the lights!"

Jerry helped her back up and placed her center sage and looked over at me, terrified like "What the fuck have I done?" I came back onstage, made a big X with white electrical tape, and gently reminded her to just stand in one spot.

"OK, Edie, stand on the X, *don't* move! Just stand in that very spot, X marks the spot, ha, and talk into the mic. I'll ask you some of the questions you rehearsed, and you can answer them. No, Edie, you don't need to put your actual lips *on* the mic, just close to it." I showed her how to talk into it.

"Testing, testing, one, two, three... That's what they say, right?"

I explained I was going back to my microphone to ask her one of the rehearsed questions. "Edie, what do you think of television?" (Her rehearsed answer was supposed to be "It's good for national emergencies.") But once I started talking to her, she looked confused.

"You're really loud; it sounds like your voice is coming from the floor"—squinting her eyes and looking down—"... are you under there?"

This can't be happening, I think. "There's a little speaker under the floor so we can hear each other," I explained, making another note—don't use the fucking monitor as it obviously makes her think I'm talking to her from under the floor. Now *I* was the one panicking, thinking *Jesus fucking Christ on a stick, what have I gotten myself into?*

Edie decided she wanted to start singing and asked if she could go ahead. I told her that was a great idea, as long as she *didn't move.* The pianist came onstage and began playing the first four bars leading into "Tea for Two," but she thought he was playing without her, so she burst into song totally off the mark.

"Edie, let's try it again. When you hear him play the eighth note is when you start singing, and he'll catch up to wherever you are."

"OK. Tea for two and two for tea..."

"Edie, wait until you hear a note from the piano, any note will do, just pick one..."

"Ohhh..."

This repeated six times until I suggested we take a little break, which was code for I need a fucking drink. I helped Edie off the stage, went over to the pianist and Jerry, and said, "Let's go to the front and talk." Jerry, looking like his mother just died, said, "We all knew this was going to be a challenge, but I think once she does it right, she'll get it..."

"Right, if she doesn't break her neck first!" I mumbled. I started to wonder if I had my emergency quaalude tucked in my 501 pocket as Little Edie and her entourage left so Edie could 'practice' for the show opening a few hours later. The set was slated to run forty-five minutes with no opening act, since we all realized an opening act would utterly confuse her. Jerry knew, as did I, that this was going to be a total zoo. She had never been onstage before—this was her debut—and we could only control so much. I suggested a stagehand, someone who could stand by for every show to help her as needed—for falls or performing to the stage wall instead of the audience. (I was hopeful with actual people in the audience she would not turn around, as she did in rehearsal, and start singing to the brick wall behind her.) They could also help when she forgot where the mic was, the answers to questions, or decided to dance (oh yes, she wanted dance to be part of the show but that was a no-go from the get-go). The possibilities for what could go wrong were endless. I was majorly freaked out but also weirdly curious to see if this was going to be car-crash bad or, well, entertaining. Because that's how Little Edie was in the movie—she was her wacky and sad, stubborn and funny self, and that's who people were coming to see. So, I chilled out and remembered that my job was to do my best to make the performer look good, sound good, get on and off the stage (as opposed to falling on and off the stage), and take the money.

An hour before the first show, I was lubricating myself with a scotch for what I knew was going to be an interesting two weeks. I decided to top off the drink with a few pulls on a joint. (And a Valium.) Reno's only had one door, and as I headed towards it, I noticed a crowd. I opened the door to about fifteen photographers and several reporters waiting for Edie's arrival. I walked down 13th Street to 7th

Avenue and lit up. Walking back, I readied myself for the night and whatever it would hold.

Loads of flowers were arriving for her (from fans of the movie—nothing from a Bouvier, Kennedy, or Onassis). The 'dressing room' at the club was an office during the day, and it was tiny. I knew with certainty that Edie would knock all the flowers over, so I took them to the basement, which was easily accessible through the kitchen. I thought I'd carefully walk Edie down the steps so she could admire the flowers just before the show to keep her mind off opening night nerves.

She arrived in full glory to a storm of flashbulbs and shouted questions. Her dream was coming true—she was a star. Edie posed, and posed, and posed, until I pushed through the front door, grabbed Jerry, and pointed at my watch. He got her settled in the dressing room with ten minutes until showtime. I gave her a single rose and went over the basics again: "Don't move, stay center, stand on the X, talk into the mic but don't put your mouth on it, don't wait for the pianist, he'll catch up to you, and try to remember the answers to the planted questions."

Surprisingly, the first show got off to a good start. She was walked to center stage and was rather charming in welcoming the audience. Edie talked a little about how it was her lifelong dream to be on the stage, but how her mother had never allowed it because of "who we were." She broke into "Tea for Two" and proceeded to sing it in a variety of keys. The pianist tried to change his key when she changed hers, but he couldn't keep up, so he just played random chords with abandon while she butchered the lyrics, making up most of them. She had such a radiant look on her face that frankly, nobody cared what she did—she was a hit! They even liked the two times she fell off the stage and when she walked into the piano, as well as the adlib monologue she did to the stage wall thinking that's where the audience was. She remembered the answers to her rehearsed questions; then I started reading a few questions from the audience, the real ones. As I fed her the first one, I could see her processing. There was a long silence, and then she said, "David, did we rehearse this part? I don't remember the answers to this part." She looked puzzled, then frightened. I think she thought she had done something wrong and had forgotten something. My heart went out to her.

"Edie, just tell these people, who love you, whatever you think about the question—you're doing great!"

The audience, for the most part, understood what I understood—that she was stumped, and they started applauding. Then she smiled and began answering the audience questions with more wit and humor than I had seen before. After that first performance, she got a long-standing ovation and she was clapping right along with the audience, which was adorable. Little Edie Beale had her stage debut and she was delighted, lit up brighter than the lights. I took her down to the basement to see all of the flowers, which she loved. Then she said she'd like to rest for a little while in the dressing room before the next show. I got her settled, and as Jerry and his partner worked the press in the room and the bar, I sat at a corner seat so I could watch the dressing room door to make sure she stayed put during the one-hour break. I was having a drink and hoping the second show would go as bizarrely well as the first when I heard a noise coming from the dressing room. Oh shit. I walked over and realized the noise was just about the loudest snoring I'd ever heard in my life. I opened the door, and there was Little Edie, fast asleep in a chair, her head back, her mouth open, holding her rose, and sawing logs big-time! Never before (or since) have I seen a performer I worked with snore. It was fabulous. It was perfect.

She never got worse, she never got better, and she fell every show at least two times. She also continued to be confused about where the audience and the stage wall were. But there was not one minute onstage when she wasn't genuinely radiating joy at finally being able to live her dream, and it was surprisingly moving and emotional to the majority of the audiences. They got their money's worth, and I didn't feel like the evil ringmaster of a Fellini movie. After her final performance, I went to the dressing room to wish her well and bon voyage, and I gave her a kiss on the cheek. She said, "I have learned so much about my *craft* from you." I don't know why, but it nearly moved me to tears. I replied, "Edie, I learned more from you than you could ever learn from me." What I didn't tell her was that I thought it was going to be a freak show, and it turned out to be such an authentic, uplifting experience for the audience and for Little Edie and for me—it was like having a daffy, off-kilter but delightful aunt over for Christmas, and it left me with nothing but warmth in my heart for her.

9.

MAFIA MULE, CARNEGIE DEBUT, AND A SHITTY AVERY FISHER

If my experience working on The Block in Baltimore taught me anything, it was how to work closely with the mafia. In the sleazy 'show it all' nightspots in the 60s, the mob blatantly used the various strip clubs and burlesque houses for money laundering—everybody was paid off the books and under the table in cash, including the cops, who were given hush-money bribes for themselves and their higher-ups so they wouldn't bust operations. (At least not too often.) The clubs also used mafia distribution companies for their liquor, laundry, and cigarette services, and all of this was no different for the 70s nightclubs and theatre venues I was working with now.

These mafia distribution companies looked like regular corporations and enterprises, but I later learned through a connected friend (the gay brother of a mafia kingpin, who was dating a singer I knew) that a lot of the crime families wanted out of the drug cartel business in the late 60s and early 70s and instead switched to companies that looked 'legal,' because it was far less violent than moving heroin and cocaine and also floated under the radar more easily.

I already knew that the mafia ran the gay bars, the cabarets, nightclub showrooms, and even the swanky, sometimes iconic, larger theatre venues. In the mid-70s, when I was hired by Columbia Records to work with some of their recording artists as a technical director and road manager, that's when I learned that the arms of the mob reached most of the record labels and even the radio stations that could turn a song into a 'hit.' (The infiltration of the record labels began in the late 50s as a cleanish way to launder money during the distribution of the actual physical records to music stores and radio stations. Occasionally a singer might read in *Billboard* or *Variety* that their record was selling hundreds of thousands of copies and inquire via their management about their missing royalties, only to be told with a wink they had only sold 40,000 copies—that phony sales number, leaked to the music press—was made up to cover mob money laundering.)

The Gambino and the Genovese families were most active with the record companies in the 60s and 70s, as was the Colombo family. Michael Franzese, a well-known name in the music industry, kept his hand in while he served time. His family still got business done, even with him behind bars. It was in the summer of 1976 that I became a legitimate cash mule for the mafia. I'd already been doing a few cash drops as favors for Steve Ostrow, the managing director of The Continental Baths. One night after the show, Ted Hook asked me if I would take an envelope to a man who was waiting for it at a bar. I asked him what this little side job entailed.

"You just have to meet a man wearing a green hat at the Acme bar in Midtown, pass him this envelope, and you're done," he explained, with a roll of his eyes. "Don't count it, don't look inside, and don't ask me any more questions, David." With that, the subject was closed. He added that if I did a good job, it could lead to a significant increase in tech and road management gigs, as 'certain people' had 'certain connections.' Well, that sounded great to me! I was in, and Ted was right. After I did a good job at the first envelope drop, albeit with sweaty palms, I was asked to do them more and more. While I was still the technical director at Reno Sweeney, I was also booking tons more lighting and road manager gigs on the side, using my backup guy to cover the Reno shows. My old pals Harry, Jerry, and Larry were very good to me in that way. I know they eventually, uh, 'recommended' me for tours involving Colombia recording artists, which in turn led to work with other labels: Arista, Capital, Atlantic, and A&M, primarily. Soon I was directly communicating with my mob connections regularly and awaiting instructions on what to do with the box office money from the shows I was teching.

The only way Harry, Jerry, and Larry communicated with me was via telephone. They set me up with a dedicated phone line that was answered by a real person (there were no answering machines back then). I'd call my answering service, always hoping the voice on the other end of the line would sound like Judy Holliday in *Bells Are Ringing* (alas, they sounded more like Zasu Pitts), and check for messages every couple of days. If there was a message from H, J & L, I called them back via a closely guarded phone number, which connected me to 'Betty,' who relayed messages and gave me my instructions. (There were several Bettys during this time—I could tell by the voice changes, but they were always called Betty.)

My envelope drops were filled with the box office revenue from clubs, showrooms, theatres, and other venues, which had been counted out to me, in cash, by the house manager. These cash drops nearly always took place in Manhattan (later it grew to include LA and Vegas), and I was advised, again by phone, to be at "Acme" bar at such-and-such day and time and to hand over my 'goods' to the guy with a hat of a certain color or with an out-of-state newspaper under his arm. The 'goods' eventually got counted by someone, somewhere. I was naïve about a lot of things during my show business career but never about what would happen to me if the money was ever short. Well, one time I was $500 short. It was after a Jane Olivor concert in a now defunct mafia showroom in Washington, D.C., when, for whatever reason, I was told to give the *sealed* manila envelope of cash to Jane's sister/manager. The next day, I was informed it was $500 short, and Jane's manager blamed me and demanded I "pay back" the $500 out of my own pocket, which I did with a lot of anger.

I called H, J, & L to tell them the story and reminded them that not once had I ever been short a single dollar, ever. They got it. Where did those greenbacks go? The manager had turned the envelope over, still sealed, to the accountant, and I suspect he must have been a magician on the side, since I was convinced *he* made that $500 'disappear.' A few days later, I was told to meet someone at the Acme bar wearing a certain hat, and he passed me an envelope and said, "Yours, kid." Inside was $500. That might be why I always had affection for the mafia. That might also be why I never heard that accountant's name again; he disappeared. Mobsters were straight-up guys with me, and of course they paid well for my troubles, on time and in cash. I was never placed in a dangerous situation (even if I was carrying $50K or more in cash in a briefcase on an airplane, which felt exciting but not really dangerous to me). I could set my clock to receiving a birthday bonus and a generous Christmas envelope. It made me laugh that twice a year *I* was the one getting an envelope at the Acme bar! Not once was I asked to rat out anything or anyone while I was on the road. As an added perk, if I ever had the unfortunate experience—okay, let's change that to *when I had unfortunate experiences* of contracting gonorrhea or syphilis—their private NYC doctor took care of it free of charge and without reporting it to the NYC Health Department. (That was the law in those days if you got syphilis, which happened to the best of us. His waiting room was a 'who's who' of mobsters, politicians, and celebrities.)

A Betty once let me know that if I ever wanted to visit 'Dr. Feelgood' to just ask. (Another perk, but I never asked. Downers were my thing, not uppers.) 'Dr. Feelgood' was Dr. Max Jacobsen, whose Park Avenue office was visited by JFK and Jackie Kennedy and oh-so-many other famous big names and politicians (he also made house calls, sometimes *White House* calls). His product was some sort of "energy formula" that erased pain and pepped up performers and government officials alike. (It turned out it was just a combination of meth and liquid steroids.) Dr. Feelgood's 'patients' included so many of the Grammy, Emmy, Tony, and Academy Award winners I worked with that I could usually tell when it was time for them to get a little liquid refill, because they'd try to schedule their tours to NYC at just the right time. Honestly, I often thought how exhilarating it was to be 'connected' to the mob but without the responsibility of having to shoot people or arson a hotspot—the best of both worlds, as it were. If the mob chose which of their clients were up for a pair of concrete shoes for unpaid bills on their own time, that was of no interest to me. Nosey as I was, I minded my own business when it came to this sideline gig. It was Christine Jorgensen, who had the first legal sex change in the world (thank you, Sweden!) and was one of the nicest women entertainers I ever worked with, who told me, looking very serious, "David, create a bubble around yourself. See what you need to see, do what you need to do, and stay out of the rest of it." It was basically a more sophisticated way of saying exactly what my stripper friends had told me years earlier, and it was a philosophy that certainly worked during my days as a mafia money mule. I estimate that all told, I carried well over a million dollars for Harry, Jerry, and Larry during my show business years. All in small bills. Hey, it helped my biceps!

———————•———————

Road managing for the record companies wasn't just an opportunity to showcase my ability to handle and transport large sums of cash. I was also honing my technical skills by working with some of the biggest names of the day, at some of the largest venues. A mere decade after my very first Amtrak ride from Baltimore to New York City, I was flying long hauls, occasionally international, to places like LA, London, Sydney, and Paris for career-making or marquee performances at Carnegie Hall, Avery Fisher, the Palladium, the Olympia, the Sydney Opera House, the Greek Theatre, and the Hollywood Bowl. I was also working with *big* names. It was a slice of life that I ate up and I was good at. It was during this career high that I fell in love with Julie Andrews. It was only a two-night gig in Hollywood, just her and a pianist. (A gay friend of hers had a nightclub that was an inch from going under, so she offered to do two shows, for 'old times' sake' while there filming a movie.) Obviously, Julie's shows would sell out, thus helping her old pal with cash flow. Julie loved to talk, to anybody, at any time, about anything. She had such a squeaky-clean image that her distinctly filthy vocabulary shocked everybody backstage, including me. I found her to be a hoot and a delight.

"Pet, love, keep the reverb low, light me as you fucking please and just know I'm not a fan of those goddamn blackouts because you can see the son-of-a-bitch performers moving in place anyway," she said to me with a smile. Julie knew all the dirty words but was a little out of practice stringing them together. I guess that's what playing a singing nun will do to you. She began her career on the British vaudeville circuit as a prodigy child singer (three octaves at age seven!) and early in her career played theatres that even burlesque dancers wouldn't touch—of course she had the same vocabulary as someone who grew up in my shitty, white trash neighborhood!

After her sound check, one of the International Alliance of Theatrical Stage Employees (IATSE) guys came over to me and said, "Julie Andrews has the mouth of a sailor. She even out-cusses you, David!" I told him, "I may have a mouth like a sailor, but what I really want is a sailor in my mouth!" I grinned. No response. My gay joke went right over his straight head. The IATSE guys usually weren't the brightest bulbs, but what they lacked in brains they made up for in brawn. (There was a joke back then that the IATSE "Nazis" wielded more muscle in the theatre world than the mafia.)

Julie brought in so much revenue during that two-night, four-show engagement that her old friend was able to save his club for several months before he put a bullet through his head—or someone did. It was never made clear, and it was one of those nightclubs where you didn't ask questions.

A few weeks later, I found myself working with Peggy Lee for a three-week show at the Empire Room at the Waldorf-Astoria. (If she liked you, she asked that you call her "Peg.") I knew Peggy's voice well since I was a rabid fan and I knew exactly how I wanted to mix her sound—very little reverb and a lot of middle, with not much bass or top. I was more concerned about the nine musicians because the size of the showroom required some amplification of several instruments, but Peggy insisted the musicians, who were all pickup players except her pianist, not be called for a sound check. Peg, I soon found out, was so tight she squeaked. She didn't want a sound check either. Her manager mailed me a copy of *Mirrors*, the concept album she had just recorded and was pushing, with a note that said, "Just make her sound like this." That was a first—a sound check by mail.

I decided to preset Peggy's lights; I was told she was not a 'mover.' I also knew her hair was platinum white, which, from a lighting standpoint, is not the best. Any overhead or back lighting on a white-haired person could make them look as if they were wearing a colored hat, and if they were not good at hitting specific stage marks, they could actually be in a down-beam that would make their nose, cheeks, and chin *vivid* from the various lighting gels. I used colored gel lights with abandon—to add definition, depth, and mood *around* the singer—but never to turn someone's face fuchsia or chartreuse. Never! I had a reputation within the industry that when you were lit by me, you looked like you, not a clown or a Halloween decoration.

When Peggy arrived for the show, I noticed she was already *very* made up. I wondered if it was stage makeup or if this was her normal look (oh please dear god let it be her stage makeup!). There are certain brands of makeup designed to basically turn your face into a flesh-colored mask, with Xermablend being the best known. Peggy's face was very shiny; that kind of makeup reflects facial lighting, which makes a performer's face look like a death mask (and her lipstick was already a 'Dying Blush' color). She wore a gauzy white muumuu with an empire waist, which she must have thought would hide her weight issues, but *I* knew that she would look like a billboard in search of an ad once onstage. It didn't take long to realize I was fucked, lighting-wise, unless I never took any of the instruments above about 65% of their potential brightness. A 'dark show,' if you will. Luckily, that can work in a nightclub as the distance from the audience to the stage is shallow.

Peggy invited me to sit beside her at her makeup mirror. ("No more makeup, Peggy, please," I muttered inwardly.) I went over the tech cues I had planned, she nodded, and then she asked me where my tux was. My tux?! I was wearing my usual 501s, so I explained that I would be tucked away in a booth where no one could see me. She studied me again and said, "You don't have on underwear." (I never wore underwear. In those days, one never knew when the opportunity for a potential quickie might arise.) I replied, "And you don't have your powder on yet." Of course, I already knew why. Female celebs of a certain age are aware how easily powder can settle into wrinkles and facial cracks—it was an issue that I was well versed in. So when Peggy told me she didn't like powder, I said, "If you don't powder, and heavily, your face is going to reflect so much light up there that you'll look like a freeway sign in a car's headlights." She paused, then, with a poker face and a flat tone said, "So you're scaring me into using powder, you don't have a tux on, and you're going to walk around showing off your dick." There was another pause, then a slow smile. "Call me Peg." I was in!

Over a three-week period, we chatted between shows and she was a delight. She was also tanked a little, and with regularity for the first show every night, and then tanked a lot, for the second show. Peg never slurred; she just got a little spacy. It was a great foil for her drinking, as she already looked spacy—she was known for that signature 'far away' look! On the third night, in between shows, she offered me a pill. (How did she know?) "It's just a little downer, lover, but it saves on alcohol 'cause they mix well with what I drink for the first show real good, and my drinks aren't comped here like they were at The Copa." I mentioned I enjoyed a quaalude after shows, thrown down with a brandy stinger. The next night, she said she couldn't get me a quaalude, but she made the hotel give her the ingredients for a brandy stinger and her assistant promptly made each of us one. What could I do? When a lady asks you to have a drink it's rude to decline. That became our ritual for the remainder of the gig—a brandy stinger between shows along with the hottest gossip about who was in the audience and what she knew about them—my Peg was a talker!

While chatting with her assistant, I discovered her many-years-old issue with alcohol and prescription meds. And her weight. Towards the end of her life, I heard from a friend still working with her that it had gotten to a point where Peg was not very functional. What put her in a long-lasting depression was her dream to perform a musical about her life. The sad outcome of that project, *Peg* (the show, starring her from youth to the present), hit Broadway a couple years later, but it was panned by the critics and closed after three performances. She was never the same, even after winning a long court battle with Disney over the royalty rights for the two songs she wrote on the cartoon-movie soundtrack *Lady and the Tramp*. Miss Peggy Lee died of a heart attack in 2002, at age eighty-one. All said, I wouldn't trade one minute of the time I had with her while listening to her haunting vocals. When she hit the stage, regardless of her altered states and dreamlike eyes, she was pure magic and a dame in the best sense of the word.

———— • ————

I first met Jane Olivor when she was showcasing at the Monday Talent Nights at Reno's. She quickly became another of my favorite artists to work with and played a hugely important part in my career. Jane introduced me to Johnny Mathis (who I later worked with and befriended) and she was the first performer I ever tech-directed at Carnegie Hall. Prior to that, she had never played anything larger than intimate cabarets and her sudden rise from small saloons to iconic venues was unheard of. Who the fuck plays Carnegie Hall as their first segue from the NYC cabaret circuit?

Jane's record company was aggressively pushing to make their 'new star' visible to larger audiences while promoting her first album, *First Night*, an ironic title for her debut album (Carnegie was the first night she performed in a space with more than two hundred seats, as I recall it). In truth (make that in my opinion), she was professionally and emotionally abused by both Columbia Records and the William Morris Agency, who threw her into the deep end for her first large audience performance in the world's most iconic theatre! She didn't have a say in the matter.

Her older sister and manager called and asked if I was free to do the lights, sound, spotlight calls, and stage management for the Carnegie gig less than a week before the show! I'd never teched any theatre that large, let alone Carnegie Hall, so I immediately said yes, thinking mostly about what it could do for my resume and fee. I confess, I was also starstruck by the famous concert hall. All I could think of was that old chestnut: "How do you get to Carnegie Hall? Practice, practice, practice!" I had 'practiced' up the ass (yeah, I know), having worked with over fifty well-known performers in my career, but those engagements had been in small cabarets or medium-sized nightclubs.

I still had a 'pals with privileges' arrangement going on with Greg, Ellen Greene's very handsome friend and Broadway stage manager. So I called and pumped him for info. I asked how to call spotlight cues and other details about Carnegie, my very first Stagehand's Union theatre.

Greg told me to "Get over here fast!" He lived on the Upper West Side, so I hopped on the #1 to his place. As soon as I walked through his apartment door, Greg scared the shit out of me with a ten-minute lecture about everything that was going to go wrong—so much so that I threw up my arms, got hissy, and headed for the exit. He did everything to prevent me from leaving, including literally standing in front of the door with his arms spread wide and shouting over and over again, *"Don't* do Carnegie, you're not ready for it, you're going to look like an idiot, it's professional suicide, David!" But I was twenty-five and thought I was invincible. I didn't believe it could be any different from the nightclubs I'd worked at: Light her up, make her sound good, tell the spotlight guys what to do, take the money. Apparently not. Once Greg realized I really *was* going to do the gig, he insisted on giving me

'Carnegie Hall for Dummies' lessons right there and then. It was probably the only thing that saved my ass in the end, because he knew the IATSE union rules and regs and how they insisted things be done. We went over union everythings until we were both cross-eyed. Then we fucked, made plans for lesson number two the next day, and ordered Chinese. There were infinite benefits to knowing Greg!

The day before the gig, I went to his apartment for my second lesson: How to call spotlights. Let me tell you something: cueing five spotlights is like solving a Rubik's Cube, but *calling* spotlight cues to the union operators handling them via headset? Nearly impossible. I not only had to call all cues and gel color changes but also sound cues, stage monitor cues, backstage cues, and more. While I was relating cues to the spot operators and the sound engineers, both my hands would also be operating the two-scene preset manual lighting board, creating the visual moods for each song, and deciding where to have a blackout, a bump-up, a fade, etc. Oh, and I'd also be talking to the sound engineer about reverb and mixing certain levels for certain songs at the same time as calling light cues. As Greg began my spotlight cue-call lesson in his apartment, I'm thinking, *A goddamn octopus couldn't do all this at once!* To say I was freaked out is an understatement, to the point that I was thinking about just packing up and leaving New York. Frozen with fear, I broke into a flop sweat and cried as Greg held me. (And occasionally called a 'time out' so I could fuck him to calm my nerves. Good old Greg.)

Here's what he taught me about calling lights in a union house: Every cue has to be called with a countdown. If you want the spots to black out, you say, "Blackout on five," and then you count down. "Five, four, three, two, one, blackout!" If you want some spots to black out and others not to, you say, "Spots number two and number four, blackout on five," and then count down. For the spotlight to go from a "Full" (full body) shot to tighten just to the upper chest, the call is "Full to tit shot on five," then count down when you want it to narrow, or "slow tighten to a waist shot on ten," and then count down for a slower, more subtle effect. Or, "Full bump up on six!" It was never fucking ending.

The whole time I took notes and practiced calling cues, song by song, having gotten the music set order (nineteen tunes) from Jane Olivor's producer. I was also wearing a nonfunctional headset Greg had swiped from the Majestic Theatre, so I could get used to having something over one ear while listening to Janie's voice and mixing sound with the other. I thought, *I'm so fucked with no lube,* but my name was already attached to the gig. I'd signed a contract with Columbia Records management, and my name was even in the *Playbill* programs. Broadway Greg turned to me and asked, "Now, what are we forgetting?" "Quaaludes?" I replied. Silence. He continued, "You're also going to be calling sound cues, remember?" I burst into tears (yet again) and ran to the kitchen looking for a bottle of liquor, any liquor. Could I do this? I had no idea. I was sweating and spooked.

I arrived at 10:00 a.m. on the day of the show to run through the tech, having convinced myself I was ready. I'd penciled out an ad hoc lighting chart for what I wanted to do with the hanging lights—overheads, rails instruments, side lights hanging from the metal trees in the wings, which color gels to use, and so forth—but I was a natural at that part. Working with two hundred lights or twenty lights was no different than blowing a big dick versus a little dick as far as I was concerned. Same process! I'd also gelled the spotlights for Janie's face skin tone, using my go-to Rosco 842.

When Janie came in for the sound and light check, the sound was fine, exactly as I wanted it to 'read' in the house. (It was mixed by a guy from a prestigious sound company that I had hired working the board from the left wing; not ideal but there was no space in the house at Carnegie for a mixing board in the orchestra area.) The volume from the stage monitors also seemed good. Singers need to hear themselves over the sound of the band in order to stay on pitch (this was before earpods took the place of monitors). The stage monitors had to be mixed differently than the house speakers, since most singers only wanted to hear the piano and/or drums. I showed Janie the center mark on the floor where she would stand and sing and the area scooped around the Steinway grand piano where she would sit on a stool while singing some ballads. I wanted to double-check the lighting for that piano space, so I ran into the wings, grabbed a stool, and took it to the piano so she could sit. Suddenly I heard seven IATSE guys scream "*Stop!*" I thought I was about to fall through a hole in the floor or something. But a union rep walked over to me and said, "Give me the stool, and you have a two-hundred-dollar violation for moving it." This union was fucking *strict*—non-IATSE members were not allowed to touch anything, literally. I was surprised they let me touch Janie! Then he asked, nice as can be, where I wanted the stool. Oh, did I want to tell him where he could put it, but Greg had warned me that yelling at an IATSE stagehand was like yelling at Harry, Jerry, and Larry—a big-time no-no. (Turns out the union requires an actual 'stool mover.' They call it something else but that was the gist of it. Then another union guy places the music arrangement folders on the music stands.) I glibly said, "So who puts the vase with a dozen red roses on the piano, the flower person?" I thought I was being funny, but they had one of those too, and it was a different person than the stool person! (Please note: It takes the stool person and the flower/prop person less than one minute to move those two things to their place on the stage, and each are paid for eight hours of 'work.') I finally got Jane on the stool to check the lighting angles and it looked stellar.

An hour before the show began, the audience started to trickle in. There were so many flower arrangements in her dressing room that it looked like a funeral. I was with Janie, who was terrified but putting up a good front, a makeup artist (supplied by the record company and then charged back to her), her sister-manager (making 20%), her mentor and music producer, her pianist-conductor, and several big-headed Columbia Record execs drinking Dom Perignon (which they then charged back to her). The next thing we knew, it was showtime. I made my way to the lighting console near the tech booth, feeling very uncomfortable in my contractual, mandatory tuxedo, donned my headset, and checked to see the union crew were all in place. The backstage union guy confirmed Jane was in the wings and that the eleven-piece band was set. The sound guy confirmed we were "hot" with the mics and monitors, so I cued them, "Dim the house lights," and called my first spot cues as Janie entered from the left wing. Everything went well! Jane managed to overcome her nerves and get through the performance with aplomb, and I was calling the spots and sound cues, while working the light board, like a pro. And then the encores happened.

I had been told, quite firmly, by the Columbia execs who were producing and therefore pulling the strings on this performance, that there would be one false exit and then three curtain call encores, followed by the house lights so the union stagehands wouldn't go into overtime, which was outrageously expensive. As Jane Olivor exited after the third standing ovation encore, I did as I was told by the record label and brought up the house lights while darkening the stage. The audience was still going crazy, and I was beyond relieved I got through it. My first Carnegie Hall show, and I did it! I thanked the spotlight men profusely and let them know their tip envelopes were with the union rep, when one of them says, "She's not coming back? You sure?" I was feeling cocky with the energy of a successful gig. I replied, "No, guys, that's it. She won't come back, thanks again, good night." I heard four headsets click off, and as I started to stand up, a Columbia exec starts screaming from backstage in my headset, "She's coming back, she's coming back, *lights*!"

Fuck, fuck, fuck! Jane hit the stage, the band turned on their music stand lights, and I froze. I'd just released the spot guys! They were gone! I felt like a deer in the headlights, so frozen that I had no clue what to do. I just sat there while time stood still. Then I heard the guy manning spotlight number five, still on a headset, say, "Quick, bring up every stage light you have and I'll roll over to the #842 gel and pick her up." I could have cried; his voice jerked me out of my frozen stupor and told me what to do. "House lights down, stage lights up full!" The left side of Jane's face was brighter than the rest of her (my savior spot guy, who had remained, had an angled shot with his spot but did the best he could). When the song was over (the same one she had sung three times now), Jane exited and I heard the Columbia guy in my headset again. "We're going into overtime, overtime! Turn off the fucking stage lights! House lights! House lights. *Now!*" In the wings an IATSE guy said, calmly, in the headset, "David, she's headed to the dressing room." This time, the show really was over. And I felt like an idiot. Why did I trust that those Columbia execs would enforce the three-encore curtain call strategy? It was fucking Carnegie Hall—the same theatre where Judy Garland said "I'll sing 'em all and we'll stay all night!" on her best-selling *Live at Carnegie Hall* LP, an album I had played so many times the grooves wore thin. It was the most embarrassing moment of my show business career (so far); all that sense of self-worth and confidence I'd built over the past two years dimmed like that last remaining spotlight. There was an after-show album release party at The Plaza, but I didn't go; I felt too humiliated. Trembling, I found my bag and walked out the front doors of Carnegie Hall to the #1 subway to head back to my apartment in the West Village, where I had the cry of my life, for being so stupid.

———•———

Unfortunately, my spotlight screwup at Carnegie was not the only problem I had during one of Jane Olivor's New York concerts. Two years later, I was tech director for her prestigious gig at Avery Fisher Hall—a 2,700-seat theatre within the Lincoln Center Complex and a very commanding place to do a one-woman show. This time things went to shit at the end again, literally. The gig was on my calendar for months, and I was looking forward to what I hoped would be a redeeming night after my Carnegie fail. I'd even studied the blueprints of the theatre closely to figure out an entirely new, unique lighting arrangement. The day before the show, I had just returned from a tent circuit in Mexico, and though I wasn't feeling queasy, I drank some

Pepto Bismol as insurance, grabbed a roll of Tums, and headed to Avery Fisher Hall for the 10:00 a.m. tech check. This was another IATSE union theatre, but at this point I was a pro when it came to working with 'the guys.' (I suspect that the union supervisors knew of my connection to Harry, Jerry, and Larry, so I felt appreciatively protected.) Everything was going great. We hung the lighting rails and poles, gelled to my specifications, tuned the grand piano, and when Jane and her pianist arrived, the sound check was flawless. My excitement mounted—I was going to blow the NYC tech community away with my artistry!

The tech had gone so smoothly that we were ahead of schedule. A bunch of the IATSE guys (yes, still a men-only union) and I were hanging out onstage shooting the shit when an executive from Columbia Records barreled through the house and up to the stage, bellowing my name.

"David Vass! Where's David Vass?" he screamed.

"I'm David Vass," I slowly replied, in a 'who the fuck are you?' sort of way.

"I represent Columbia Records. I was at Carnegie Hall the night you released all the spotlights before Olivor's final encore. Listen up. I want you to tell me, song by song, *exactly* what you're going to be doing with the lights, and then I want to inspect them and talk with the spotlight operators because there aren't going to be any fuckups tonight! I'm here to make sure! One wrong move, one mistake, Vass, and you'll never work for Columbia or in this town again!"

Wow. *Wow!* I stood there open-mouthed while the twelve IATSE muscle guys stared, waiting for me to respond. What I wanted to do was call my mob connections to come break this prick's legs, but I made myself calm down.

"Well, hello to you too! Sorry, I didn't catch your name, but this is a union stage, and without prior approval, you're not allowed to stand on it, which means you're in violation right now. I'll check with the supervisor to see how much the fine will be, and I assume you'll want that charged to Columbia?" I said quietly, then continued. "The situation you're referencing happened two years ago when I was still green and called to the gig a few days before it happened. I've worked with Jane Olivor for over eighty performances since then, and many other Columbia singers. In fact, I'm booked for seven upcoming Columbia gigs. Two of them are international. Everything here is set, professional, and like I said, you're in a union house and illegally on a union stage." I couldn't help myself, so I added, "So I suggest you get your ass off it, you little piece of shit." That *really* set him off. He moved a few inches closer to my face.

"Do you know who I am and what I can do to your career? You can't talk to me like that. I'll knock your faggot face off!" Oh dear, so we were going down the "faggot" road, were we? I laughed—and it was a genuine laugh, because I had those giant IATSE guys behind me, and all twelve looked like former boxers. I turned to my union buddies. "I knew Columbia had a lot of pretentious, stupid execs, but what kind of business school garbage bin do you think they pulled this homophobic asshole out of?" They laughed, shared a collective look, then wordlessly formed a protective ring around me. I looked through the IATSE muscle circle at the Columbia stooge.

"I think this might be a good time for you to, uh, exit stage left." He was redder than a bottom's ass after a good spanking. One of the union guys chimed in: "Look, you rude little jerk, everybody has to learn their craft and David has clearly learned his, so why don't you go back to wherever you came from and learn yours, which would include how to talk to people. Start with a lesson in please and thank you." The exec, looking rattled, did a 180 and ran away fast. I turned to my IATSE friends to thank them for their support and the supervisor of the group turned to me.

"Don't worry about him or what just happened. We deal with assholes like that all the time. But for the record, if anyone *ever* calls you a faggot again, hit first, and ask questions later."

The Avery Fisher show went brilliantly. Janie sang brilliantly, she looked great, there was not one musical or technical hiccup, and the audience was frenzied by the end. Until the encores. Again. The lighting board at Avery Fisher was actually in the house on the balcony above the dress circle, meaning I was surrounded on three sides by audience members. And it was when the first encore began that my Mexico trip hit my body without warning and with full force. I suddenly had to shit so badly, so uncontrollably, and with three encores to go I knew I wasn't going to be able to hold it, but I was trapped calling the cues and working the board solo. I used the head mic to ask if anyone could come fast to relieve me—run, don't walk—but no one could elbow through the audience, and realistically, *I'd* set up the intricate lighting rig and only I knew the cues and what the various sliders were connected to. What to do? Maybe turn all the stage lights up, tell the spotlights to go full and follow Janie while I ran to the bathroom? Then Montezuma took his revenge. My body muscles were defeated and ... I shit myself. Three times. In fast succession. Jesus fucking Christ.

I barely controlled my panic. I didn't detect an odor, not that I noticed anyway. So while the audience was standing and sitting, standing and sitting, cheering and bravoing for Jane's endless encores, I sat there with shit all over my ass, my tuxedo pants, and probably the chair seat. Full disclosure: The shit alerted my bladder that it was full, *really* full, and I thought, *What the fuck, I've already shit myself, why not piss too?* So I did. Piss ran down my leg, collecting in my rented patent leather shoes. I was at a total loss what to do. So I stayed put until the show ended and the audience left, figuring I'd make my break when the hall had fully cleared out. Well, at least I didn't freeze like at Carnegie. The balcony was finally empty when the house manager strolled over and smiled.

"You shit yourself, didn't you?" He said it so nonchalantly, like he was talking about whether it was going to rain tomorrow. "Um, yes. I did. And I think I pissed myself too." I wanted to curl up and die. This was the most embarrassed I'd ever been. In a kind, sympathetic voice, he explained it happened at Avery Fisher all the time. "Mostly to audience members," he said. Apparently, many of the shows attracted senior citizens who couldn't always control their bowels, so this was *not* a first. Except maybe to a technical director running a show from the house while surrounded by 2,700 people. He explained the seat cushions came off easily; they sent them to a dry cleaner who knew what to do, and they were returned a few days later good as new. He offered to fetch me a robe—they kept a few backstage for this type of situation. "I'll go get you one to wear over the tux, and when you're ready, I'll call you a cab and you can go out the stage door." He said all of this without a hint of judgment. I wanted to kiss him. Actually, he was super handsome, so I really did, but I figured my timing was, uh, a little off that night.

———•———

Life went on and I continued my booked gigs. I was getting used to the emotional highs and lows of show business and of being on the road, but I was also beginning to wonder how long it would last before I grew tired of this experience too, just like all the others in my life. The travel was beginning to wear me out and a new music trend was taking over—disco. The offers I got for those kinds of gigs held no interest for me. I was a Great American Songbook kind of guy. I got my kicks listening to a vocalist soar, not hearing the ear-splitting bottom notes of a synthesizer on endless repeat. It was disco that first made me realize how dumbed down the music industry had become and I was ready to wash my hands of it.

Another significant crossroads in my life. I opened my mind to try to hear, I don't really know, the Universe maybe? In the past, whenever an end was near, a new beginning always seemed to be waiting in the wings. I had faith in that and waited. As it turned out, I wouldn't have to wait long.

10.

THE FOG LIFTS

Three weeks later, opportunity knocked. A well-known entertainment mogul in the Bay Area, Lawrence Simms, offered me a new job and a new beginning in San Francisco. It was an offer I couldn't refuse, but first, I had one last contract to fulfill: a one-nighter at The Greek Theatre in LA.

The Greek had a career-making reputation; it was the most prestigious booking on the West Coast, just as Carnegie Hall was on the East. I put my excitement about starting over in the city by the Bay on a mental shelf and focused solely on making this last technical gig a testament to everything I'd learned, every stage trick I'd picked up, during my years as a tech director and road manager.

An Evening with Jane Olivor was going to be a lavish, spare-no-expense production, underwritten by her record label to add some muscle to her latest album, *Stay the Night*. The Greek was a 6,000-seat outdoor venue with a huge, covered stage. Handling this event seemed like a fitting farewell to my years working in the technical end of show business. I'd done my homework and knew exactly what I wanted for the staging of this special night. Now it was time to roll up my sleeves and turn my vision into reality. Make that a stellar, spectacular reality!

I arrived two days before the performance to eyeball the stage and the equipment and to meet the technical management director, who was a deliciously handsome young man. Our meeting went flawlessly and with heavy flirting occurring on both sides. My goal was to talk him into letting me paint the entire stage floor white, something that had never been allowed before at The Greek. I pleaded, I cajoled, I begged. I won! Okay, it wasn't just the flirting and pleading, we also fucked until his eyes rolled to the back of his pretty head. My secret weapon got me the result I desired and a classic down-low good time, too.

Jane and the conductor-pianist arrived the day prior to the show for rehearsals with the eleven-piece pickup band, while I focused on sound and light details before the IATSE guys arrived for the performance day tech. I even found time late in the afternoon to go shopping with Janie on Rodeo Drive. I talked her into an all-white stage ensemble. "David, this outfit is just too expensive, we can't...." I cut her off. "Janie, remember when the Columbia execs drank bottles of Dom Perignon in your dressing room at Carnegie Hall and charged it back to you? Well, it's payback time, sweetie. We're re-charging this to Columbia," I said, grinning! In fact, I wanted my colored gel effects to 'pop' on parts of *her*, as well as on the flooring and orchestra platforms. The goal was to create the visual ambiance of a color palette inspired by the work of Monet.

Seating at The Greek was extremely steep; the seats looked 'down' on the stage rather than at the usual audience angle. I was armed with four super-trooper spotlights to light Jane so she could be seen a mile away, and three hundred lighting instruments hung as overheads, on front rails and side tree-pipes. I hoped the audience would feel like they were watching a performance within a rainbow.

Of course, Janie had sold out all 6,000 seats in record-breaking time. As the arena lights dimmed, the stage lights came up in a lavish splash of colors while the super troopers picked her up walking to the center of that all-white stage. Before she even began singing, the visuals had already stopped the show and my eyes teared up. Jane Olivor gave the best vocal performance I'd ever heard her sing—and that's saying something after working on over eighty of her performances. Five standing ovations and encores later, the audience filed out, but the atmosphere within that now empty theatre space still buzzed with energy. I stood alone on the darkened stage, unhurriedly took in the 6,000 empty seats, and blew a kiss to the end of this chapter in my career.

As I was being driven to the Chateau Marmont, I pondered why I was leaving yet another lucrative career to risk trying something completely new. Why was I never content with my existing success? Why was I always drawn to new, dicey chances? Here I was walking *away* from money, a sterling reputation, and my choice of the world's best performers. But I sensed there was another unknown chapter waiting in the wings—the wings being just four hundred miles to the north. Closing my eyes as the limo pulled into the hotel's cul-de-sac, I pictured the fog rolling in from the sea, the Golden Gate Bridge, Nob Hill, and Irish coffees. As I opened my eyes, another thought occurred to me— Hello, maybe I'd find someone to love there!

———•———

I'd met Lawrence through a friend of mine, Zohn Artman. Zohn was the chargé d'affaires for Bill Graham, the most powerful and connected promoter of singers, bands, and other music acts in San Francisco and, later, New York. Zohn and I had first met when he was traveling through Manhattan keeping an eye on a hot new band with drug problems, some group Bill Graham was promoting. They were doing a three-night stint at The Palladium on 14th Street, which was the premier rock and roll palace in NYC. I was invited to the show but, hating hard rock, I passed. However, I did decide to pop in for the after-party to see if there were any cute, fuckable guys or a famous face or two. Zohn and I started talking in the backstage green room, and the conversation took a direction it usually did with gay men his age; he wanted to have sex with me. He hardly held my interest physically. He was about fifteen years older, but he *did* seem like a genuine, nice guy. Zohn told me he had a problem with sex; he couldn't get an erection.

Well, I do love a challenge and the remainder of my night was free, so I popped into Zohn's limo and went back to his hotel and put on my 'Mr. Fix-It' hat. I figured if he's lying, I'll know it when he gets a hard-on. And if he's not lying, I'll get him hard, because at this point, I could have written a book on the art of blow jobs. So while it took some doing and a few skillful tricks, I got him there and he even climaxed. Zohn was thrilled, and the look of relief on his face was worth my effort. He said it was the first time that had happened in months. I think he'd felt broken, a feeling I'd struggled with since I was five. If only I could find such an easy solution, like a magical BJ! We never hooked up sexually again, but I suspect I gave him back some confidence, which helped him normalize his sex life, and we remained friendly. It was at the post show party that I'd also met Lawrence, who Zohn had introduced me to. We chatted briefly and he told me about his nightclub complex in San Francisco (a two-hundred-seat showroom on one floor and a late-night, primarily gay disco on the level above) and how desperate he was to make the showroom *the* number one nightclub for big-name talent in the Bay Area.

Lawrence had a huge ego and a funny, competitive but likable personality. He was also *very* gay and very, *very* rich. He visited me in NYC for a business dinner meeting a few weeks later and offered me a position—the talent booking agent for The City Showroom. I would be the person who scouted, found, and contracted the talent. No tech responsibilities, I just had to use my connections and once more work with record labels, agents, management companies and the mercurial, often drugged-out artists that would play the nightclub. Easy! The job came with a little carriage house apartment, which Lawrence also owned, sitting atop Pacific Heights near Nob Hill. He even offered to match the money I was making as an independent contractor in the music industry. The best part? I wouldn't have to travel nearly nonstop anymore. By that point, the exhaustion that came with being on the road all the time was starting to really wear on me, not to mention the jetlag. Plus, I was drinking a ton, and knew it was getting out of control—the last thing I needed was yet another addiction! A few weeks earlier, my ad hoc mom Anita O'Day had even warned me that I was getting in too deep with the sauce.

"Anita, it's Avid-day," I said, when I called her for one of our regular late night gossip sessions. "Sometimes I can't remember what happened after a show. I'm drinking too much booze, feeling like shit, and dealing with too many headaches the next day. And when I drink, it's not making me feel better; it's making me feel nasty—low and worthless. Any advice?"

There was a pause on the line, which was unusual for Anita, as she had immediate opinions about everything. One of the many qualities I admired about her was that she thought as fast as I did, faster actually. So if I heard the 'Anita pause,' it was always a cause for concern.

"Avid-day, do you realize how fucked up you are right *now*?"

"Huh?" I mumbled.

"You're slurring," she said. "Did you do a gig tonight? And did it go well?"

"Uh, yes, it was great as usual, and I didn't start drinking until after as usual, and I'm not shurring, uh stirring, uh *slurring*! Shit. Okay, I'm fucked up." I could always count on Anita for tough love. She never held back with me.

"Avid-day, your next step is going to be junk. I think that's all that's left for you," she warned. "You've described over the last few months the drugs, the paying for sex, alcohol, hookups out of control, and all of it leaving you empty. Exactly how I felt when I started using. Do you really wanna go down that rabbit hole? You've worked with enough of us hypos to see where that leads. You have got to stop, reset, get off the merry-go-round. Right now." She added, "You're bored with what you're doing, and I get it, hell, I've *been* it! It's just like I can't sing the same song the same way twice. You feel like you've used up your box of tricks and you're on auto-repeat. Avid-day, *don't* do what I did. Don't keep going down this path, because it's a hard road back, and a lot don't make it. I think it's time you changed your career, and fast. Get away from the temptations, do something different with your talents and your knowledge of our business. You're a smart cookie, so for fuck sake figure it out—time for a tempo change, kiddo—stop with the three quarters and switch it up to seven eighths!"

I knew she was right. I *was* a shitty drunk; it was not an addiction I liked, unlike all the others which I *did* like. I was tanked nearly every night, and based on her experience, and knowing how much we were alike, it definitely could have led to me dabbling with heroin. Actually, I'd been toying with the idea—just a teeny poke, a tiny snort. Finally riding the dark horse? Me? After all I'd seen, pushing celebrities onstage and jerking needles out of their arms? I had an instant epiphany—I was teetering on the edge of oblivion. I told Anita that I'd been offered a booking job at a club in San Francisco, and she thought it would be a great move. Or as she put it, "Your scat is stale, Avid-day, and you've already got the shakes, I can hear it in your voice, and you haven't even shot up yet, for fucks sake! You'd make a shitty junkie! Switch it up before you do something stupid that could check you out."

Three weeks later, I'd accepted the job offer, given up my New York City apartment, and disconnected my phone line to Harry, Jerry, and Larry. I'd thanked them for their business and loyalty, and they understood my decision to make a change. I suspect theirs was a revolving door of money mules, probably theatre execs and technicians like me; they were used to change. My mob family offered an open invitation to work for them again if I wanted to return, then wished me well. My last phone call was from a 'Betty' who gave me info for one last Acme bar meeting where I was given a good luck envelope, filled with *lots* of good luck! And then I was headed to the Bay Area.

Lawrence called a few nights prior to my arrival and said he'd meet me at the airport, asking me, "Which color?"

"Which color what?" I replied, totally stumped. "Which color Bentley, David. I have eight, you know." Uh, no, I didn't know. So I said, "What are my color choices?" and he replied "Just pick a fucking color, okay?!" I told him to surprise me. It was purple. Not so surprising; it *was* San Francisco!

———•———

My first stop was the carriage house apartment, to check out my digs and see what I needed. It was a beautiful little place, loads of character: plaster around the ceilings and some stained glass atop the front windows, one huge room, a pullman kitchen, and full bath. I went shopping with Lawrence's driver and purchased an *actual* mattress—not a roll of foam!—although I didn't bother with a bed frame. I picked up a small table with two chairs, a bookcase, a beautiful vintage beaded Victorian standing lamp, and enough kitchen stuff to cook a simple dinner and make coffee. It wasn't that I was a minimalist; I just didn't really care about having 'stuff.' I'd lived in crash pads and on the road for so long that a pretty lamp and real mattress did the trick.

The neighborhood was upscale and beautiful, filled chockablock with Victorian houses, wild calla lilies growing in their front yards, and views of the Pacific Ocean from the hilltops. Visually, San Francisco spoke to me. It was gorgeous and walkable, which I loved. In fact, my most vivid memory of those first two weeks was how fucking sore my calves were from walking *up* hills and *down* hills. And when the fog rolled in, so dreamy and relaxing, it was like the first ten minutes after a quaalude hits. The ambiance was completely different from New York; it was laid-back, soft and gentle, like Mel Tormé's voice. (I used to call Mel "The Velvet Fog;" everybody in the business did.) I had never learned to drive, so it took me a while to figure out the city's public transportation, but nearly everything I needed was within walking distance, up and down those hills. Two blocks away, a cable car picked me up and dropped me off one block from The City Showroom in North Beach. How I loved hanging off those cable cars, singing old MGM songs. ("Clang, clang, clang went the trolley!") No one stared at me when I did things like that, because everyone in San Francisco back then was usually *way* more stoned than I was.

The City Showroom was a black box space—the walls were black, the ceiling was black, everything was black. There was a stage with no curtain, and the tables and chairs were on four tiers, with the lowest tier on the floor closest to the stage and so on. That gave everyone an unobstructed view of the show. The tables were covered with black cloths and lit candles. There was a baby grand piano, a state-of-the-art sound and lighting system, plus a good tech director who listened when I made the occasional suggestion. There was no food, only drinks, served by really, really cute male waiters. While some club managers might do a 'glove check,' to make sure a uniform wasn't too dirty, Lawrence would conduct a 'pants check' with the waiters, occasionally saying something like "You couldn't find anything tighter?" He'd even sent a waiter home once, saying, "Come back in tighter pants, or don't come back at all!"

Lawrence was a character. Gay, flamboyant, and as I said, powerfully rich. (He collected Bentleys—who does that?). If he liked you, he liked you. If he didn't, he didn't. He was funny and he always thought big. Lawrence would never turn down an act I'd suggested just because the fee was too high, so long as it brought in a crowd and a good review. He was in his early fifties, slightly overweight, and had an acne-scarred face—not an attractive man. He said his money came from his wealthy family, but whenever I squeezed him for details, he'd change the subject. One night I was hanging out with Zohn, who was very high after eating a mushroom brownie, who said, "David, you know Lawrence's money is from drugs, right?" Um, no, I didn't know that!

"Like, he's a drug dealer?" I asked.

"Oh, he's *way* more than a drug dealer; he's a kingpin," Zohn said thoughtfully. "He has an entire business empire, a kind of umbrella spread, complete with managers and full-time staff, all along the West

Coast, and he's at the top of the umbrella, pulling all the strings. How do you think he got eight Bentleys?"

"He told me it was family money," I said, shrugging.

I'd already worked with the mob, so I wasn't put off by this information in the least. Just a new note to myself: Keep your mouth shut and don't ask about his family again. If I *had* wanted to connect the dots, I wouldn't have been surprised if they had led to Harry, Jerry, and Larry. It's a small world.

My days were soon busy booking singers and acts, most of whom wouldn't normally work a two-hundred-seat club, but they knew me and I was calling in favors. Within the first three weeks, I had booked the nightclub for the next six months: Charles Pierce (the foremost female impersonator and gay comedienne in the USA), Wayland Flowers and Madame, Nina Simone, Sarah Vaughn, Carmen McRae, Morgana King, Phyllis Diller, Nancy LaMott, 4 Girls 4, and my beloved Anita O'Day ("Only for you, Avid-day, because I hate fucking San Francisco—couldn't they have rebuilt the goddamn place somewhere flat after it burned down?!"). Lawrence was delighted; we had to add a second box office phone for advance reservations.

The first performer I booked for our reopening was Nina Simone, who had oddly enough never played San Francisco. She'd played Oakland (or maybe Berkeley), but never San Francisco. It created the kind of buzz I needed, to introduce The City Showroom as the new *premier* nightclub. On opening night, a who's who of San Francisco turned out to hear Nina. Zohn booked a table for twelve and brought in Bill Graham and Jann Wenner, the founder of *Rolling Stone*, who brought a bunch of other *Rolling Stone* execs. Herb Caen of the *San Francisco Examiner* was there, as was Joan Baez with a couple of her gal pals. The house was packed with all the 'right' people. Honestly, there should have been spotlights out front.

The day I met her, Nina Simone scared the shit out of me (not literally, to clarify). She wasn't trying to, but her energy was so up-front fierce, and she'd glued these crazy long 14K gold fingernails on that looked like they could take your eye out. The first couple of nights, she was quiet around me and then she opened up and we talked about lots of things between shows. She was fascinated about the nuts and bolts of gay sex (the only woman besides Anita who wasn't frazzled when I explained fist-fucking and glory holes to her) and Nina shared with me she never really wanted to be a singer. She always thought of herself as a pianist; she'd studied classical piano for many years.

During her solo shows, she accompanied herself on the baby grand and threw in as much piano showmanship without singing as she could—and that's when her face really lit up. But to put food on the table at the beginning of her career, she had started singing as well, mostly in dives, once sharing, "I never liked my voice—sounded like I was opening a can with a church key." After "I Put a Spell on You" hit big, she signed a three-album deal, and not knowing the ins and outs of contracts, like many singers in the business, she got screwed. Nina never saw any royalties from those albums, and it made her bitter towards the music industry. I got the feeling that she was living hand to mouth (she was generous with her men, I learned). I also got the impression she really didn't understand just how big of a cult following she had, and how with savvy management, she could make some serious big bucks. But really, she wanted to play piano and be left alone. The last night of the gigs, I hugged her goodbye, and she handed me an envelope. I knew it was a tip, and I knew she was struggling financially, so I gave it back and told her to buy herself something fun or silly. Nina was moved by that. I don't think she was used to kindness, and like me, she was most definitely a loner.

After the performance, the reviews for Nina Simone and the reworking of The City Showroom were stunning. Herb Caen even wrote about *me* by name: "I have a feeling The City Showroom's new impresario, David Vass, is aiming to make this nightspot the premier nightclub in town, and that same feeling tells me he's the one to do it!"

Right after Nina played, I had booked **Charles Pierce**. He was Hollywood's most famous female impersonator and iconic to the San Francisco gay community. He normally played small clubs for a week, but I booked him for a six-week run and it was standing-room only every show. Aside from nailing the looks and movements of legends like Bette Davis, Tallulah Bankhead, and Katharine Hepburn, Charles also did a two-woman cat-fight routine between Bette and Tallulah, playing both characters. He contorted his face to actually look like each one during a series of rapid-fire one-liners ("You must speak good of the dead, and I heard Tallulah was dead. Good!"). It brought the house down.

Anita O'Day, of course, came out, and unbeknownst to Lawrence, I tripled her usual weekly appearance fee. After her last performance, she looked at me, gave me her crooked grin, and said, "Avid-day, this triple the money thing? That's an addiction you can keep, Daddy-O!"

I was riding a high, and not from booze. I was actually engaged in what I was doing, this new craft, in a way I hadn't felt in years! I took stock of my life yet again. Exciting new job that I was good at and paid great? Check. Drinking and most of my other addictions under control? Check. Beautiful place to live in a fancy neighborhood? Yup. All my material needs within walking distance, including a very small and uber-chic gay bar with a pianist (no loud music!). Yes! I had it all! Oh, wait. The lonely part; I was still lonely. Cripplingly lonely, and there was nothing I could find that could fill that specific hole. I started to wonder what the fuck was wrong with me that I couldn't find a boyfriend? Was I putting out a vibe that I only wanted to conquer and split? Was there something so broken inside of me that I couldn't start a conversation in a bar with a man that didn't begin with "I wanna fuck you 'til you hurt?" With my work responsibilities running smoothly, I decided my new goal was to work, really *work*, at finding a relationship. There *had* to be a way for me to develop boyfriend skills and not just generate sex vibes.

Nearly every night after work, I would go to my chic local bar, nurse a drink, and make goo-goo eyes at anyone who looked like boyfriend material. I had even rehearsed my opening dialogue (I guess most people called it conversation?) so that it didn't sound like my usual smutty self. Still nothing! I could cruise; I could find a fuck buddy in five minutes. But I couldn't engage a man in a conversation over a brandy stinger. I even dusted off lying, pretending to have done or read or experienced things they had done in a feeble attempt to get someone to like me or to be who I *thought* they wanted me to be, but apparently, I didn't sound interesting enough for anything but sex. And here I thought my move to San Francisco was going to improve my sense of self-worth. Inside I remained that fucked-up, insecure little boy from Baltimore with the speech impediment, just disguised as a grown man who could now speak correctly, but with no one to speak *to*! I realized I still didn't like who I was, and if *I* didn't like me, how could I expect anyone else to?

One night, after watching Charles Pierce bring the house down, I grabbed a cable car back to my hood wearing my fabulous new Burberry trench coat that would blow in the wind as I rode up and down the hills. I was sitting at my chic bar counting peanuts in a crystal mini-bowl when there was a tap on my shoulder. I turned, and there before me stood a real-life Adonis. A stunningly handsome man my age, just my type, who was looking at me with blue eyes I could have swum in and with a smile that could light up a room. My first thought was, *He's selling something, probably his body. Why else would he want to talk to me?*

He introduced himself and asked if I'd mind if he sat on the stool next to mine. Mind?! I wanted to put my hand on the stool seat so when he sat down I could grab a feel, but I reminded myself this was genuine potential boyfriend material, and it would be gauche to just grab his ass. His name was Hunter. I nearly said "Hi, Hunter, my name is Prey," but instead I played it cool. "Hi, I'm David and I live two blocks from here." Suave, real suave. Hunter laughed and said something about my being frisky, and then a miracle happened. He *actually started talking and I started listening*. One drink and thirty minutes later, and I knew he was going after his master's in marketing, was working as a driver-guide for a tourist mini-bus service, was sweet and surprisingly shy, and had all his teeth. Here it was. I'd met a man who turned me on not just with what he had to offer visually, physically, and sexually, but in conversation too. I genuinely was intrigued by his personality, his honesty, the way he was approaching what he wanted to do with his life, the focused look he got in his eyes when he spoke of his future plans, his dreams. He was sharing with me hopes and aspirations and his vision of what he wanted to become. And in return I gave him...nothing. Fuck, I was so frustrated—I couldn't talk about what I wanted out of life, because I didn't *know* what I wanted. I was comfortable with my ability to fuck Hunter six ways to tomorrow, but my ability to converse comfortably, discussing politics or future plans or dreams of *mine*—there was nothing in my head; my thoughts turned empty, poof, gone.

I could not share even one simple emotional experience, one dream, maybe because all my attempts at verbalizing emotional experiences had been shut down when I was a kid. I hadn't come from a 'normal' family where anyone cared about my emotions, my thoughts. As I tried to open my mouth and say something, anything, I remembered feeling invisible as a child, that even when I talked, I felt like no one heard me, and it was *exactly the same feeling* I had now. It hit me like a slap on the face, realizing that my mind couldn't stray from what I wanted to *do* to Hunter physically, I could not express what I wanted him to *know* about me.

I pictured what would be in the cards if we went home together: me lying beside another Adonis-type, having had yet another night of sex. And for what? Yet another climax? Perhaps a superficial exchange of phone numbers, knowing I'd never call because the conquest contest was over, and what would be the point of a second meet-up? In a mood and mindset unusual for me, I said a quick good night to Hunter and bolted out of the bar and hustled myself home, except it wasn't *home*—so, what was it? I was camping out, passing through, another place, another experience. The same pattern I had been creating and re-creating for myself the past decade.

Unlocking my carriage house door and hanging up my Burberry trench, changing into the same tee shirt I slept in when I was alone (which was always), I thought about my sex addiction. Because that's what it was. How was I even going to find 'love,' when as soon as I met any attractive man, my mind instantly turned to sex and turned off emotionally? I had zero sense that I could ever share something other than my cock with a man. I may have, as Anita said, "gotten off the merry-go-round" as related to my drug and alcohol addictions, but the other amusement park ride, that sexual encounters with strangers carousel? I was still circling on *that* ride.

That night, I felt the lowest depths of lonely, broken and empty, surrounded by my many thoughts and things that looked and felt like success. Another job well done, another accomplishment for *someone else*, organized by *me*, while I continued to feel empty, staring at a wall thinking, *now what?* Thoughts and emotions swirled for most of that night, puzzle pieces of my life caught up in the tornado of my brain, and I knew where this destructive storm could land. Back to where I always seemed to land—embracing addictions again to take the place of loneliness. I *had* to make a change that didn't involve pills, sex, lies, alcohol. I was bored yet again—each time it was happening faster, and boredom brought out the worst in me and activated my habits, my addictions.

Sleeping was not an option; I spent time looking through some of my diaries from my past, rereading about earlier life incidents: breaking through gay stereotypes, being rejected as a deviant at school, retraining myself how to speak, the Chelsea YMCA, that Jane Street studio apartment as part of the four musketeers, strippers, running mob money, all the various addictions and the thought they would be fun only landed me in dark and desolate places. The drunken night I had, just before I left New York, stumbling towards my apartment and thinking I would just take a tiny nap, lying down on the sidewalk, and waking up some hours later being kicked by little girls in pigtails and Catholic school uniforms shouting "Mister? Mister?" who were waiting to see if I was dead. The humiliation I felt for being a drunk in front of a school at 7:00 a.m. I even read about the sweet coat check girl at The Ninth Circle bar, who gave me her poetry one night towards the beginning of my professional show business career, asking me my opinion:

I did him in a doorway

I did him in a hall

I did him in an alleyway

I did him in a stall

Fast food, fast food, New York treat

Eat it, forget it,

Fast food can't be beat

I remember laughing at the poem and asking her what inspired it, to which she replied, "*You.*"

Was that me? Was my life going to be reduced to a line in a poem, a 'lived fast, died young' anecdote at a dinner party? Suddenly, I was *very* awake and *very* terrified. I'd been Band-Aiding my life for so many years when what it really needed was a heart transplant. In that powerful moment of clarity, I knew my change had to be swift, all encompassing, and *now*! A new everything, a do-over. But how? What? Where? I'd been thinking if I found 'love,' found a 'boyfriend,' I would feel full. But how was finding that even possible when all I had to offer was an empty *me*? Who wants someone empty? How could I possibly expect a relationship to change my life before I changed my life for someone to *want* to be a part of it?

By sunrise I was ready to leave everything behind: my career, finances, my old way of thinking and living, and use what was left of my energy to start from the ground up and rebuild a new me *I* would want to date. The kind *I* would want to love. My entire life I had worked on fixing myself, and I realized as I fixed one part, another part went to shit. I was playing emotional Whack-a-Mole. This was not something to discuss with Anita, with anyone. This time it was up to *me*—time to take stock, throw out everything that weakened me, and teach myself to embrace everything left, if there was anything, that strengthened *me*. No one could do it but me. The last decade I spent fixing everyone else. I needed to take the time to be my *own* road manager and hand-holder now. As sunrise lightened the room I was ready to embrace a new focus to deliver on what I had discovered, uncovered, this long night: Get the hell out of show business, shed my addictive personality and my self-pitying lack of self-worth act, and build a new foundation that would really work. It was time for little David to finally grow the fuck up.

———•———

I spent the next day at the office, twiddling my thumbs, and trying to figure out exactly what I needed to do next to change my life. That night, I'd been invited to a dinner party on Nob Hill, where the host happened to own the second-largest cuckoo clock collection in the United States. Having been deep in thought all day, at sunset I taxied to the party, and sitting in the back seat I silently asked the Universe for a sign, any sign, that it was time to *really* change, whatever that meant and whatever it took—I asked for clarity. Then I stood at the door of the posh Victorian home, thinking I really didn't want to be around people tonight at all, but maybe the distraction would stop my brain for a while, so I knocked. Pretending to be my usual, pithy self and rattling off stories about celebrities, between the entrée and dessert, there was a 4.9 earthquake. I was stoned, and when all two hundred of those goddamn birds in the cuckoo clocks went off—all at the same time—while it felt like a subway was rumbling under me, *that*, brother, was that. The Universe gave me a sign all right, and not a subtle one! I booked a flight back to New York the next day.

I called Lawrence just before boarding and explained. We both knew I wasn't leaving him in the lurch because the club was so far booked out, and he took the news like a champ and just like Harry, Jerry & Larry, let me know I was always welcome to work for him again (I think he saw this coming before I knew). The club was now a well-oiled machine and Lawrence was thrilled to have the premier nightclub and most popular gay disco in the Bay Area—I had made good on my promise.

For me, it was time to return to the one place that always somehow energized me, New York City. I had hoped New York would offer me a clean slate to create a new and better me, a life change I was finally ready to embrace. I had no idea what I was going to do next, but as I sat on that plane and watched San Francisco disappear below the clouds, I knew there would be *something* waiting in the wings—there always was—oh God I *hoped* there was. I ordered a bourbon and watched the clouds float by, waiting once more for my next chapter to begin.

———•———

My return to Manhattan in 1979 was a time to work on myself and a much-needed pause in my professional life. A tech friend let me sublet his place for four months while he was away on a gig, and I had nothing but time on my hands. So I took walks. I read books. I spent hours at a time in the stacks of the NYC library on 5th Avenue. Many afternoons I spent sitting on a bench in Central Park and simply *thinking*. After years of being on the road, of taking quaaludes, of doing five dicks a night, lying to be liked—this sudden combination of mindful and mindless contemplating, it evened me out. When I thought about what was next for me, my mind went blank, still. In a way that was a blessing because I *needed* time to regroup and come up for air after years of hand-holding everyone else.

Moreover, for the first time in my life, I no longer had an interest in sex. It was a strange, new feeling. The few times when muscle memory took me to a street corner and I went into automatic cruising mode, it just seemed, well, silly. I'd had every type of man, in every type of position or place, countless times. Even the *thought* of a physical hookup bored me—no interest. Instead, I'd find a nearby ice cream shop and ponder my biggest decision of the day—Rocky Road or Funky Fudge?

This lack of interest in sex coincidentally came at the same time tragic, deadly clouds were darkening the skies of my community. All anyone I knew could talk about was the 'gay cancer' or the '501 disease' that most everyone in my tribe seemed to be getting. There were rumors galore but few facts. It was the blue dye in Levi's that caused it. The Reagan administration released it as a genocide to rid the planet of gays. God was pissed and punishing the fabulous—who the fuck knew? The few friends and acquaintances I had left in Manhattan began to develop skin lesions—purple and red bruise-like areas on the arms and face. This condition had a name: Kaposi's Sarcoma. When it appeared, it meant you were soon to check out, and there was nothing you could do about it. A gay man would walk into a subway car with a lesion showing, and within the minute the car cleared out. Horrible doesn't begin to describe what was happening to us.

I made a decision to volunteer with ACT UP, the organization playwright Larry Kramer started out of outrage, because the government was really dragging its feet when it came to their response to AIDS. The ACT UP meetings reminded me of The Gay Liberation Front meetings I'd attended at the Firehouse all those years ago—we were pissed off and wanted the world to know that we weren't expendable. Much has been written about those years and documentaries abound, but my own experience with the AIDS crisis is something I still find hard to revisit. There will never be the right words to accurately describe how it feels when two-thirds of the vibrant people you once knew or dated or laughed or danced with or loved are suddenly just…gone—cross outs in an address book.

A few months after I was back in Manhattan in 1979, I'd read about a five-man gay ballet company from the Netherlands that was performing for a week at a tiny theatre on Greene Street in SoHo. The piece mentioned an elder dancer, who was in a wheelchair. Wheelchair choreography, huh, it captured my interest, and I walked downtown that night to see the show. The wheelchair dance number was inspiring, but it was a dancer in the troupe who caught my eye. For the first time in months, I felt a physical spark. I waited at the stage door (which was also the front door), and when Leon came out with his dance bag slung over his shoulder, I introduced myself and asked if he'd like to have a bite to eat. He did. Over dinner Leon explained he had choreographed the wheelchair piece. The poor guy was looking forward to getting back to Amsterdam as all five of the dancers were sharing a studio apartment and things had turned tense. "Leon, I'm subletting a one bedroom on the Upper West Side and you're welcome to stay with me for your remaining week in New York." A little unsure why I even offered, I explained, "When I first moved here, I shared a studio with three other guys, and luckily, we got along great. But if we hadn't in such a small space, two of us would probably be dead." Leon laughed and then probed further, trying to determine if this was going to be a sex romp or if it was a simple generous offer. Trying hard to be honest (I was shedding my addictions and lying was one of them), I said, "No strings, Leon. You take the couch. The only rule is don't bring anyone home with you." He looked genuinely relieved to have a better living situation. We walked to the East Village studio apartment where he was staying, grabbed his suitcase, and took the #1 to 79th Street.

The first night, we did indeed sleep in separate rooms. The second night, Leon climbed into bed with me around 3:00 a.m. and I didn't say no. We had careful sex and while it felt good to have a warm body to cuddle, he didn't light my fire; I could tell I didn't light his. Later that morning, Leon traveled by train to Philadelphia to teach a master class at Pennsylvania Ballet, where he also had a friend. A day later he returned. With two nights until his flight back to Holland, I asked if he had made any pals while performing in the Big Apple and he said he'd met a few. I suggested he invite them over for his last night in New York. We'd have an informal goodbye party, and I'd supply some wine and cheese. Leon liked the idea and asked if he could invite his ballet friend from Philly, some guy named Paul. I said sure.

Around 6:00 p.m. the night of the party, there was a knock on the door of my sublet. I opened it, and there stood Leon's friend Paul. I took one look at him, and I knew.

Holy fuck. Here he is. Mr. Right, I thought.

Two things happened simultaneously—my eyes took in a handsome young man with olive skin and a chiseled chin and classic nose. He had chestnut brown hair, full lips, and a sweet, genuine, happy smile—plus a gorgeous dancer's body. While I was processing all of that, I also had a kind of psychic premonition that his energy and my energy were connecting, that we were an instantaneous fit, that I was staring at my future. I *knew* he was the one. And my brain turned back on.

Some years earlier I was in a car accident, and although the accident only took a few seconds, while it was occurring, it felt like time stood still and I had all the time in the world to process what was happening. "Was I going to go headfirst through the windshield, or was I going to break my back sliding over a seat, or were these my last moments on Earth?" I could see it frame by frame, and that's how I felt when I laid eyes on Paul. I saw all of him, the physical and the emotional, and the potential of *us*, frame by frame, and I just knew he was the one. I knew it like I knew the Earth was round. My head wasn't blank any longer. The fog had lifted! With all my being I knew it was love at first sight. I remember praying he'd feel the same about me. Three months after we met, I moved to Philadelphia to live with Paul.

OK, so it was *kind* of love at first sight for him. He was exceedingly disciplined, because he'd been studying ballet professionally since he was fifteen, and he was somewhat naïve when it came to personal life experiences. Paul had been to Germany once for two weeks with his cousin, while in high school, but other than that had never left the country. He'd never known the inside of seedy strip clubs or seen women shoot Ping-Pong balls from their vaginas. He'd never gotten scabies at the Chelsea Y, never pulled dope needles out of celebrities' arms, never did money drops for the mafia. He'd never seen the inside of a bathhouse hundreds of times, and when we discussed our sexual past, it turned out I was … only the third man he'd ever slept with. Blushing (something new for me) I told him my number was, uh, a little higher than his. (I'd estimated it was somewhere between two and three thousand.) But Paul didn't seem to care about my past. He only seemed to care about *me*.

For the first time in my life, I allowed myself to *be* myself, and miraculously, it didn't scare him away. Finally, I learned what this love thing was truly all about, and fuck, it was beautiful, and it felt right. I was smart enough to know that now that I had it, I was *never* letting it go. Paul was patient in helping me overcome my insecurity and addictions, and I learned by his example. He dotted my i's and I crossed his t's. Over time, we became a team. Paul offered me stability and kindness, and I gave him excitement and a worldly view of how things worked. And *we* just worked. We will be celebrating our forty-sixth anniversary in 2024.

EPILOGUE

When Paul's contract with Pennsylvania Ballet was up for renewal, he was also offered prime spots with American Ballet Theatre and Feld Ballet. He decided to sign with Feld based on his love of Eliot Feld's choreography, having already mastered the technique of Balanchine, who'd founded New York City Ballet. We moved to Manhattan, and I used my knowledge (and a few connections but *not* my knees) to get us a charming apartment on the top floor of a brownstone on Morton Street, in the West Village. Paul began racking up great reviews in the *NY Times* (he was one of senior dance reviewer Anna Kisselgoff's favorite dancers; she was fond of referencing him as the next Edward Villella) and the other dailies were equally generous—creating a serious buzz in the NY dance community for Paul. Meanwhile, I was trying to figure out *my* next steps.

We decided to take an extremely chic cruise on a small ship, and just like sound and lighting design had, all those years ago, 'talked to me,' so did the possibility of working with a deluxe cruise brand. Thus, my successful career in luxury travel began. It morphed over the years from onboard and shoreside management of ship brands (Sea Goddess, Cunard, Seabourn, Holland America, SeaDream, The World) to the travel industry's *most discreet luxury destination management company*, with a clientele reflecting celebrities, royalty, and the wealthiest families on the planet. Many, many years under my belt later, and with a Lifetime Achievement Award for my contributions to the luxury travel industry hung on my wall, I had traveled to 141 countries and racked up seven million air miles. I'd been around the world more times than two-thirds of the United States astronauts. I met royalty, heads of state, hung out with Princess Grace and Prince Rainier (they despised each other, at least while I was with them), got arrested in three different countries for being a queer and refusing to lie about it, played elephant polo with Nelson Mandela and Desmond Tutu, set up the rental and security team of a small village in a southern Africa country for two of the world's hottest movie stars to have privacy while she had her baby, and got the skinny from a 'fence' on Camilla and Prince Charles, about how their (not so) secret trysts were *really* organized. I even knew which male members of the Royal Family liked to dabble in some very, uh, kinky sex with other men and what a certain closet just off Queen Elizabeth's formal meeting room was *really* used for. But those are stories for my memoir, part two: Dishing all the dirty travel secrets of the rich and famous. Oh, fuck me in first class with a privacy screen … you know you want to read it!

11.

Celebrity Profiles (Bonus Chapter)

(Based on my diary entries: some of the best-known clients I have worked for, with, and around. This chapter is a 'mash-up' of verbatim words from my diaries and my filling in parts from memory, for context)

Sarah Vaughn
<u>Mischievous Miss Sassy</u>

A three-week tent circuit (three cities) as her road manager, tech director and handler. Sarah liked liquor and her pills, and occasionally more. She had an ability to perform onstage regardless of her altered state, and as a result, the performances were rather, uh, fluid—always interesting in one way or another. There were good nights, a few great nights, and the occasional sad night where her chops just weren't in good enough shape to soar into her top octave. Sarah didn't like to move much on stage, possibly because her evening condition made her unsure about balance. For the life of her, she could never find her excellently designed hotspots, meant to make her look fabulous. I realized right away she was a 'spotlight performer.' Many of the celebrities I worked with were. A few could find a ray of light anywhere on a stage—they just had 'lighting radar' (see Ellen Greene, Chapter 8).

Sarah, her trio, and I were playing a summer tent circuit in Long Island. One night, mid-show, it started pouring rain. The 'tent' had a tin roof and it sounded like a gatling gun! She stopped mid-song and went into a rant, "Who the fuck puts a tin roof on a theatre? Oh, it doesn't take Miss Sassy long to figure THAT out—the fucking Mafia, that's who!" She did not have filters on her best days and by nightfall was altered enough not to remember what she had said when she woke up the following morning. Of course the summer tent circuit was run by the Mafia, they *all* were. Luckily they rarely cared about these kinds of cracks—look at what Sinatra got away with!

Sarah told me she needed a car service to take her to a NYC recording studio after the late show; she was cutting tracks for an album the following morning. I inquired what time the session was (early morning) and if she had a NYC hotel of preference. She said, "Honey, I don't need a hotel. I have a standing rule that when I record, I hit the clubs til they close and have a few drinks and whatever else I can find—hopefully some good sex, so I'm mildly fucked up, and hopefully sore ha—when I hit the studio doors. I sing best when I'm altered. That's how I roll." I suggested she try a different way and show up sober for the session—I was being paid to nursemaid as well as road manage. Her then manager was 'connected' and wanted her clean as much as was possible, as it was her high register that made her 'Sarah.' When she was altered her low and middle were still great, but the high was subpar. Laughing, Miss Sassy said, "You've heard my albums, right? Why do you think I don't sound like Ella? I like singing fucked up, I'm better that way—relaxes me." I tried my best a few more times but it was obvious she was going to do what she did. Her pattern had already been established for years. Sadly, she *didn't* sound better that way. I came to realize that Sarah was afraid of being *compared* to Ella ... that's why she fortified herself with juice and pills before recording. And her body of work? Compared to Ella's there was not an abundance of albums for someone of her stature and with *that* voice (her range was actually better than Ella's). Ella, on the other hand, recorded nearly the entire Great American SongBook—over 200 albums, while Sarah recorded forty-eight, plus a few in Japan.

Sassy chose her career managers based on their looks, and told me one night when I went out drinking with her after a show, "I love a big dick. That's why I go through managers and agents. If they're not good in bed and don't have the right equipment, it's time for ol' Sassy to make other arrangements. Hopefully they are clever with a contract, but hey, no one has everything." I adored her, in spite of her altered states resulting in extra hand-holding before and after performances. Sarah got that 'spooked' thing some of them get when they're in the wings. Not stage fright—but some mysterious vibe that freezes them—I never heard a name for that kind of frozen in time moment. Stage fright usually takes place pre-show, and it can be shaken off enroute to the stage (especially if you can distract the performer). But Sassy, like some others, always needed a little push from the wings. One thing's for sure, she was her own woman, and unlike Frank Sinatra, she really DID "do it her way …"

Frank Sinatra

He Did It *His Way* Which Sure As Fuck Wasn't *My* Way!

Everyone in the business had heard the rumors about working with Frank: a gentle touch with musicians and a jerk with stagehands and management. I only worked with him for one night—private gig—a Mafia birthday party. Vegas, of course. Lucky me.

I'm in Vegas doing a three-week gig with **Wayland Flowers & Madame** in a 500-seat lounge on The Strip. I teched Wayland's show a lot in N.Y.C.—we got on swell—we both had raunchy senses of humor. He hated Vegas, but it was good for his career; he always sold out. Wayland was shy—the sinister undertone of The Strip scared him. He knew I had 'connections' and asked me to do his show whenever he played Sin City, and that contract usually extended to LA as well; those gigs were often booked one after another for travel cost reductions. Wayland thought of me as a lubricant between himself and the IATSE stage union guys (they were all guys in those days—straight, or pretending to be, and hooked to the mob if you followed the dots). Wayland was openly gay and effeminate—Vegas and the IATSE union guys spooked him.

His show was an easy one, technically: a stool, a mic on a stand, a piano for his accompanist, cluster lighting around him, his puppets, and a spotlight. No real cues or lighting changes, just a fast-lighting bump every now and again for variety, or to highlight a punchline.

Wayland really didn't need a road manager. I was more so his go-between, so he didn't have to deal with what he perceived as 'mob guys.' Being brought up around violent and iffy characters, I never gave a second thought about the Vegas mob, but he was frightened by their aura of menace. Poor Wayland, he simply couldn't get comfortable during the Vegas gigs.

I had a week off between Wayland and a San Francisco Fairmont Hotel circuit of *4 Girls 4:* **Rosemary Clooney, Rose Marie, Margaret Whiting and Helen Merrill**, a fun act I had done the year previously on a summer tent circuit. The four of them were a hoot, and I was looking forward to it.

I got a call from a Vegas tech friend on Saturday, "What are you doing on Monday? I'm sick." After the why and the how much money and, "Really, how do you know you're gonna be sick on Monday?" part, I agreed to road manage/tech a special appearance by Frank Sinatra at a Mafia private birthday party for, let's say, uh, Larry the Lion. It was in a hotel showroom—dark on Mondays with good existing lighting and sound. Holy shit, the money was *serious*, my diary says $2000 for showing up at 3:00 p.m. and leaving at 10:00 p.m. (These days, that would equate $10K at least). I said yes. For the money and because I wanted Sinatra on my resume, and I figured not much could go wrong in seven hours and five songs, even knowing his horrible reputation and the stories of flash anger bouts due to *serious alcohol issues*. I was the guy who could "work with anybody," right? Ha.

I asked his management company, by phone, if he would please come to the showroom at 4:00 p.m. for a short sound check. They said they would pass the info along, and told me he was working with a trio—piano, bass and drums, and the musicians already had the (music) charts. So, I let them know I didn't need a sound check for the trio, I only needed to know if they were not going to do the usual stage arrangement—piano on the left, bass in the middle, drums on the right, SOP. Check.

I arrived at the showroom at 2:00 p.m. and sussed out the lighting. Okay, a quick survey and I determined with just a couple lighting angle turns, and a few different gel colors (ones that evened out liver spots), it was workable. The sound system was state-of-the-art, and I was told he only used one mic, and wanted a long cord (no cordless in those days), as he paced around the stage a lot and sometimes even trotted into the audience. Sound wise, I miked the inside of the piano and used a boom mic and stand for the bass—the drums in that sized showroom didn't need to be amplified.

All of that took ninety minutes, then I grabbed a bottle of water and a glass for the sound check and put them on the stage for Frank. 4:00 p.m.—no Frank. Then it was 4:30, then it was 5:00. Come on, I knew he was staying in the hotel, so for him it was a fucking elevator ride down in five minutes. As the wait staff started to set up for the birthday party, which began at 7:00 p.m., I phoned the rooms division manager of the hotel to connect me to Frank's suite—no answer. Okay, five tunes and a trio—hardly any possibility of something going wrong, right?

He's to perform at 9:30. The room is buzzing, filled with big-breasted dames and guys I wouldn't want to meet in an alley, all laughing, drinking, and having a blast. A deejay is there as the iffy looking crowd starts dancing and nibbling on the passed food. 9:30, no Frank. 9:45, no Frank. Then it was 10:00 p.m. and a "biggie" who obviously was controlling the party says to me, "Where the fuck is Frank?" I said, "I don't know, he didn't show up for the sound check either." This guy, who I found out later was the birthday boy himself, Larry the Lion, makes a beeline back to a house phone.

Five minutes later, Frank, in tux and trailed by a bodyguard three times my size, enters via the main lounge door and starts shaking hands and gabbing with a lot of the approximately 100 people there. He slowly makes his way towards the stage. The trio has been there for an hour, checking their watches and looking at girlie mags tucked in their music stands. I read the room and thought, *no way am I going to interrupt his slow chitchat with the attendees*. So, with a headset on to call spot and light cues, I waited by the stairs leading up to the stage.

Finally, he is in front of me. "Frank, before you go on, I want to confirm the reverb…" That's as far as I got. He said "It's Mr. Sinatra. I want full lights, and have the spot follow me. No cues, no blackouts, let's go!" So, I hop up the steps after him to my backstage mic and say, "Ladies and Gentleman, Mr. Frank Sinatra!" He's center stage by then, the spot is on him, the lights are up full. I cue the house lights down, and he opens with *The Best is Yet to Come*—it seemed like a good choice for a birthday celebration. There's a little echo on his voice, so I communicate to the sound guy to turn off all reverb.

I'm watching and listening, and it is apparent to me that Frank is tanked. Not stumbling or slurring, he just *sounded* tanked, meaning his tempo was a little off that of the trio. He stopped and restarted the song several times to crack jokes about how everyone gets older. The trio, with no rehearsal, only sheet music sent over, did a great job of following along. With the drummer even throwing in a few rim shots for the jokes. (Much as I hated Vegas, they had the best pick-up musicians in the USA). Frank talks and sings, talks and sings. He's at the end of the fourth song (my notes say he's doing five). He unexpectedly sprints into the audience (the spot follows) and says, "Ladies and Gentleman, watch this!" Waiters start to roll out a huge birthday cake on a wheeled stand—five huge tiers, like in the movie *Some Like It Hot*—the one where a machine gun guy pops out and kills everyone. I'm getting nervous and yelling in my headset "House lights, house lights!"

Frank: "Hey tech guy, we're not paying you for your looks, turn up the fucking lights!" The lighting operator (I guess Frank thought *I* was running everything, like an octopus) turns the house lights up, Happy B'Day is sung, shoulder slapping and kissing ensued. Frank starts back to the stage but gets too close to a side wall sound monitor by the stage steps, and there's a loud, brief blast of feedback. He knew what happens when you pass too close to a speaker with a hot mic, same as what happens onstage with monitors—feedback. He'd have remembered that had he been sober—all he had to do was lower the mic in his hand a bit. It only lasted a few seconds before he was back on stage: "I guess this is the last performance for our blondie tech guy," and everyone (but me) laughed.

Then he croons his last tune, "Strangers in the Night," with some changed words for the crowd. He exits, waving, into the wings and towards me.

"Is there a dressing room back here?" I point and say, "The first door, Frank, and I have some..."

"It's Mr. Sinatra, and shut up!" He and his goon head for the dressing room. I'm thinking he probably wants to pee and wipe the 86% alcohol sweat off his face. Did I mention he had asked to have a bottle of Johnny Walker Black and a tall glass with ice placed on stage next to his stool? He was carrying that off with him, smiling and pointing to it, yucking it up—the party crowd ate it up.

It was obvious he wasn't coming back, so I thanked the trio, the light and sound guys, and dismissed them all. They were dissembling their instruments and packing up to leave. The stage was dark, the party was at full-speed, loud and happy. Then the goon off-stage flagged me over with his hand. I walk into the wings and he says, "Mr. Sinatra wants to see you in five minutes." Well, a tech only gets called after a show for one of two reasons: a tip envelope or to get a new asshole torn.

Five minutes later I knocked on the door. Nothing. I do it again. Nothing. But I hear his voice, "I tell all the Vegas bimbos the same: 'talk *bad* and fuck *good*.'" So, I open the door and there is Frank, standing over a sink by the dressing table, the goon in a chair by the door. It was obvious my knocks were heard. (There is something to be said for youth. I really did think I was invincible in my early 20s). The rest went like this:

Frank: "You should wait til someone opens the door."

Me: "I knocked three times and your, uh, colleague was right next to the door, surely I was heard?"

Frank: "Hearing doesn't mean I want you in here."

Me: "Then why did this guy tell me to come back in five minutes?"

Frank: (to the goon) "Did you tell him that?"

Goon: "Boss, you told me to tell him that!"

Frank: "No I didn't!"

(The goon looks at me and gives me a subtle eye roll, and I notice the scotch bottle is empty already.)

Me: "Mr. Sinatra, sorry for the feedback hiccup out there but, candidly, if you'd shown up for the sound check, none of that would have happened."

Frank: "You are an unprofessional asshole, how did you get this gig?"

Me: "Your normal tech was sick and called me as a sub. I cleared it with your management. I, uh, know a lot of your…"

Frank: "I don't give a fuck who you know, I could make you disappear if I wanted to."

Me: "Harry, Jerry and Larry all knew I was doing this party, and I've worked for them and your very own record label for *three years*, and you're the first singer I've worked with who told me I was unprofessional and an asshole."

Frank: "Well you are."

Me: "I heard you were difficult, but no one warned me how rude you are."

Frank: "Go fuck yourself!" (Bunching his fists and turning redder while his goon is giving me not so subtle head motions to get out.)

Me: "Ella told me you were wonderful, Sarah too. Peggy said you were fun to work with, Rosie Clooney told me you were a gentleman…"

Frank: (screaming) "GET OUT!!!"

Goon opens the door.

Me: "Kiss my gay ass!" (I exit.)

I ran immediately into Larry the Lion, who was coming back to thank Frank, I guess. He was laughing his (straight) ass off as I said, in a meek voice, "Did you hear that?"

Larry: "Don't worry about it, kid, he's drunk and when he's like that he gets mean, just like his mom." (Hairpin Betty, in case you've forgotten.)

Me: "Thank you, and a very happy birthday, sir."

I proceed to leave the stool on stage, hang my headset on a lighting tree, leave the trio arrangements on the music stands and walk out the front door of the casino, thinking, *fuck this whole thing.* The next morning, an envelope was delivered to my hotel room with $2500 cash in it (the gig fee plus a $500 tip) and no note.

About a week later I got a call from Harry, and he said, "I've spoken with Jerry and Larry and I need to tell you, if you ever work with him again, don't talk back. He IS Frank Sinatra and he's a handful, but he brings in the cash." Not being completely stupid, I said, "I've never been spoken to that way before and you know who I've worked with, and a lot of them bring in the cash too. I lost my temper but I'm not sorry for what I said." There was a pause, "It's over and done now. Maybe it's a good idea you don't work with him again—I'll make a note."

Flying to my next gig, in San Francisco, I took stock of Frank: Pros: world-class arrangements, excellent phrasing (especially for a drunk), charisma on stage, ability to work well while tanked, thanked the musicians for all his gigs. Cons: overrated, mostly used up and lazy voice with just a barely okay middle range, no real lows or highs, can't sustain notes, no vibrato, and a genuine egotistical jerk who thinks changing out words from the Great American Songbook to ones he thinks are 'hip' just reinforces how very *unhip* he really is. "That's why the lady was a *chick*" was never gonna work for me! I saw Rosie Clooney a few days later—she said, "I hear you worked with Frank." I said, "Uh, yeah." Giving me the arched eyebrows look she said, "Well, you're still here so I guess he liked you," and laughed. I laughed too—fuck, why not? At least I had him on my resume now, which upped my fee. So, I'm making more money while he's losing his voice. I think I won that one!

Afterthoughts on Frank: During live performances he always made a point of mentioning and thanking the arranger of the music, and sometimes the composer. That's a plus. Rarely did he mention the lyricist, as he constantly changed their words to make them 'more current' or 'funny,' which only made him seem stupid and angered so many lyricists that they didn't *want* to be mentioned by Sinatra. The arrangements became critical to Frank—after his fourth album his voice was nearly always stuck in the middle range; he had limited breath control and little vibrato. These weaknesses could be covered with clever arrangements. The arrangers and composers kept the secret of his limited pipes and their smoke and mirrors approach to his music for the most part, doing their best to cover his vocal weaknesses.

Frank's strengths were his phrasing, another rogue technique for weak "pipes," hence his careful choosing of arrangers. I told Nancy Wilson of my Frank debacle, and she confided that she was asked to be 'the girl' on his team when he was doing his colosseum tours with not much voice left (propped up by other singers: Judy and Dean, Ella and Como, Peggy and Sammy). She responded no, politely but firmly. "I have never approved of lazy singers, or drunks, onstage—rather be a little poorer and not have to listen to him."

Peggy Lee told me earlier in my career, "If autograph hounds want your signature, Frank will show you respect, but if you're below that level, I've watched him play kick the can with too many behind the scenes pros. Not a nice man, but too connected to cross—unless you're a Kennedy."

Tony Bennett

The Perfect Gentleman Who Sang Me A Rainbow

Tony Bennett. Only one-night, last minute, and for twenty minutes at The Hollywood Bowl as part of a huge roaster of legendary singers. The lights were preset by someone, and you worked with what was there (not unusual with so many names on a shared stage or for a charity event). His tech guy suffered from migraines and had been with Tony for years. I got the call for the twenty-minute job the morning of. I was working with Wayland & Madame, but it was a dark night for us, and I *seriously* wanted any experience with Tony, one of the few I had never heard a single bad thing about. He was what Frank Sinatra *should* have been, in my head. I said yes with a capital Y, and it was organized that we meet thirty minutes prior to his twenty-minute spot in this three hour, heavy-hitters benefit show. Some of the other performers I had worked with already, and I figured if I could hang backstage a little before and a little after Tony, I could have a reunion with a few I knew. He was primetime, 9:00 p.m.

I knew the lighting wasn't a problem as The Hollywood Bowl had five Super Troopers, the strongest spotlights made, it was an IATSE (union) theatre, and their spot guys were always above average to great. I heard the sound guys were excellent too. And the outdoor audience section, facing the covered stage-shell, between the actual seats and the rolling hills used for blankets, held 17,500 audience members. So no sweat, no pressure—ha.

When I met Tony in the huge green room backstage, he told me immediately about his vocal cord problem, which rendered him an iffy voice. I asked him why he didn't cancel with so many other big names and he said the charity was dear to him, and he could control his voice so long as I would 'ride' the mic. Most singers hated that, as did I. So suddenly, I was to take over a sound board I hadn't set up and also call the spotlight cues. Tony said to me, "My voice is gonna be like a rainbow tonight, I don't know which colors I'm gonna hit so please just ride me and if I start to sound scratchy, up the reverb and I'll speed up the tempo. And thanks." Such a gentle, nice guy. He also told me he would talk for five of the twenty minutes to save some of his voice.

I was lucky—I knew the company doing sound; I hired them on occasion, and their lead mixer, who I knew, was okay with me running the board. The orchestra levels for the sound didn't even need to be touched, so I only had to 'ride' Tony's voice. With the spotlights that bright, they could see the stage from a plane landing at LAX, and Tony and I decided no light cues, just everything full bright and follow him. This was the usual standard operating procedure for big charity events.

We got through it, and he was amazing for a singer that had very broken chops that night. He knew all the tricks, and I helped on my end, dabbling a little with the bass and middle where needed. Afterwards I went backstage (no easy trip through 17,000 people) and he was still there, talking to Lena Horne, who I had also worked with. Tony was such a delight. He thanked me, said he thought he sounded great, at least in the monitors, and that he hoped we could work together again sometime. He mentioned something about a showroom in Vegas later in the year, but it never came to be.

Tony Bennett—the genuine thing; a perfect gentleman and a sweet person who knew his craft and voice so well, he even pulled it off with minimal vocal cord function. He did what I've seen other real pros do—he relied on his phrasing and sped up his tempos. As I was being driven back to my hotel, I couldn't help but compare his gentleness and kindness to Frank Sinatra's shitty voice, lazy phrasing, and horrible attitude. He could have taken a few etiquette lessons from Tony.

And 'one for the road'—Tony agreed with me that Frank was difficult except with other big names, but he also shared that in 1965 while being interviewed for *Life Magazine,* Sinatra said his favorite singer and the best all-time male singer was Bennett. Tony said his album sales doubled within the week and his live engagements tripled. He said to me, "Frank showed me a generosity that moved my career forward by a decade at least. And my checkbook too."

Ann Miller

Tap Your Troubles Away, Sweetie And A Purse Full Of Contracts, Sweetie

Ann was 100% a 'the show must go on' trooper. I did a Fairmont Circuit with her, nearly six weeks in five cities and she was chatty, before and after each show. She sang and tapped. The tapping was an issue as it required putting a sprung-wood surface over part of the stage floor so the taps didn't damage the real wood. It was sixteen feet long by nine feet wide. We began in San Francisco (SFO) and the show was flawless, selling out along the entire circuit. It was a two a-night, five nighter—then on to the next Fairmont. The second to last night in SFO I said to Ann, "What's in your contract about your tap floor? Is it Fairmont's responsibility to provide it in every showroom?" She said, "I don't know, sweetie," and a minute later pulled the entire twenty-page contract out of her huge purse and said, "Would you read through this about the floor, please sweetie, it should be around page fourteen?" I thought she'd check with her manager or agent—and who carries a twenty-page contract around with them? I read it, and there was no mention of the floor except for SFO. I told her, "No way they're going to travel this huge piece of wood floor by truck for you." I was slightly freaked. She smiled and said, "Leave it with me, sweetie." The day before the last night of the SFO gig I asked about the floor again. I didn't want to walk into a tech in the next city for a song and dance show with no floor! She said, "Listen and learn, sweetie." She called in the GM of The Nob Hill Fairmount, and when he arrived, she suddenly *looked* ill (how someone could turn on looking ill—well, I guess only Ann Miller (with a little help from all that MGM training and movies). In what sounded like a genuinely hoarse voice she said to him, "I think I can make it through tonight and tomorrow, but I'm probably going to have to cancel the other Fairmont's because I'm sick. There's a clause in my contract for that, isn't there, sweetie?" The GM said he didn't know, and yet again, she pulls the fucking contract out of her magic bag, coughs, and says, "Page eleven, sweetie." She had made a fortune for that GM Fairmont, standing room only (SRO) for every show, and that was with drinks and dinner as add-on revenue to the cover charge. Serious money for a nightclub gig. Then she says, with a cough and that faux hoarse voice, "Well, it's just as well cause they're probably not going to build a dance floor for me and we can't travel *this* one, can we sweetie?"

He left "to make some calls." She looked at me, and with a wink said, "I told you just leave it with me, sweetie." The next morning, we got word the dance floor would be built for every Fairmont on the circuit. She was one smart cookie and had 'been there, done that' with every show biz situation imaginable. A delight to work with, and a good tipper!

Julie Andrews – *See Chapter 9*

Debbie Reynolds

She'd Have Done Her Act, An Encore, And Signed Autographs, While The Titanic Sank!

Exactly how I thought she would be—a perky, funny movie star doing a circuit of big clubs because her movies were drying up and so were her Vegas gigs. Debbie was professional and easy. Her ability to impersonate the voices of other performers was masterful and something that surprised most people, including me. Seriously good chops, too. She traveled with her own tech director, and I was her road manager, primarily because there were money transactions at play (she probably didn't even know about them and wondered what the fuck I was doing backstage all the time). But Harry, Jerry & Larry wanted me there, to, uh, check the box office counts, so there I was. Six weeks of easy for me, and I watched her show from the wings each night, and it was always perfect. She was a 'broad' at heart, had a salty mouth, and left an envelope. I'm sure she had no idea *why* she was tipping me, but as I was there in the wings every show, she knew I did 'something,' I guess. Or maybe her tech crew clued her in that I represented 'connections.'

Blossom Dearie

A Little Ray Of Pitch Black

Blossom thought the music industry sabotaged her career, and in a way, they did. Her voice was light and whimsical, a human version of Betty Boop, so in essence she was a novelty singer. And we all know what happens to novelty acts. One of the best pianists I ever worked with, I suspect if she had concentrated on her piano skills, she would have received more acclaim. While accompanying herself for gigs, most of the audience didn't have the trained ear to recognize she did not just play chords when she sang, but also the melody, and often counter-counted it with her pitch-perfect voice and phrasing. The only other person I can think of who could do that was Nat King Cole. It is a fucking hard thing to do and is rarely noticed except by other musicians. John Lennon and George Shearing (iconic pianist and composer) were both fans and frequent audience members.

She was, uh, challenging. It was a good gig for me when I was in NYC as she played from 5:50 p.m. to 7:00 p.m. four nights a week, which allowed me my regular gigs later in the evenings. She worked covers and I was paid $100 a show; I frequently made more than her on slower days. After the two sets she'd sit at the bar, throwing back scotch courtesy of the club, and hawking her self-produced LPs for $25 a pop, which she would grudgingly sign if asked. One show, when she was already two sheets to the wind, she came to the booth after the first set and told me never to use reverb on her again. "Blossom, I am well aware your songs are stories and reverb would not compliment how you sing them, I didn't use reverb on you at all, ever."

"Oh yes you did!" She slurred back. All right then, here we go. "Blossom, how many of *me* do you see? If it's more than one, maybe you've had a few too many and maybe you're hearing two of *you*!" Good fucking grief. Fun gigs, ha.

Charles Pierce – see Chapter 10

Craig Russell

<u>Can You Perform If We Carry You Onstage?</u>

Craig Russell was a trip, if you were traveling on a train that wrecked. When he was sober (sometimes the first show of two), he was focused and did impersonations of Mae West, Carol Channing, Judy Garland, and Peggy Lee, with deadly accuracy and an equally deadly black humor. He loved the women he impersonated but it didn't stop him from his over-the-top dialogue coloring them in the least flattering light. He differentiated himself from Charles Pierce— really his only genuine competition in the 70s—because he used his voice to sing. Pierce didn't lip sync and couldn't sing, so he didn't go there. Craig did. His career began at seventeen when he was hired as

Mae West's 'Guy Friday.' He studied her carefully, practiced in the mirror, and realized he had a natural talent to impersonate. He left Mae nine months later with the beginning of his act, fifty stolen lipsticks, and a wig.

His vocal takes on his celebs, especially Peggy and Carol, were correct, key perfect, and his Mae singing was also as she performed, more a musical talk. Unfortunately, he needed to do Judy in a key much higher than Garland, so while the cadence and vocal mimicry was there, without the correct key, it wasn't even close to the Garland sound. Craig often cut the bit from the first show because he knew it was the weak spot of his otherwise laugh-out-loud funny, sometimes off-putting performance. By the second set, he was always, and I mean *always* wasted on alcohol and downers, and that's when his Judy snuck out.

I worked with Craig four times in three cities, and it was always the same for the first show, and progressively more frightening for the second. One night in NYC he was so fucked up he couldn't stand up from his dressing room chair. He kept all his wigs but the entrance one on stage on a coat rack, with dresses that he could Velcro around his SOP stage outfit—black tights and a leotard. Trude Heller, who owned the club he was playing, came back, saw his condition and said, "I don't care if you have to crawl through the audience to the stage, you perform this SRO show, or I pull your contract for the remaining performances and don't pay you a nickel." Craig had such a bad reputation around money. His pianists were a revolving door of freelancers, demanding their pay before the start of each night's show.

Craig slurred to me, "I'll show that bitch, I WILL crawl out. I'm do my fucking show on the floor!" I couldn't allow that, I liked Craig. When he was on, his talent was explosive, and it was obvious his addictions were winning, and he had not a dollar in his purse/pocket. I got an idea and suggested we get two waiters to lift him and the chair he was sitting on and walk him through the club and place him on stage in the crook of the piano. He looked at me, said "Great," and tried to blow me a kiss, but ended up slapping his face.

This was not unusual behavior for him, and a few shows happened with no wigs or costumes, just Craig doing 'his ladies.' Somehow, he always could make that part of the show work. There was an additional issue—he was a mean drunk and with good vision. When he was in that altered state, his eye would scan the audience looking for types he could wipe the floor with: "I hope you dick's smaller than your nose, asshole, you haven't laughed once," or "I don't know how much you paid for that ugly hooker practically in your lap, but take a table in the back next time, she'll look better and I won't have to look at bad teeth and a cheap wig." It was meant to hurt, and humor was secondary to his verbal darts. Slowly, he alienated nearly every club owner and manager on the nightclub circuit, because no one ever knew which Craig would show up.

It was too sad for me to watch, and I broke connections with him—I just couldn't watch such talent burning out, but I heard it got worse. In 1977 he filmed a movie as an actor/actress, *Outrageous*. It played the film festival circuit and developed a cult following of sorts. He was in good shape for the impersonations, but Craig was not an actor or an actress and the movie was an uneven mess. Shortly thereafter he returned to Canada. Then one night at a large showroom, started tearing off his clothes and throwing wigs and jewelry at the audience while jabbering incoherently. The police were called and that mostly finished his already almost finished career. He died of AIDs in 1990.

Peter Allen

<u>Please Louise, Get Your Ass Off The Piano Lid! – Well, Never Mind, It's Been Everywhere Else...</u>

Peter was not easy for me to work with or watch, especially in a small venue. His personality and performance style were big, and I never thought it worked to lay on top of the piano in a 120-seat cabaret. I found him difficult; he lacked professional manners (like please and thank you). His voice was not great, sometimes not even good—he had a tendency to go flat. His songwriting talent and his excellent piano work were way better than the singing part, but his sense of importance was off-putting. I never understood what the big deal was about Peter, on stage. I never liked him and I think the feeling was mutual. My guess, as he was not an attractive man, he envied me my looks and didn't want me around. Too much crowing for such a little cock, I often thought. Good songwriter though. And he sure knew who to 'marry.'

Johnny Mathis

<u>Gentleman, Peacemaker, Consummate Pro, One Of The 'Good' Ones</u>

If Johnny liked you, he politely asked that you call him John. I asked him why once and he said, "Johnny is a child's name and I always hated it, but Columbia [his label] insisted, they were playing off my youth at the beginning." If he didn't like you, he was still extremely courteous, almost courtly, in a professional way. He often wore headsets, as a barrier to keep fans from talking to him. He used this trick on planes a lot—it was his way of not having to deal with the public, I think. John was one of the nicest artists I worked with. His only insistence—all hotels for his tours had to be booked near the best golf courses. John played golf daily, up until a few hours before performances. As his entourage we stayed where he stayed, and the golfing left us in a suburb somewhere with the only cruising possibility, be you straight or gay, the hotel bar. We were all too busy pre-show and intermission to 'lobby flirt' and John insisted his bus, with his team, pull out of the parking lot immediately after his last encore. All of us were gone before the crowds stopped applauding.

There were alcohol demons during my tenure with him. I usually couldn't tell if he had too many 'glasses of fizz' as he called it—Champagne, which was his drink of choice. John loved to 'roam' the apron of the stage when he sang, rarely standing still, like a boxer. I heard from his long-time tech that when he met Nancy Reagan, (I still can't figure out that attraction, as he was not impressed by power and her husband was so homophonic, he never uttered the word AIDs until one week before the end of his last term. She knew full well, while her *gay* hairdresser was fluffing her 'do' and her *gay* make-up guy was packing on the foundation, that because of 'Ronnie's' homophobia, nearly an entire generation of gay men suffered a flat-out genocide. Doubtful she asked her *gay* astrologer what she should do about that.) One night at a charity function in LA, she pulled John aside and told him he drank too much, point blank. Her timing must have been good, as the next day she had arranged a car to take him to The Betty Ford Center where he got clean. (I think it was Betty Ford but it may have been a similar one—I didn't write the details in my dairy.) He stayed that way thereafter—clean. They remained besties until she died, while I scratched my head, wondering how he could keep her company given he was casually out his entire career, just not announcing it officially until 1982 when an article to be published would have outed him. He did it first to better control the response. John was never really in the closet, he was just a private person and didn't see a need to discuss his personal life.

He traveled with a hot plate and used it in his hotel suite to make yummy southern food. He'd whip it all together before leaving for the show and on his return it was ready. Sometimes, he'd invite a few of us over for an after-show dinner; we sat on the floor eating out of throwaway bowls with plastic forks. It was fun and gossipy. I'd crack him up with my stories of other singers, he'd share some zingers in a gentlemanly fashion, sip on his 'fizz,' and we'd all decompress from the energy rush performances generated post-show. We're lucky that fucking hot plate didn't burn a hotel or two down!

He did not gossip about his personal affairs and was always the gentleman, the peacemaker, and one of the 'good guys' in the business.

Lena Horne

Professional, Kind, Bruised By Hollywood And Walked Away

I had good fortune with the Lena Horne engagement falling in my lap. She had just come off a Broadway run and a multi-city national tour of "Tony Bennett & Lena Horne—Together." Tony had taken ill with throat problems, and with two cities remaining (Seattle and Portland), the tour dates were changed to "An Evening with Lena." The tech director for the Tony/Lena combo show was a nice guy and our paths crossed frequently. He called and asked if I was available to do the Lena solo gigs (ten performances total with a fifteen-piece orchestra). I only had one week's notice, but I shifted my schedule as I was such a fan of Lena and always thought she was underrated as an actress and a singer. I found a way to make it work within my schedule and her management approved me. She had requested a talk by phone about her lighting and sound, which I had never done before. We spoke for about thirty minutes and were both on the same page, as I had seen her on stage twice before and knew she was a heavy sweater and a mover. Just like Johnny Mathis, she liked to move constantly across the stage while singing. And just like Ella, she kept a thin towel on a stool and in her hand to wipe her face.

We met the morning of the first show in Seattle. I had set the lighting per the chart from the guy I was replacing, although I was not onboard with what he was doing with the angles of the pipe and side lights. I suspected as he had to design for both Tony and Lena, he had made compromises to try to please them both. When Lena came on stage for the light and sound check she was graceful, friendly, professional, and a little leery of working with someone 'new' to her show after three months on the road with a different tech. I would have felt the same way, so I did my best to put her at ease and decided just to be honest with my thoughts on her solo shows. I told her vocally, I thought her an easy mix as her voice was right in the middle range and she knew how to use it and had great mic technique. Both times I saw her live, I was impressed with how she handled her mic (which was how a singer should handle it), keeping it at the exact same distance from her mouth, always, and not moving it closer or further away based on the intensity of her notes or breath control. That means a good sound man is free to do the work and make her sound uniform throughout. I complimented her on that technique, which put her more at ease. It helped her realize I knew my stuff, though she had also been forwarded my resume by her management and had seen the other 'legend' singers I had worked with, many of whom she knew.

I just laid it out for her, explaining I wanted to change the lighting since she 'traveled' the stage, and with Tony not a part of the show, I could refocus and use more flattering gels for her skin tone and cover a wider space on the apron of the stage with color effects. She was onboard immediately, and I had preset a gel I thought would work with her skin tone for the spotlights, which as a 'mover' would be her primary lighting source for face and body. Because she was more a 'chocolate' color than a darker skin like Ella, Sarah, or Cab, I opted for Rosco 841 (Surprise Pink). We tested and it looked great on her. It was not what her normal tech used, and she could see immediately it brought out the warmth of her skin. Pro that she was, she asked the spot to close tight and just light her arm—with a sleeveless blouse on, she could see what all of her skin would look like. She loved it, approved it, and asked me how I knew so much about skin tones. I told her I grew up lighting strippers of assorted colors. Lena was intrigued and said, "Tell me about that during the intermissions."

Lena Horne was a formidable force on stage, and a delight to work with. She did all of it letter-perfect every night. And by the Portland gigs she had opened up to me about how disappointed she was with her Hollywood years, and her missed opportunities because of her color, and so many of her scenes in 'white' movies being cut in the southern states. She was still angry that the studios allowed the theatre chains to do that in the 50s and 60s, and that was why she switched to nightclubs and theatre appearances. "David, MGM had me wear Max Factor 'Egyptian Tan' pancake which made me darker, then they cut me out of movies because I was *too dark,*" she whispered almost to herself, shaking her head. Lena said she couldn't continue with Hollywood and not get angry. "David, getting angry isn't good for your health and gets you nowhere." There was once an MGM casting incident—she said to me specifically, "I wasn't bitter, I was sad, just sad, because I knew the movie machine wasn't personal, it was about ticket sales." She was talking about the movie version of *Showboat*, and the role everyone in Hollywood thought she would get: the female lead, but it went instead to Ava Gardner (extremely hot at the time, and a ticket mover) with a dubbed singing voice. All the MGM leads, including Ava, thought it was Lena's role, and Ava and Kathryn Greyson even went to Louie Mayor to try to change his mind. His response, Lena told me, was he asked her if she would like to be the singing voice that 'dubbed' for Ava! That was the day she broke her contract and told

MGM to "kiss her ass." She told me she was managing her not getting the role fairly well until that came up, and she felt so demeaned by the suggestion, she just walked away from that part of her career; switched to live stage work and TV. I asked her if she saw the movie, and she shook her head, replying she was never able to bring herself to do that, but she hoped, *maybe one day*.

I had held so many hands, dealt with so much attitude, put-up with so many inflated egos and drugged out personalities, that to have these 'straight up' talks with Lena was like a fresh breeze. She really *wasn't* bitter, just sad, and bruised up by the Hollywood system— MGM really worked her over. I thought it took an extraordinarily strong and special woman to see it that way. And onstage, she shone like the brightest star. Movies and television never really captured Lena Horne—she had such a big, radiant personality—it needed to be seen and felt live. She was 'present' for every performance; she delivered 100%. One of my favorite gigs, nothing but perfection and the joy of watching a true pro turning it out night after night, and enjoying it!

4 Girls 4

Rosie, Rose, Helen & Margaret, And A Surprise Appearance By Jack Wrangler

Rosemary Clooney: As part of the 4 Girls 4 act, Rosie had found a good niche for a singer who had little voice left. She only had to carry 25% of the show and knew her name was at the top of the marquee both for ego and ticket sales. She kept to herself mostly, not liking to talk backstage or at post-show dressing room invites, and was rather cool (nice way of saying a fucking ice cube), even onstage. I think she was doing the gig out of boredom, and the audiences reacted to that, as her part of the act was indeed boring, and robotic. She *could* draw a mean set of eyebrows over those chilly eyes!

Rose Marie: Everyone was relieved when the hysterically funny Rose Marie (Dick Van Dyke Show fame and a Vaudeville comedienne in the old days) came on with one of the bluest comedy acts (i.e. dirty) I've heard outside of strip clubs. She was a bawdy delight, which was just up my alley! We were sometimes after-show drinking buddies. She liked to go to gay bars, and once said to me, "I wear so much make-up, they all think I'm a drag queen anyway so why not!"

Helen Merrill: Still had good chops but seemed vacant a lot, on stage and off. I didn't know about early onset Dementia then, but I suspect her memory issues (remembering lyrics, sadly was a downfall for her) and a vapid stage manner came at times when she just seemed to 'check out.' She was replaced with a series of other big band singers after the first-year circuit gigs.

Margaret Whiting: Had only her low vocal register left and used it like a Mack truck. Subtle songs were *not* her specialty. Ballads were a stretch. Her novelty tunes worked well, at least. She sang "On the Good Ship Lollipop," one of her famous songwriter father's tunes, and I giggled when Rose Marie said to me, "It's not the good ship lollipop she wants to be licking." La Scandal had broken just as *4 Girls 4* started touring—Margaret and gay porn superstar Jack Wrangler, had fallen in love and were planning to get married (which indeed happened later, in 1994). Margaret had a smile on her face *all* the time, and I thought it would be cruel to tell her that Jack aspired to have his own singing act, and that most porn stars, gay or straight, could get it up on cue ... and that I had had sex with him two weeks before, while he was scouting out the performance space, and I understood her smile...

Jack Wrangler, note, had a tube of hemorrhoid ointment in his Dobb kit, and as I was able to, uh, look carefully and see no need for it, inquired. In his 'teacher' voice he said, "Apply it to your face wherever there are wrinkles and poof, they're gone!" Well, blow me over—oh wait...

Butterfly McQueen

<u>A Sad Story</u>

Worked with her at the Paradise Room in Reno Sweeney, circa 1975. Butterfly's famous line from *Gone with The Wind* was, "I don't know nothin' bout' birthin' no babies!" Well, she didn't know nothin' about the talents needed for a nightclub act either. She couldn't sing, and she just wasn't a good storyteller. This was before these kinds of actresses' 'personalities' could put together a digital tape and use their appearances in movies to reference their personal stories.

She was not chatty with me but twice. Her story was that she felt abused by Hollywood for her stereotypical roles as maids, slaves, and fetch-its in movies for nearly thirty years. As she put it, "I was never offered a single role that didn't require me to wear an apron or have straw in my hair."

Butterfly shared with me that while making *Gone with the Wind* (GWTW) she made $350 a week and Hattie McDaniel (Scarlett's maid) made $400. Neither received any royalties, although they both sued some years later and lost—they had stock 'Negro' contracts. McDaniel went on to become the first Black Actress to win an Oscar—Best Supporting Actress. The MGM commissary was segregated during the filming of GWTW and neither were allowed to eat with the white cast members. After the Oscar win, MGM opened the commissary to all film actors with speaking roles. Butterfly said to me, "I never wanted to eat there anyway, that Clark Gable? Ohhh, he had terrible bad breath from those false teeth." She died broke in a rent-controlled apartment in Harlem.

Barbara Cook

<u>Working With Her At Her Lowest And Relishing Watching Her At Her Highest</u>

Towards the end of her singing career, and when she started teaching at Juilliard and had gotten her addiction monsters under control (just like me), Barbara Cook was a beacon of show business expertise and inspiration, helping so many talented young singers and offering up her occasional victorious and smashing concerts in iconic theatres. I was happy for her—even though I only knew her from our nightclub work—proud of her turning addiction and her career around. This late career success also helped me realize that Barbara Cook needed a proper stage; a theatre, to really bring out her magic. Nightclubs did not inspire her—I think they made her feel trapped. What they say is true, hindsight *is* twenty-twenty.

The first time I worked with Barbara, she was hitting her bottom. I didn't know it at the time, but I figured it out later. I found I adored Barbara exactly one night after working through a horrific first encounter and what had to be one of the nastiest tech days of my career. We hated each other within the first thirty minutes of that tech. I showed my ass and she showed hers— it was a rudeness draw. She had a three-week gig at Reno Sweeney around 1976. I knew she won a Tony in the 50s for *The Music Man* and had done a lot of other Broadway roles, and loads of television. And I knew of her pianist, Wally Harper, who had his finger in a lot of current Broadway shows and various singer's career arcs. Candidly, I was more interested in working with Wally than with Barbara, having never been a fan of sopranos. They were hard to mix; hard to make them not sound squeaky. But having heard Wally was a brilliant pianist and accompanist for 'all' the big singers at one time or another, he was of interest to me.

He and I talked a lot during Barbara's gig. He had so many show biz stories to share 'on the downlow.' There was no sexual interest, but we exchanged singer stories the way little boys traded baseball cards.

I hadn't seen recent pictures of Barbara or heard much about her. She played the occasional club, but I was 'whatever' about it. Turns out, she was at the lowest point of her career—money concerns brought her to Reno's along with a lack of demand for bookings as word had spread of her alcohol issues.

The sound and light check was for 3:00 p.m. on a Tuesday, with her opening show five hours later. Wally couldn't make it, but I didn't need a piano check and he didn't sing, so I only needed to mix Barbara's voice and explain to her the eccentric lighting at Reno Sweeney—low ceilings, no spotlight, important to hit light marks as there were no movable lighting instruments.

It was a fucked-up beginning. It's 3:20 p.m. and no Barbara. I'm starting to get pissed, Tony winner or not; my time had value too.

A big woman with a scarf on her head walks through the front door and I think *oh please dear god don't let that be her.* It was her. "Barbara?" I say. And she says, "Hi, sorry I'm late, my lunch ran long." I thought it looked like her lunch ran for several years, and her dinner too, but I escorted her to the showroom and thought, *well at least she won't have trouble hitting the hot spots for lights.* Big Barbara, little stage. Yes, I know that's mean, so sue me.

She was in a muumuu, and I asked her to please lose the head scarf as I wanted to see the overhead fresnel's on her hair color. She replied her hair was a mess under the scarf and no dice. I said please, *again*. She took it off with a huff and I could tell she already hated me. I then asked if she had a specific costume she wore for the shows. She explained it was a loose-fitting long black dress with a beaded short black jacket.

I helped her up on the not very high platform stage and I smelled alcohol on her breath and thought, *oh, okay, got it.* I had the mic on a stand, center, and the piano was to her side with a stool and a boom-stand. She said, "I don't need the boom, I hold the mic with my hand, mostly, and do you have a stool without a back?" Then she said, "Would you hand me my purse?" I did and she pulled out a candy bar, opened it, and started chomping away. I'm thinking, *how the fuck am I going to adjust the sound to her voice if her mouth is full of Almond Joys?* So I wait for her to finish her 'snack' after her long, late lunch. She looks at me, clearly irritated, and says, "Well, what are you waiting for, let's do the sound check!" I'm starting to lose it and say, "Would you mind swallowing your snack so I can HEAR your voice?" Oops. She gingerly steps off the stage and says, "I can't work with you!" and heads to the front of the club, shouting, "Where is Lewis?" (the owner) and I say, "He's on vacation. Looks like you're stuck with me unless you want to bring in your own person? Doesn't matter to me, I get paid either way." She stomps back to the stage, having swallowed the candy bar, and starts singing an iconic song from *The Music Man*, for which she won the Tony, and then, of course, she sings the hit song from another Tony winning show, She Loves Me, ironically titled "Ice Cream!"

Hers was the usual soprano voice, slightly tinny at the top as they all are, but when she went into her lower head-voice, it was quite rich (unusual for a soprano). I didn't add reverb as my experience was it never improved a full-on soprano voice. I knew in ten seconds how she needed to be mixed, made a minor adjustment, and said "There you go Barbara, you sound great."

Her: "You don't have any reverb in the mix."

Me: "You don't need it and in your highest range, which is, uh, a little reedy, you'll sound like a trio."

She mutters something, shakes her head and says: "Where's my monitor?"

Me: "Barbara, it's a small club and the two main speakers are behind you on either side of the wall, no one has ever complained they can't hear themselves."

Her: "I don't work without a monitor."

Me: "I looked over your contract before you arrived, and it clearly states we don't have a monitor or a spotlight. I didn't see a rider attached that said you required a monitor. I could call the tech rental house we use and rent you one, but it would be around $600 for the three weeks and the cost would be on you, and frankly, a monitor would be louder than the house sound, and give the effect that you're yodeling."

Then we had a stare-off contest, and she blinked first. Grabbing her coat, scarf, purse, and snacks, she turned and left. I called after her, "Uh, nice to meet you, the first show's at eight, see you then!"

A few hours later she arrives all in black and with her hair nicely fluffed, I see her and wave, but she heads straight for the dressing room. Following her in the door was who I thought must be Wally Harper, as he had a folder of sheet music and was in a dark suit. He heads towards me. I welcome him, tell him I am a fan, and that there is a music light and a special 'inky spot' for him focused on the piano, which was tuned late in the afternoon. He takes a quick look as there are people at the tables eating and drinking already. I confirm he doesn't need a mic. He gives me a sweet smile and says, "Barbara says the two of you didn't get off to a good start. Don't worry, she gets really nervous during a sound check, but she'll be great onstage." I thank him and jump in, ass to the wind, and say, "Wally, there was a strong alcohol smell on her breath, are we going to have a problem getting her on stage on time for the shows? She stormed out before I could ask her my usual questions."

He informs me that Barbara has a 'little' alcohol problem, but it never interferes with her stage work, and that everyone has trouble getting her on and *nobody* has trouble getting her off, and laughs. I think, *I like this guy* and say, "I'd love to talk between shows, I know you are having such an amazing career," and he says "Sure." There were a few eye sparks between us, but as he was nine years my elder, no dice—I liked them young.

Showtime and I go through the kitchen, the only way to get to the dressing room without walking through the bar area, which is usually packed. Knocking on the door: "Barbara, Wally, showtime! Follow me as we have to go through the kitchen to get backstage for your entrance." Wally comes out while at the same time Barbara yells, "I need ten more minutes!" He mutters, "I told you so," and heads to the piano to preset his music. Okay. Time to earn my money. I knock loudly on the door and say, "Barbara, I'm coming in," and I do. She's sitting there with a rocks glass that looks to be full of scotch, or bourbon or whiskey—that color. And I can smell the alcohol—it's the *first* show, for fuck sake! I make a mental note that there are five packages of Twinkies on the dressing room table. I try again, "Barbara, I will only do this once. I'll hold the show for ten minutes now. But starting with the 11:00 p.m. show, you are backstage next to me ON TIME when I call it, or as God is my witness, I'll announce you, and Wally can segue on the piano until you decide to get on stage—I'll do it Barbara."

A couple minutes later she showed up backstage, and thus began our first show. Barbara was letter perfect, charming on stage, sounded incredible, got a standing ovation, and came back past the equipment boards and me enroute to the dressing room. Her eyes met mine, she smiled, and said "Good job, David!" I said, "Good job to YOU, Barbara, they were on their feet—you're amazing!" She was a different person on stage.

The rest of the three weeks were fun; no head-butting, no late starts, with her getting nicer and nicer to me every night, and my respect for her growing with each show. Plus I'm hanging between shows with Wally, and we're having a ball gossiping about singers we've worked with.

Barbara did lose a fair amount of weight over the next few years, and she also called me about a year later and asked me to stage manage a NYC Town Hall concert a well-known producer booked for her. I was already engaged for that date or I would have gladly said, "my pleasure." Her onstage persona and vocal talent were top of the talent ladder stellar, and I'm so glad I was able to see her on stage where she belonged. Her days during that period may have had serious lows, but the nights when she took that stage, she was the very embodiment of a star, and one who delivered.

Bette Davis

Shut-Up And Get Outta My Way

A one-week gig in LA at a 400-seat black-box theatre, and she talked about her movies, not her life—in a wheelchair while chain-smoking. My instructions from her mouth: "Turn the lights on bright, have the mic live and on a low stand, and a boom pipe. When I wheel off I don't come back, no autographs and no one but you knocks on my dressing room door—don't knock 'til you call the house lights down, I'll be ready." The first night, early show, I knocked on her door, wheeled her to the black velvet wing curtain, spoke into my headset to the booth (she's ready—lights!) and said, "Break a leg!" She looked at me and said, "Shut up," with that voice only she had. Probably not the best good luck phrase to say to someone in a wheelchair on reflection, but I was buzzed on something that entire gig, probably Quaaludes. She had moments of clarity and moments of rambling. No envelope, no goodbye, no fuck you. Actually, it went better than I expected, and the lighting looked exceptional. As she chained-smoked, the effect was similar to having a fog machine on stage, which always dramatizes lighting.

Morgana King

The Godmother With A Killer Voice And A Heart Of Gold

Most readers will remember her as the mother in the Godfather movies I suspect (Marlon Brando's wife). Too bad, as she was one of the best jazz singers in the business, and I loved that she talked in the dressing room and told me stories about Nat King Cole. (She called him 'the panther' and I suspect...) She was of dark-skinned Italian descent; many audience members thought she was mixed. Morgana told me Nat would have been in more movies and that his TV show could have lasted longer, but his skin was so black he absorbed almost all the lighting and reflected back to the cameras only a little of it, and the advertisers complained nobody could see him! Television was primitive in those early days and black & white filming did his skin tone no favors.

Morgana was the first singer I worked with who had a rider clause in her contract stating: no smoking while she was onstage, with a mandatory pre-show announcement and a 'no smoking during the performance' card on all the nightclub tables, which she had printed and traveled with. This was a big deal in the mid 70s as smoking was just taken for granted when playing clubs. She lost some gigs over it. Her sound was husky, low and deep by nature, and I don't think the smoke would have impacted her voice. I think she had a crush on Nat King Cole, and as he died a painful death from chain-smoking leading to lung cancer, which crashed his career at its peak, it spooked her. She also gave me the recipe for a brew she made before each show and sipped on stage. (See recipe on page 261.) Said she got it from Nat. I can't tell you how many of those 'voice toddys' I made for various singers after learning that miracle recipe. Morgana performed with a trio combination which was unusual for nightclubs: a percussionist (not a drummer), a bass that bowed as much as plucked, and a guitar. It perfectly suited the cadence of her voice. She knew exactly how she sounded, Morgana did, and which instruments complimented her vocal quality—rare for a singer. She was one of my favorite performers. She took no bullshit but was kind, professional, unassuming, and knew her craft. She made me feel the way I felt when I smoked hashish. ust floaty and mellow. Morgana hugged me a lot, an unusual backstage physicality. Her smile was radiant and her manner was sincere. The last night of the gig, I told her if she ever wanted to work with me again, just call and I'd do it for free. I enjoyed her voice *that* much.

Manhattan Transfer

<u>A Story 'Tucked' Into A Story</u>

Manhattan Transfer was riding high on the release of their first Album, *The Manhattan Transfer*, on Atlantic Records, and playing a three-week gig at Reno Sweeney was the cherry topping off the album release in 1975. Many of those early songs were tributes to past eras, and this talented quartet of singers had been on the scene a while. But with this album they became white-hot, even hosting a Sunday night CBS variety show within the same year of its release.

The four of them needed to squeeze into Reno's tiny 'dressing room,' which was the box-office during the day. Mornings found the box office person frustrated, having to clean up red glitter galore from the two desks which acted as make-up tables at night, (they glittered their lips during this early period). Wearing tuxedos and gowns, and recreating the feel of the Deco area, they brought the house down every show. Pros from the get-go: excellent mic techniques, fun choreography, and a perfectly paced musical set. Stellar was the perfect word for their product.

The group kept to themselves while I was teching them, I suspect so busy making career plans for their sudden and huge success arc, it left no time for gossiping between shows.

My tech gigs often crossed their circuit gigs and we would nod at each other and throw a smile.

In 1977, Janie had a big, one-nighter outdoor concert in Philly. It was a huge theatre, and with a split bill: Jane Olivor and Manhattan Transfer (or maybe it was the other way around—either way it was a fifty-fifty split of stage time). While teching for Jane's half, a really, and I mean *really*, cute young guy with an amazing bubble-butt was hovering around the stage for the sound check and blatantly cruising me. After a bit I went over to him and said, "Hey pretty eyes, who are you?" He was the younger brother of one of the Man Tran singers, was living in NYC, and came along to this gig 'for the ride.' He was as blatant as me and said, "You wanna fuck me after the show tonight, don't cha'?" Oh God, that bubble-butt! I said "Is pig pussy pork?" (duh) then remembered I already had a hook-up with a stagehand (an IATSE stagehand so he was probably the outcast cousin of Harry, Jerry or Larry—you don't cancel those kinds of hook-ups without getting your fingers broken), so I asked bubble-butt-cutie-guy for his phone number in NYC and said I'd call him a few days later. I only had a Sharpie marker pen on me—he wrote his number on my Levi 501s underwearless crotch, (much to the laughter of the IATSE stagehands) which I thought was very inventive and also a real turn-on—and it showed! The next day and back in NYC, I left those 501s on as that phone number on my crotch was like a candle catching moths to the flame, and I had my share of handsome West Village guys the following few days before calling bubble-butt cutie-guy, having 'the icing on the cake' sex with him, and then had to wash my jeans. Ah, show biz...

Nina Simone - Chapter 10

Eartha Kitt

A Legend In Her Own Mind

'Miss Kitt' had all the moves of a huge star, and the talent of a tiny one. I'd score her stage presence ten, vocal talent four, ability to say please or thank you, one. I'll credit her with the capacity to be unintentionally camp, which she sadly confused with talent. I was looking at two miserable weeks for me; she was a diva who lived in her own dream world.

You got what you saw and heard—drama, attitude, snobbery and a dismissive personality. I don't know what was on her shoulder, but it was heavy. She was a "Call me Miss Kitt" type, and I can't recall one kind word I heard come out of her mouth during the nightclub gig I was hired to do in SFO. Harry, Jerry & Larry—who else would want to deal with her except money launderers? She barely bothered to sing, which is challenging when you aren't a good singer to begin with; off-pitch, lazy breath control, an entitled sense that lyrics were secondary to the way she thought they should be. Eartha "didn't want to use her vocal energy in a shitty little club." (I heard her say that through her dressing room, while attempting to get her on stage somewhat on time.) She was distant and dismissive of her audiences—wore a watch and checked it every five minutes or so to see how much longer she 'had' to be on stage, per her contract. She wore one aging gown, which hadn't been dry-cleaned in so long I invested in a spray bottle of room freshener (this was pre-Febreze) to give it a go-over before she arrived. The costume was odorous, and she didn't give a fuck. A living example of the worst of show business.

Nell Carter

A Powerhouse Looking For A Plug

Her voice put me in a tailspin of happiness. Nell was magnificent. This was before her Tony win in *Ain't Misbehavin*; she was in junior roles in various shows on the Big White Way. After that Tony win, and her appearance with full vocal balletics in the movie version of *Hair*, she landed the TV gig *Gimme a Break,* which ran for many years and garnered her several Emmy nominations. Nell was cast as the original 'Effie' in *Dreamgirls*, but left after two weeks rehearsal to take a one-spot guest gig on TV. In reality, she hated Michael Bennett, the choreographer and director, and likewise, they each wanted the other gone. Too bad, she'd have won a Tony for that too.

Coming off the stage of The Grande Finale having played to twenty to thirty patrons a night she'd wrap her arms around me and cry like a baby. "Why aren't people coming to see me? Why?!" She was a powerhouse belter but at that point in her career, she simply didn't have name recognition. It hurt her deeply, and I felt so badly, as she always gave a great show and the lack of recognition fueled her drug and food issues. I suggested she look for a new manager and agent, as someone needed to work on her visibility. She was way too talented to play in nearly empty clubs.

Nell did change management, and her career blossomed on warp speed. After the eight-year TV gig, she opened for Joan Rivers for a while, then began another spiral downwards due to alcohol and drugs. She died too young, at fifty-four, but no one in the business was surprised. Her addiction to food probably killed her more than the (many) other vices which she had tried to control, to varying degrees of success for some years. A lot of people found her 'difficult.' Not me! She was always friendly and funny, maybe because I genuinely cared about her and she reacted to affection. And what a voice!

Dudley Moore (and Peter Cook)

We Don't Pay You And You Don't Pay Us, Kay?

They had a two-man comedy act and for Dudley, this was before his major movie gigs, especially with Liza Minelli in *Arthur*. They were nice enough, always performed drunk, were hard to get on stage, did as they pleased, considered the entire gig "some spending money and some wasted time" as Dudley told me. They closed their gig at the club, owing several thousand dollars of bar tabs—they bought so many of their NYC friends drinks, and for themselves, bottles every night—they were their own mini rat-pack. The bar tab was never repaid, and their 'held' fee was never delivered to their managers. Two monkeys in a bird cage.

Peggy Lee – *See Chapter 9*

Nancy Wilson

You Can Make Me Sound Like Dinah!?

I was contracted at the last minute to do a one-week engagement at The Venetian Room in the Fairmont Hotel in San Francisco for Nancy

Wilson. I was thrilled—she was one of my all-time favorite singers and I actually broke a different engagement to take this one. She was very loyal to her tech director and he had taken ill, hence this opportunity. I sure wasn't going to let it pass me by!

Our tech was at 3:00 p.m. on opening day, and she came with her pianist. Nancy was on time to the minute, and when I introduced myself, she said, "I know you!" As much as I wanted to remember, I didn't, so I replied, "I am so sorry, I am a fan of your voice and your song choices and it has been a goal of mine to work with you; I think you have me mixed up with someone else." She laughed, gave me a warm hug and jumped right in, "I'm friendly with Miss Sassy [Sarah Vaughn] and Ella and that's how I know you. They both said you knew your stuff. So, I'm already comfortable. I know that you know I am good at what I do and you know that I know you are good at what *you* do, and I just flew in from Japan where I taped a live album and I'm jet lagged So tell me what you want, let's do it, and then I'm going for a long bath and nap."

I told her I just wanted a quick sound check mix of her voice, that I didn't even need a piano or full song, and she jumped up on the stage and grabbed the mic. She started singing a tune I'd never heard, and one where she did a lot of what she was famous for, note-bending. A singer without perfect pitch can't do that. You begin on a note, twist it above and below where it belongs without it being discordant, and end up back to the exact note on the exact same pitch you started on. I knew within twenty seconds she needed a strong middle foundation on her mix, a low bottom, and practically no top. After about eighteen bars she stopped and said, "Got it?" and I replied in the affirmative. I asked her if I could keep the pianist for a few minutes to go over the song set and the placement of her five-piece band, please. She nodded.

But as I was mixing her voice, I heard something I'd never heard on one of her albums and I just threw it out there. I said, "Nancy, I bet I can make you sound just like Dinah Washington, I've never heard it in your voice on your albums before, but if I take out all the bottom and middle and up the top a little, I think you could sound just like her."

Bang, fuck jetlag, her face lit up and she said, "She's about my all-time favorite singer, honey, let me hear." I asked her if she knew any of Dinah's tunes and she said, "All of em'," so I suggested, "Give me a pig's foot and a bottle of beer." I dialed my mixer accordingly, and suddenly if you shut your eyes, Dinah could have been on that stage. She heard it too and was floored! "No one's ever done that with my voice before!" Nancy turned to her pianist and said, "Let's put in a Dinah song for these shows as a tribute!" He readily agreed and added that he could do his best to get a honky-tonk sound out of the baby grand.

We left it with her confirming that I could make her sound that way again and I replied, "Absolutely." I threw in that the audience was coming to hear *her* (the gig was already SRO), but if she wanted to throw in a Dinah tune I thought the audience would eat it up, and that's just what we did. Damn, did that get us off on solid footing!

Before the first show, she asked me to introduce her as "Song Stylist, Miss Nancy Wilson." That's how she heard herself. But she could have used any phrase she liked, Nancy was a powerhouse singer that had the whole package—chops, vibrato, looks, stage personality, and exquisite taste in song choices. What a fabulous week it was for the audience, and for me. A consummate pro. On time, happy, loved to sing live, radiant on stage, smiling and enjoying herself.

She stayed away from the Great American Songbook a little more than I would have suggested had I been her management team. With that voice, she could sing *everything,* but a serious amount of her body of work were songs that someone thought would have radio appeal, keep her 'contemporary.' Many with bossa nova beats and the 'lyrics of the day' which were a waste of her powerhouse voice. Her choice of material often was no match for her talent, and when that happens, it usually means a manager or record company is thinking *for* you. Still, she could sing a phone book and get a standing Ovation, as her attack on a song was always wondrous.

Nancy was starting to appear more on television in non-singing roles, and for a few years that's all she did, by choice. I realized on top of her ridiculously perfect singing voice, she was a natural actress. This lady had it all and used it, regardless of some uneven arrangements. Stellar, whatever she touched, even with often iffy management.

Jane Olivor (also *mentions in Chapters 9 & 10*)

<u>Her Meteoric Rise And What Can Happen When You Flame Too Bright And Too Fast</u>

A complicated career launch and the ensuing flame out, Jane was a dazzling bright light in the night that disappeared, like a shooting star. Of all the celebrities, singers and performers I worked with, ours was the most complicated and in some ways, parallel alliance. I tech directed and road managed for her more than any other artist in my show business oeuvre. Many of Jane's first triumphs at iconic theatres were mine too. Olivor's core audiences weren't just enthusiastic, they were fanatical. Of the more than 200 top names I worked with, none could match the intensity of adoration that swept from the concertgoers across the footlights. Those performances in the early arc of Olivor's career were a tsunami of love for her voice and her stage presence; so intense, so authentic, so in the moment. It was special, rare, and everyone could feel it. This made it all the more heartbreaking when it began to crumble right before my eyes.

She was compared to Piaf and Barbra, but I never saw the resemblance. She had her own sound. Her phrasing and approach were mesmerizing. Jane (I called her Janie) also had an almost psychic sense of which songs would work for her, and she didn't care what genre or time period they were from. One of the few performers I worked with who brought me to tears at least once for every performance, even on those gigs later on, where we were barely speaking. Janie was magical on stage. When you could *get* her on stage, which was an issue that developed later and was the beginning of the end of her recording and live performance career, at least with Columbia.

She was managed by her sister, an aggressive but sweet (at least to me) woman with no serious show biz management experience, who didn't realize this growing stage fright, fear of forgetting lyrics, would overpower Janie in the ensuing two plus years I traveled with her. It got so bad that the last circuit gig I did with her, when she was opening for Burt Bacharach, well, it overcame her, and she feigned being ill so she didn't have to go on. I knew she wasn't physically ill, but I called her sister-manager and said (lying), "Janie is really sick and can't go on to open for Burt tonight. I tried to get a doctor, but it's too close to curtain." I let Burt's manager (traveling with him as it luckily turned out) know, and Burt started working with his back-up singers to fill in as the opening act. Cissy Houston, Whitney's mother who I worked with and profiled elsewhere in the book, was one of the three back-ups. I remember her saying to me (we had worked together in various gigs before), "So the nerves, they finally got the best of her, huh." Cissy knew everything about everyone because she had worked with every-one. I just nodded yes.

I should have realized well before that night where this increasing issue with stage fright, this fear of forgetting lyrics was headed. How I wished I had figured it out better and reached out to someone to try to get her help. This talented young woman, who I had grown to really care for, was simply too spooked to perform anymore. Or at least that was my take.

But before her stage fright got that bad, we had many good or at least better times, because for most of those 'on the road' gigs, she was opening for Johnny Mathis, who she adored, and who adored her in return.

Columbia Records, who Johnny had recorded with since his first album in 1956, was literal gold to that record label. His following was reliable and large, and Jane was an obvious, excellent opener for his fans. It was a smart move for all concerned because just as Jane gained traction and was building her own audience base, Disco hit. It hit fast and big. Many nightclub and smaller circuit vocalists were impacted almost immediately. Bookings started drying up for large venues and contracted circuit runs for the smaller venues and clubs were reduced from three weeks to two, or from two to one. Performers with actual chops who sang the American SongBook and other serious tunes, were 'out.' So many genuinely good singers suddenly had a lot of time on their hands. It was sadly bizarre to watch The Village People or Gloria

Gaynor sell out two-week gigs in one day, while so many iconic singers—the Tony Bennetts, the Lena Hornes, the Peggy Lees, were left with only their loyal fan base. But that didn't move ticket sales the way they needed to secure large houses. A few were immune to this 'Disco Disease' killing off songbook crooners. Mathis remained golden, thanks to all those years of record sales and a clever marketing team that built his fan base over two decades with a full-time employed fan club team who sent birthday cards, newsletters, advance opportunities for best seats—loads of sales smartness that most of the others just never put in place. This was before the internet, before computers and texts.

William Morris and Columbia, who had spent a small fortune on Janie, did not want to see her career get reduced back to cabarets and medium-sized clubs, so they paired her with Mathis. It was a double bill, and so complementary; his older fan base, who could be turned on to Olivor (thus selling her albums and building a larger fan base for her) and her base, a younger demographic but with a love for real singing, which expanded Johnnie's sales as well. It was a smart strategy, disco proof, and one of the few clever actions I saw Columbia take.

Jane Olivor sold her records the way a politician wins in Iowa. One person, one club, one concert at a time. She was never aggressively pushed by her label on radio nor had the help of serious interviews; it didn't take the A&R label execs long after signing her to realize she was an acquired taste. Jane sold her albums—not Columbia. They just pressed them and put them in paper jackets. I knew even then, having now been around the record labels and various levels of singer 'stardom' for a while, that Janie was going to get screwed by her record company. I sensed it long before she figured it out and tried telling Janie towards the end of our working arrangement to get a good lawyer and renegotiate with her record label, because I road managed a lot of her solo concerts and counted ticket stubs, signed off on final attendance/revenue sheets, and knew that her box office appeal was significant.

Towards the end of my road management time with Jane Olivor, I started to feel distant and was not comfortable talking to her. I suspect she felt the same about me. The last few months of shows I worked on, she started doing what I call "languorous singing." I'd worked with loads of the biggest names who did it from time to time. True fans know your albums and songs and anticipate that 'high note' or the 'sustained note' or the 'that specific phrasing.' Often fans knew the songs better than the performer. When you perform live, comparisons occur between what you sounded like and did with your voice on the albums. Sometimes a singer had to take a high note to their middle range because they lost their high-end singing voice to nerves, or had a cold, or were just having a scary night, emotionally. Some nights they created a different tune ending not requiring sustaining a note for as long as it usually was, or back-phrasing to get that extra breath intake, that kind of thing. Janie started doing that, especially at the high end of her range, and I could tell it was out of fear mostly—fear her nerves were going to close her throat and she wouldn't reach it, fear that she would freeze on the words. A variety of fears, and she actioned them in an emotional way.

I could usually even read when it was going to happen before it did. When you light someone for so many months and years, you become a body language expert to that performer and their face—you're seeing it every performance. Janie's fear started affecting her vocal attack, her approach to some of her songs, and I didn't know quite why it was or how to help her. She started speeding up the tempos of her songs, which is a definite indicator of fear; you sing it faster so you don't need the same breath control and can get through your show more quickly.

I started noticing disappointed looks on the faces of some fans who expected the high note, the correct tempos. Janie seemed broken to me and I was no longer a real friend. Unable to help, I realized it was time for me to move on. All said, my memories of working with her are good ones, filled with moments when she could soar with the music, dig so deep in the song she became the lyrics, and had her unique way of uplifting an entire audience with, often, a surprisingly sad ballad. That's talent.

Jane Olivor and I worked together on summer circuits, tented arenas, large clubs, and iconic venues like Carnegie Hall, Avery Fisher, Philadelphia's Academy of Music, the Greek Theatre and the Dorothy Chandler Pavilion in LA, the Masonic in San Francisco, Boston's Symphony Hall, The Kennedy Center, and most of the other biggies across the country. Janie has always stayed in my thoughts, and in my heart. Had she been better treated and mentored by Columbia and William Morris, her 'career freeze,' which I am convinced came from an emotional reaction to her (too) sudden success, could have been avoided.

Marc Shaiman

Are You Even Out Of High School, Jailbait?

I wish my diary weren't so vague about working with Marc, and even who he played piano for at Reno Sweeney. I'm fairly certain he was working with *Formerly the Harlettes* (Bette's original back-up group of three girl singers, all with powerful pipes). What I do remember is him walking in for a tech rehearsal the afternoon of opening night and my thinking, *I hope he's not looking for work as a waiter because he must still be in high school.* While these days he looks agelessly cute with his rather funny, sparse beard and still cherubic face, my first encounter offered up a short, obviously gay teenager who looked like he couldn't wait to grow up.

Diary says he was eighteen and did some kind of magic to get a high school diploma at sixteen because he couldn't wait to hit the scene. His vibe was, 'I'm gonna be great and I know it.' Once he sat at the piano, I found him arrogant, but I also was blown away at his musical prowess. He seemed almost bored playing as a musician backing singers, and after the tech he pounded a couple out on the piano (tunes) while I was readying the stage for the 8:00 p.m. show, and I asked him what he was playing. He replied, "Just a couple things I'm working on." I knew I was gonna see this kid go places—what he was "working on" was better than most of what I was hearing in the pop genre on the cabaret circuit.

I scribbled down, after the show that night, "When he hits twenty-one, he'll start to look grown-up, and he must be fucking frustrated because he looks like a kid, a gay kid, and who is gonna want to fuck him right now except pedophiles—ha." I sensed his arrogant and aggressive dealings with most everybody was a front for a shy boy transitioning into manhood, and his talent excited me. He just had that aura of greatness around him, and I made a note to keep track of his career. Little did I know just how brilliant and prolific he would become—as of this writing, a Tony, Grammy, Emmy, and seven Oscar nominations. I should have fucked him, I guess.

I'm happy for Marc and wish I had offered myself up a little more. Looks like he hasn't lost that aggressiveness I sensed in him—all the brilliant music aside, his hard and unflinching honesty and support of LGBTQ+ rights makes me feel like I should have mentored him a bit, but his age and attitude put me off and I wasn't mature enough to dig a little deeper. I could have offered him the support I needed but didn't get when *I* was eighteen. But instead, at nine years his senior, he looked more like jailbait than a gay youth in need of a pal.

More Celebrity Musings in the following book chapters:

Ella Fitzgerald – Chapter 4

Ellen Greene – Chapter 8

Anita O'Day – Chapter 2

Cissy & Whitney Houston – Chapter 8

Holly Woodlawn – Chapter 8

Little Edie Beale – Chapter 8

Peggy Lee – Chapter 9

Julie Andrews – Chapter 9

Charles Pierce – Chapter 9

Nina Simone – Chapter 10

David Vass comes from a long line his mother once foolishly listened to. He is an accomplished Monologist, Performer, Diarist, Writer, and Activist, as well as the creator of the one-person play, *What Could Go Wrong: Musings of an Eccentric Raconteur Who Happened to be at the Right Places at the Right Times.* His one-man show is performed at intimate theaters, clubs, private engagements, and festivals in the United States, the UK and Australia. He has been partnered with his soulmate and husband Paul for forty-six years, the last sixteen of which have included a marriage license, finally. David's hobby is explaining everything to everybody.

During his years behind-the-scenes in show business, he was a road manager, technical director and/or lighting and sound designer for 200+ clients, including over fifty Oscar, Emmy, Grammy, Golden Globe and Tony award winning legends and celebrities.

A proud member of The Authors and The Dramatists Guilds, David believes there is no such thing as a politically incorrect or unusable word—a word is a word is a word. It is how a word is *used* that creates its true meaning and can make it glowingly positive and reinforcing, or hateful, demeaning, and mean-spirited. Nipsy Russell, Larry Kramer, Lenny Bruce and many others knew this. He feels our First Amendment rights are in jeopardy and wishes those in the "Woke Movement" who embrace censoring words without taking into consideration how and why they are used (or using one letter and some ***s) would rethink their position.

David's personal website, www.davidvass.com has a pictorial history of his life over the decades.

His LIAR, ALLEGED website (www.davidvassbook.com) affords readers an opportunity to keep abreast of current endeavors by joining his mailing list. He adds the occasional pop-up short story and has links for his speaking engagements, book signings, one-person show schedule, and his next book. As a hybrid-published author, he urges readers that enjoy his writing to support him by making their friends aware of his book and via reviews on Amazon, Kindle and Goodreads. Five-star reader reviews look like this ★★★★★ and will bring you great fortune.

Morgana King's throat tonic recipe for getting yourself on stage and sounding good when you have to and your throat is shot, as told to her by Nat King Cole, as told to him by Billie Holiday as told to her by Louis Armstrong:

- 12 mentholated cough drops (she used Hall's and so do I)
- Around ½ cup water
- Around 1 cup honey
- Around ½ cup brandy, cognac or bourbon

Bring the water to a soft boil and throw in the cough drops. Stir a little til they are melted into the water. Add everything else and give it a few stirs til it is warm and becomes a little thicker and has created a syrup. Don't let it boil again and lose the alcohol! Cool to room temperature and sip it before and during your music sets. Emphasis on sip!

I've shared this iconic potion with more singers than I can remember. A few had the recipe already, most not. No complaints and instant positive results. Guaranteed to get you through a couple shows 'til you can visit a "Dr. FeelGood." If you have alcohol issues, jump off the wagon til your throat is better and pray you don't stumble off the stage. No NOT substitute wine for the booze—the tannins will do a number on your vocal chords. You're welcome.

Thanks to my colleagues who helped me cobble this book together — some of whom are actually still talking to me!

Ian Corson

Sabrina Young

Gillian Telling

Lauren Carsley

Roger Brooks

Michael Leonard

Claire Trasorras

Roger Harvey

Eva Myrick

Katie Ressa

Gina Butler

The Authors Guild Legal Team

Amber Lewis

Tara Mager, Esq.

Bejamin Koenig (Audiobook - what a voice!)

www.ingramcontent.com/pod-product-compliance
Lightning Source LLC
Chambersburg PA
CBHW050325010526
44119CB00003B/105